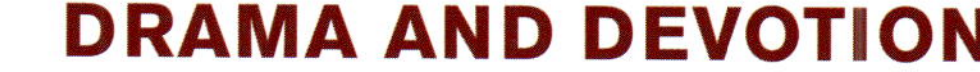

DRAMA AND DEVOTION

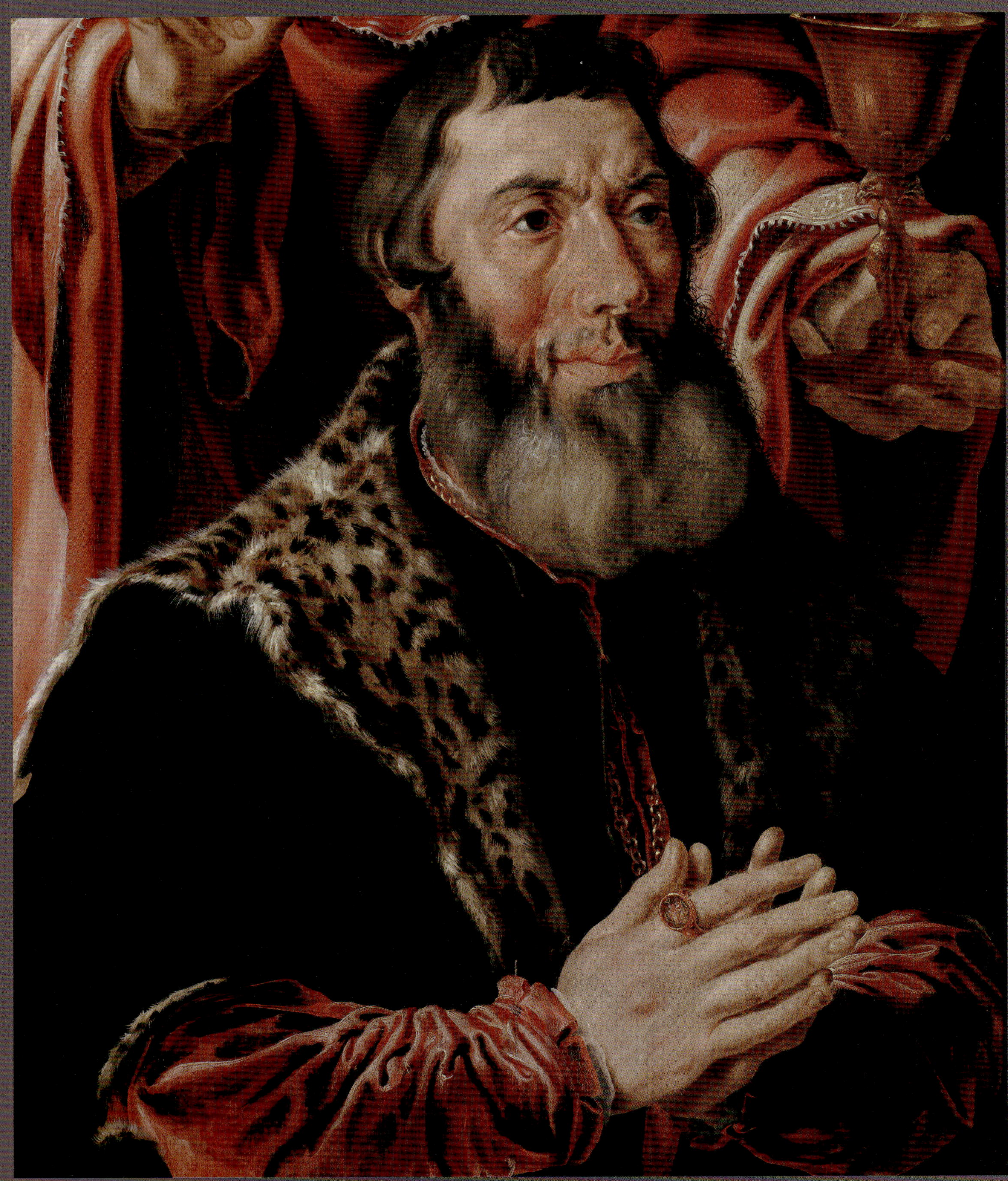

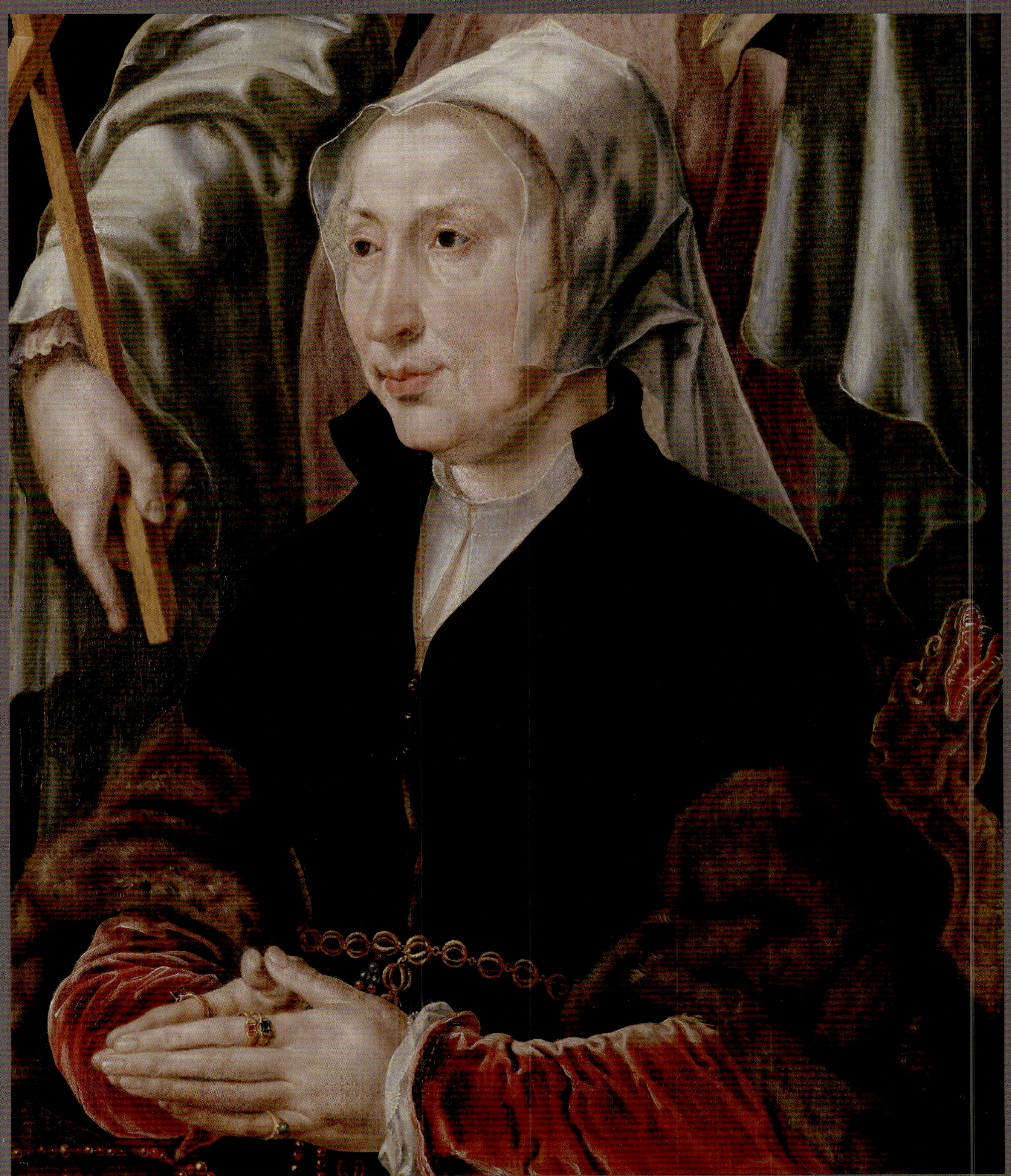

DRAMA AND DEVOTION

HEEMSKERCK'S *ECCE HOMO* ALTARPIECE FROM WARSAW

ANNE T. WOOLLETT

YVONNE SZAFRAN

ALAN PHENIX

THE J. PAUL GETTY MUSEUM

LOS ANGELES

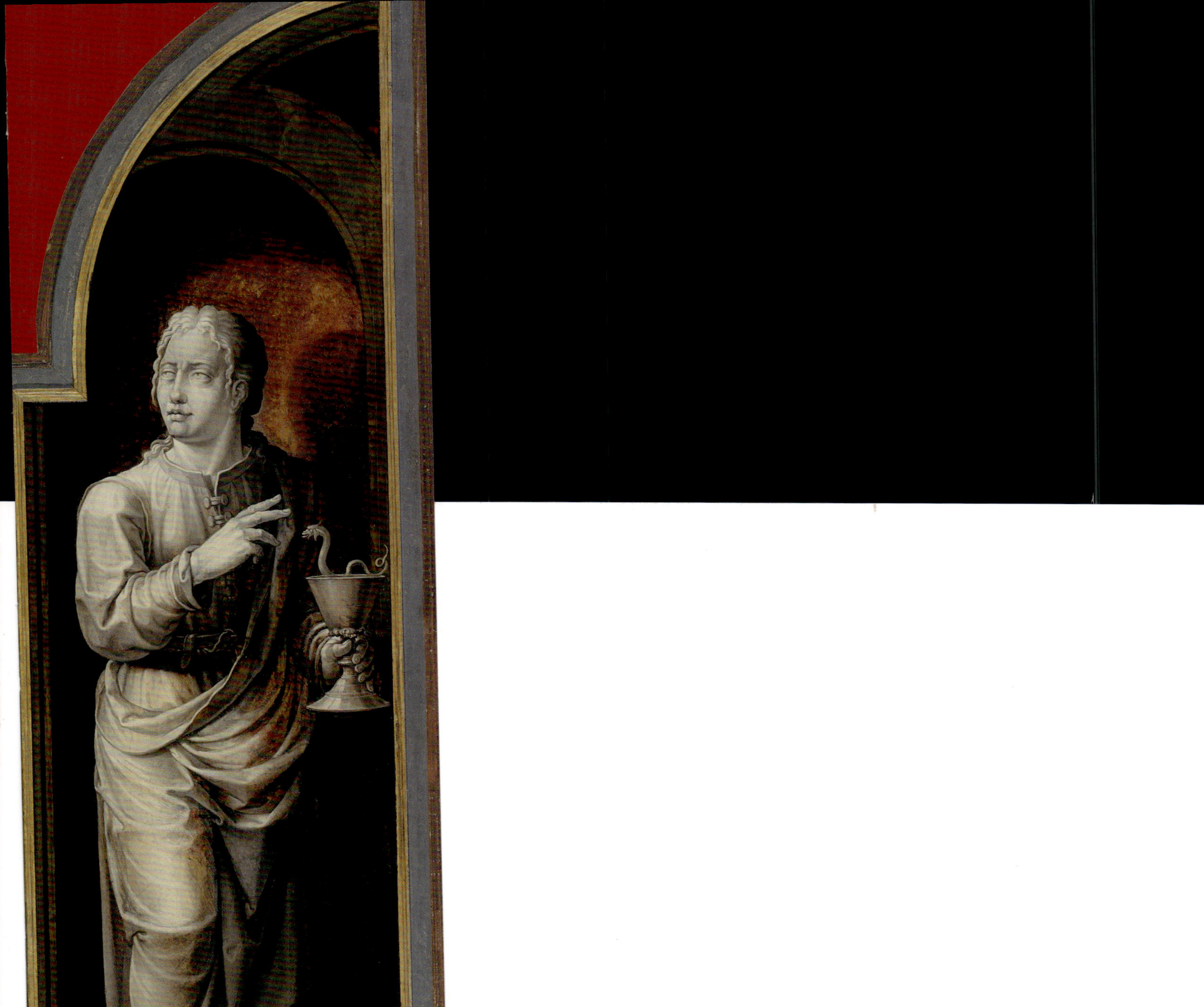

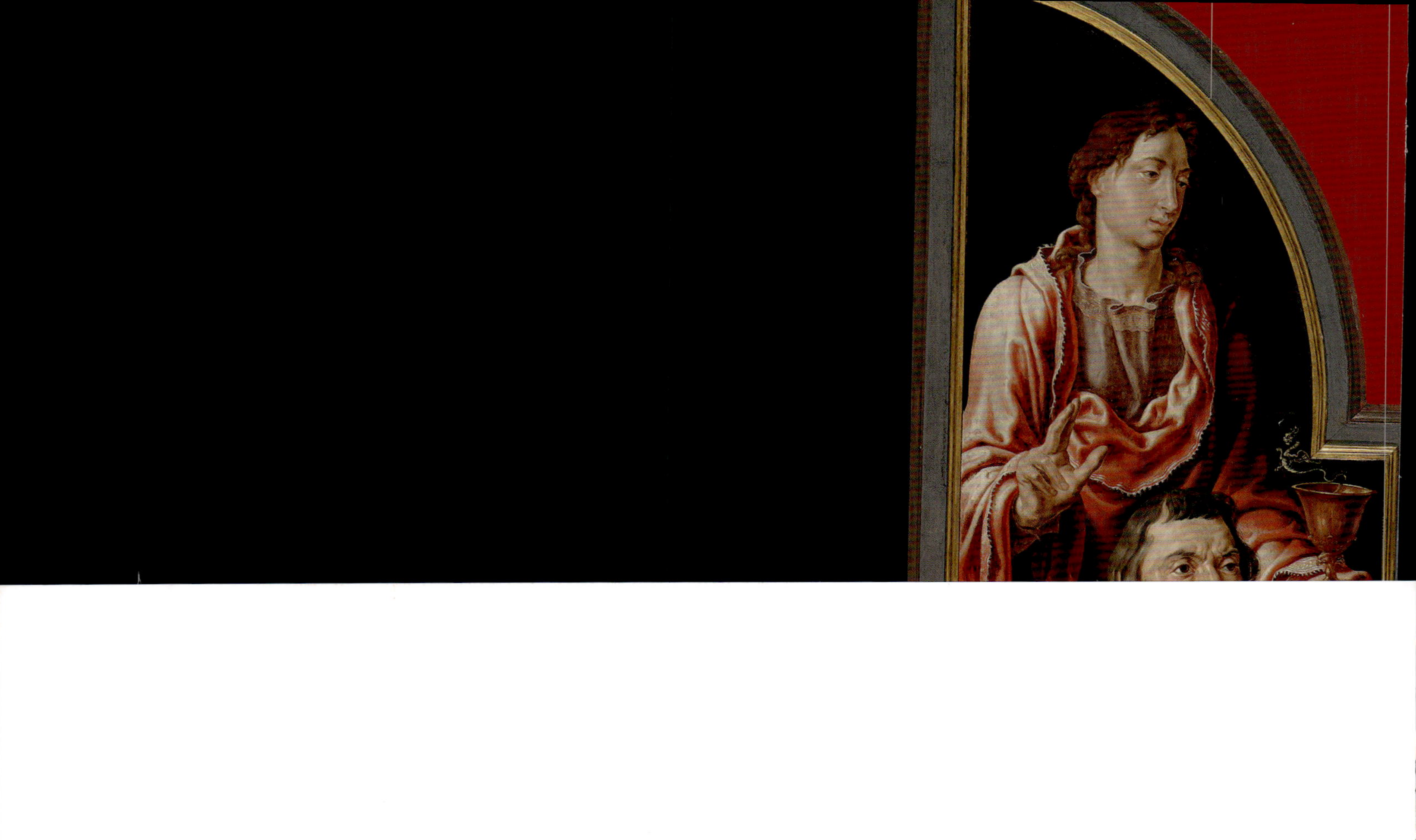

This publication is issued on the occasion of the exhibition *Drama and Devotion: Heemskerck's* Ecce Homo *Altarpiece from Warsaw*, on view at the J. Paul Getty Museum at the Getty Center, Los Angeles, from June 5, 2012, to January 13, 2013.

The Paintings Conservation Council of the J. Paul Getty Museum generously supported this book and the related conservation project and exhibition.

Second printing

Published by the J. Paul Getty Museum
Getty Publications
1200 Getty Center Drive, Suite 500
Los Angeles, California 90049-1682
www.getty.edu/publications

Elizabeth S. G. Nicholson, Editor
Jim Drobka, Designer
Elizabeth Chapin Kahn, Production Coordinator

Printed in China

Library of Congress Cataloging-in-Publication Data
Woollett, Anne T.
Drama and devotion : Heemskerck's Ecce Homo altarpiece from Warsaw / Anne T. Woollett, Yvonne Szafran, Alan Phenix.
pages cm
Includes bibliographical references and index.
ISBN 978-1-60606-112-1 (pbk.)
1. Heemskerck, Maerten van, 1498–1574. Ecce Homo altarpiece. 2. Altarpieces, Renaissance—Netherlands—Dordrecht. 3. Panel painting, Renaissance—Netherlands—Dordrecht. 4. Panel painting, Dutch—Netherlands—Dordrecht. 5. Altarpieces—Conservation and restoration—California—Los Angeles. 6. Panel painting—Conservation and restoration—California—Los Angeles. I. Szafran, Yvonne. II. Phenix, Alan. III. Title.
ND653.H4A69 2012
759.9492—dc22
2011048520

Front cover and pp. ii and iii: Maerten van Heemskerck, *Ecce Homo* triptych (details of frontispiece)

Frontispiece: Maerten van Heemskerck (Dutch, 1498–1574), *Ecce Homo* triptych, 1544. Oil on panel, central panel unframed 167 × 88.9 cm (65¾ × 35 in.), framed 188.6 × 132.7 cm (74¼ × 52¼ in.), left wing framed 183.5 × 62.5 cm (72¼ × 24⅝ in.), right wing framed 183.5 × 64.8 cm (72¼ × 25½ in.). Muzeum Narodowe w Warszawie

Back cover: Left: Maerten van Heemskerck (Dutch, 1498–1574), *Self-Portrait, with the Colosseum, Rome*, 1553. Oil on panel, 42.2 × 54 cm (16½ × 21¼ in.). Fitzwilliam Museum, University of Cambridge, UK / The Bridgeman Art Library. Right: X-radiograph of the central panel of Heemskerck's *Ecce Homo* triptych

CONTENTS

viii **FOREWORD**
James Cuno

x **ACKNOWLEDGMENTS**

1 **A RENAISSANCE ALTARPIECE REVEALED**
Anne T. Woollett

29 **THE *ECCE HOMO* TRIPTYCH: HEEMSKERCK'S MATERIALS AND METHODS**
Yvonne Szafran and Alan Phenix

83 Bibliography
89 Illustration List
91 Index

FOREWORD

For more than a decade, the Conservation Partnership program at the J. Paul Getty Museum has encouraged the valuable exchange of ideas and technical expertise among museums in Europe, the United States, and South America through the study and conservation of major works of art. Now made possible through the generous support of the Museum's Paintings Conservation Council, the varied projects have enriched our understanding of extraordinary objects and served to forge closer relationships with our colleagues in other museums around the world. Our colleagues in the Getty Conservation Institute have also had significant involvement in a number of important treatments and technical studies.

In September 2009, at the invitation of Bogdan Zdrojewski, Poland's minister of culture and national heritage, David Bomford (then acting director), Yvonne Szafran, senior conservator of paintings, and Scott Schaefer, senior curator of paintings, traveled to Poland on a marvelous journey organized by Malgorzata Cup, consul for culture at the consulate general in Los Angeles. They were warmly received by the country of Poland as they traveled to various museums, including the National Museum in Warsaw (Muzeum Narodowe w Warszawie), where they met with Piotr Piotrowski (then director), Antoni Ziemba, chief curator, Hanna Benesz, curator of early Netherlandish and Flemish paintings, Maciej Monkiewicz, curator of Dutch and German paintings, as well as chief conservator Dorota Ignatowicz-Woźniakowska and other curatorial and conservation staff. Founded in 1862, the museum's wide-ranging collection houses the national holdings of Polish painting from the sixteenth century onward, as well as significant collections of European painting and ancient and contemporary art. *Drama and Devotion: Heemskerck's* Ecce Homo *Altarpiece from Warsaw* coincides with the National Museum's 150th anniversary and represents the Getty's most recent collaboration with the museum in Warsaw, following the treatment of Pieter Saenredam's *Interior of the Saint Bavokerk in Haarlem* (1635) in connection with the 2002 exhibition *The Sacred Spaces of Pieter Saenredam* at the Getty.

The dramatic and beautifully preserved *Ecce Homo* altarpiece, by the remarkable Dutch artist Maerten van Heemskerck (1498–1574), was immediately selected for treatment and to become the subject of a focused exhibition in Los Angeles. One of Heemskerck's most distinguished private commissions in the triptych format favored in the Netherlands during his time, it not only survived the religious upheavals of the late sixteenth century intact but retains its original carved frame. Conservation treatment began in the fall of 2010, with the arrival at the Getty of Hanna Benesz and the painting, followed by guest conservator Iwona Stefanska, who worked with Getty conservators at the beginning and end of the project. Treatment and analysis continued over the winter months and included research in the Netherlands, notably Dordrecht, where the altarpiece had originally occupied the chapel of Jan van Drenckwaerdt in the Augustinian church. We thank our colleagues in the Netherlands who shared their insights into the artist and his working methods. Julia Burdajewicz, our guide in Warsaw and a paintings conservation graduate intern (2010–11), facilitated various aspects of the examination and helped overcome linguistic hurdles.

This book documents the treatment and research carried out by Yvonne Szafran (with Getty Museum conservators Laura Rivers and Tiarna Doherty) and Getty Conservation Institute scientist Alan Phenix (with Joy Mazurek, Catherine Patterson, and Karen Trentelman). Their research corroborates the contemporary sixteenth-century view of Heemskerck as an innovator and a master of Italian practices. Anne T. Woollett, curator of paintings at the Getty Museum, discusses the cultivated program of the altarpiece and frame, revealing Heemskerck's material and iconographic ingenuity on behalf of his Dordrecht patrons.

I would like to thank Agnieszka Morawińska, current director of the National Museum in Warsaw, for continuing the support of her predecessor for this project. Finally, we gratefully acknowledge the enthusiasm of the Paintings Conservation Council, whose support made this exciting partnership project possible.

James Cuno
President & CEO
The J. Paul Getty Trust

ACKNOWLEDGMENTS

The research presented here originated from a collaborative enterprise among the J. Paul Getty Museum's Paintings Curatorial and Conservation departments, along with the Getty Conservation Institute's (GCI) collections research laboratory, and we warmly thank the following colleagues who have so kindly shared their knowledge and provided indispensable help during the project: Laura Rivers, Gene Karraker, Julia Burdajewicz, Tiarna Doherty, and Laura Satterfield in Paintings Conservation; Karen Trentelman, Catherine Patterson, Joy Mazurek, and Peter Reischig, our partners in the GCI; Michael Smith, Jack Ross, and Rebecca Vera-Martinez in Imaging Services; and Rozemarijn Landsman, in the Paintings Department. This investigative endeavor could not have been undertaken without the enthusiastic commitment of the Museum's then acting director, David Bomford, and senior curator of paintings, Scott Schaefer, who were greatly involved in our initial conversations in Warsaw and have provided encouragement throughout the project. Acting associate director of collections Thomas Kren gave willing support as well.

Our colleagues at the National Museum in Warsaw have been especially supportive, and we thank Agnieszka Morawińska, Piotr Piotrowski, Antoni Ziemba, Dorota Ignatowicz-Woźniakowska, Hanna Benesz, Iwona Stefanska, and Maciej Monkiewicz. Bogdan Zdrojewski, minister of culture and national heritage, and Malgorzata Cup, from the Polish consulate in Los Angeles, were essential partners from the very beginning.

Many colleagues generously shared their files and thoughts about Heemskerck's works. During the course of our research in the Netherlands, we were graciously assisted by Gwen Tauber and Matthias Ubl at the Rijksmuseum, Amsterdam; Anna Tummers, Liesbeth Abraham, and Mireille te Marvelde at the Frans Hals Museum in Haarlem; and Christi Klinkert at the Stedelijk Museum in Alkmaar; as well as the staff of Erfgoedcentrum DiEP in Dordrecht; and by Aart de Boon of the Augustinian church in Dordrecht, the original home of the triptych. Eva Nyström Tagesson of the Östergötlands Museum and Peter Lundborg, dean of Linköping Cathedral, Sweden, were instrumental in enabling us to study Heemskerck's *Saint Lawrence* altarpiece in situ. At the Lakenhal Museum in Leiden, Christiaan Vogelaar provided insight into installation practices. Lynn Roberts in London was also extremely generous in sharing her thoughts about the frame.

It was a great pleasure working on this volume with the enthusiastic Getty Publications team. Acting co-heads of Publications Rob Flynn and Carolyn Simmons played key roles from the beginning, and we thank Ann Lucke for her support. Senior editor Elizabeth Nicholson deftly and patiently guided our collaborative efforts, while Pam Moffat swiftly assembled the illustrations and Catherine Comeau and Ruth Lane brought a keen eye to the text. For the care and inspiring creativity brought to the design and production of the catalogue, which so marvelously captures the essential character of Heemskerck's *Ecce Homo* altarpiece, we especially thank Jim Drobka and Elizabeth Kahn, as well as Karen Schmidt and Deenie Yudell.

In realizing the accompanying exhibition, we gratefully acknowledge the contributions of our colleagues at the J. Paul Getty Museum. The exhibition was skillfully implemented by Quincy Houghton and Amber Keller in the Exhibitions Department, John Giurini and Amy Hood in Communications, and Sally Hibbard and Carole Campbell in the Registrar's Office. Merritt Price, Robert Checchi, Donna Pungprechawat, and Christopher Coniglio gave the installation its handsome design. Kevin Marshall, Michael Mitchell, Cary Stehle, Tracy Witt, and John Jacoby handled the logistics of installing and lighting the *Ecce Homo* with aplomb, while Tony Moreno with Loren Vincent, David Glickman, and Butch Green fabricated the crucial support and mount for the triptych. Our thanks to Toby Tannenbaum, Clare Kunny, Maite Alvarez, and Chris Keledjian for their wise counsel on the gallery texts. The ingenuity and expertise of Stanley Smith, Erik Bertellotti, Nina Diamond, Heather MacMillan, and Gary Hughes resulted in enlightening media and online presentations to accompany the exhibition.

Finally, we are tremendously grateful to the Paintings Conservation Council of the J. Paul Getty Museum for generously supporting this rewarding research partnership, the exhibition, and the publication of this book.

Anne T. Woollett
Yvonne Szafran
Alan Phenix

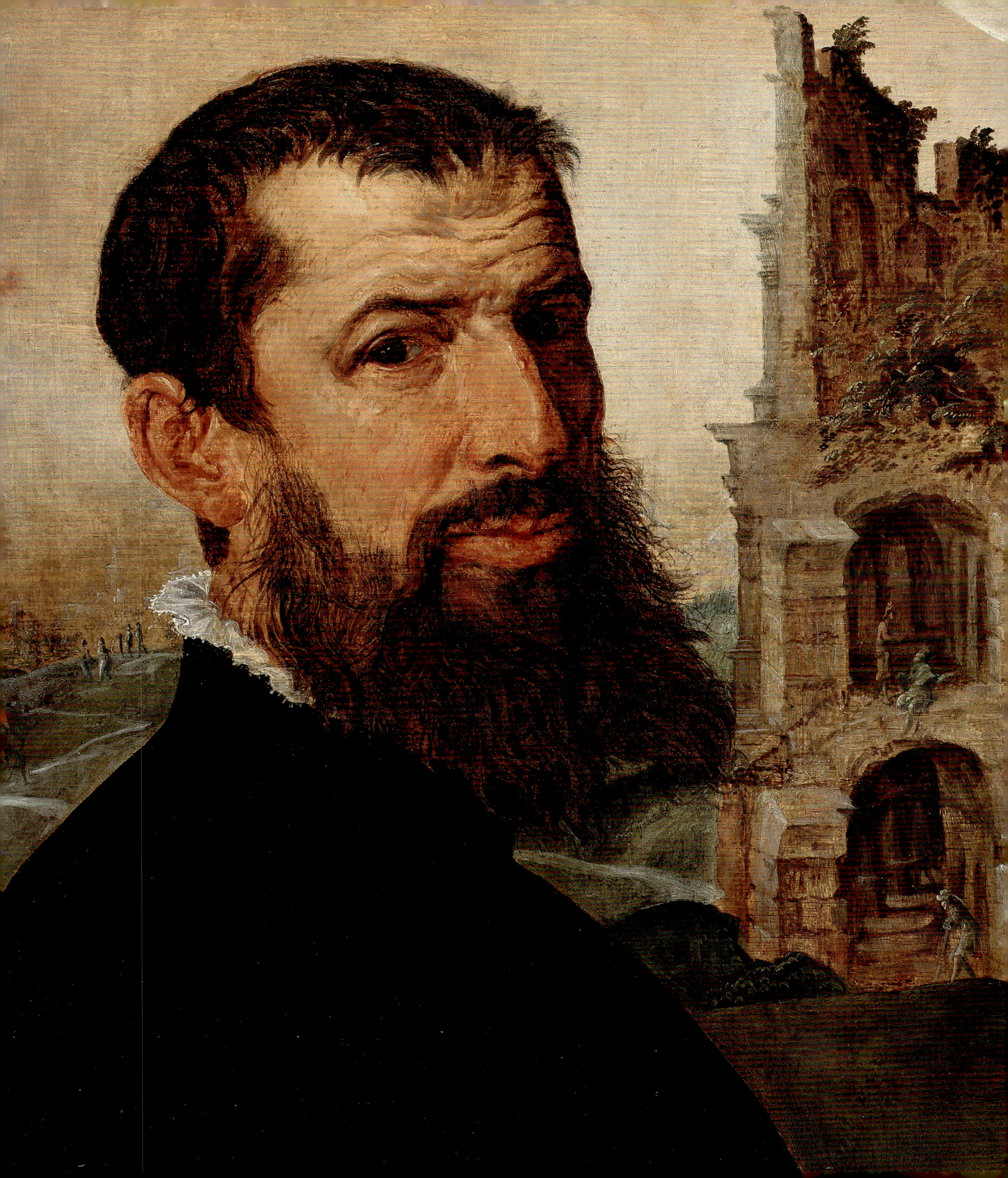

A RENAISSANCE ALTARPIECE REVEALED

ANNE T. WOOLLETT

MAERTEN VAN HEEMSKERCK IN RENAISSANCE DORDRECHT

During a period of extraordinary artistic achievement, the Dutch painter and draftsman Maerten van Heemskerck (1498–1574) (fig. 1) was one of the most celebrated (*vermaert*) artists of his day.[1] His distinguished career began during the third decade of the sixteenth century, as the eminent lives of Albrecht Dürer (1471–1528), Jan Gossaert (ca. 1478–1532), and Lucas van Leyden (ca. 1494–1533) were nearing their ends. One of the great artistic personalities of the Renaissance Netherlands, Heemskerck devised an immediately recognizable style characterized by luxuriant color and an aggressive—and, for some modern viewers, uncomfortable—physicality that distinguished him from his contemporaries. Abundantly creative, he playfully reimagined antiquity, rendered the fervor of his religious subjects, and captured the sophistication of his sitters. From his studio in Haarlem, Heemskerck attended to numerous private and corporate commissions in cities across the region. Sadly, a great number of his altarpieces were destroyed by iconoclasts in 1566 during the Revolt of the Netherlands and the transformation to the Reformed faith.[2]

One of the rare survivors of the destruction, the *Ecce Homo* triptych (see frontispiece) has long been recognized as a highlight of the collection of Netherlandish paintings in the National Museum in Warsaw.[3] The altarpiece originally decorated the private chapel of the prominent Drenckwaerdt family in the church of the Augustinian monastery in Dordrecht. Dated 1544 but unsigned, the triptych displays Heemskerck's dynamic style and versatility as a painter of devotional subjects and as a portraitist. Remarkably, the triptych retains its original frame, which features an unusual carved architectural surround for the central panel. As a unified ensemble, the *Ecce Homo* triptych is an extremely important example of a large-scale private altarpiece to survive from the second quarter of the sixteenth century.[4]

In the fall of 2010 the *Ecce Homo* altarpiece made the long journey from Warsaw to Los Angeles for treatment and study at the J. Paul Getty Museum as part of a new Conservation Partnership project with the National Museum generously supported by the Getty's Paintings Conservation Council. Investigation of this beautifully preserved work has affirmed the brilliant technique of a master painter and permitted further exploration of some of the unusual materials he employed in his pigments to achieve dazzling effects, which have since been altered by time (see Yvonne Szafran and Alan Phenix's essay in this volume). Cleaning of the panels also revealed many details that show the complexity and thoroughness with which Heemskerck carried out his commission. Although always considered a significant work in the artist's oeuvre, the *Ecce Homo* triptych now emerges more clearly as one of his most sophisticated private altarpieces. He not only masterfully addressed the spiritual requirements of his patron Jan van Drenckwaerdt but also articulated the cultured milieu of the proud city of Dordrecht through his unique blend of Italian and native artistic modes. A very important undertaking for the artist, the *Ecce Homo* triptych was highly prized by later generations, who kept it intact over the course of more than four hundred years. Originally intended for private devotion, it tells a powerful story of creativity on the eve of regional upheaval.

Detail, figure 1

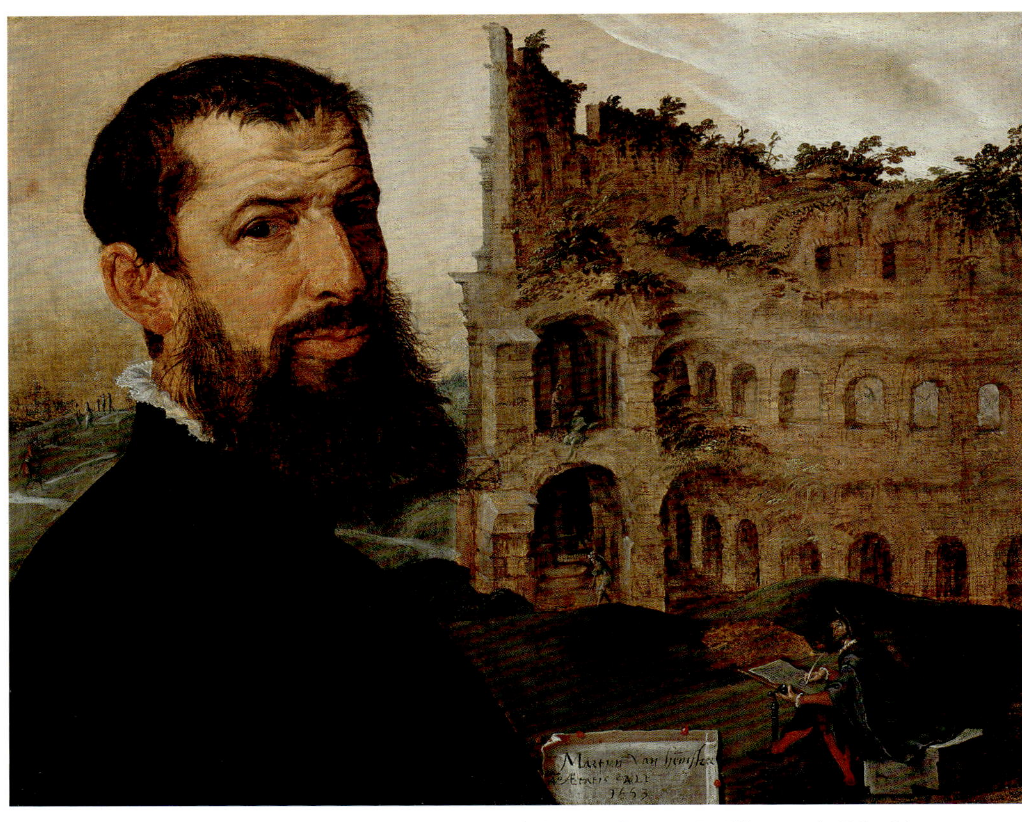

FIGURE 1 Maerten van Heemskerck, *Self-Portrait, with the Colosseum, Rome*, 1553. Oil on panel, 42.2 × 54 cm (16½ × 21¼ in.). Cambridge, Fitzwilliam Museum

HEEMSKERCK'S TRAINING AND CAREER

One of the most innovative and prolific artists of the sixteenth century, Heemskerck developed a distinctive style of restless contours and vibrant color that invigorated traditional subject matter and formats. Born in 1498, the son of a prosperous farmer in the village of Heemskerck, north of Haarlem, Maerten van Heemskerck first studied in Haarlem with Cornelis Willemsz and subsequently with Jan Lucasz in Delft, according to the biographer Karel van Mander, before entering the Haarlem studio of Jan van Scorel (1495–1562) as an apprentice in about 1527.[5] Only three years his senior, Van Scorel had already traveled to Venice, Jerusalem, and Rome (1518/20–23), where he served the Dutch pope Adrian VI (reigned 1522–23) as Keeper of Antiquities in the Belvedere, a post held previously by Raphael (1483–1520). The Italian ideas Van Scorel introduced through prestigious commissions after his return to the North in 1524 profoundly influenced the course of painting in the Netherlands. Heemskerck quickly mastered Van Scorel's novel manner, characterized by monumental forms, references to antique sources, and painterly brushwork, and he then developed his own strongly sculptural idiom after Van Scorel's departure for Utrecht in 1530. As a gift to his fellow painters and a lasting testament to his skill,

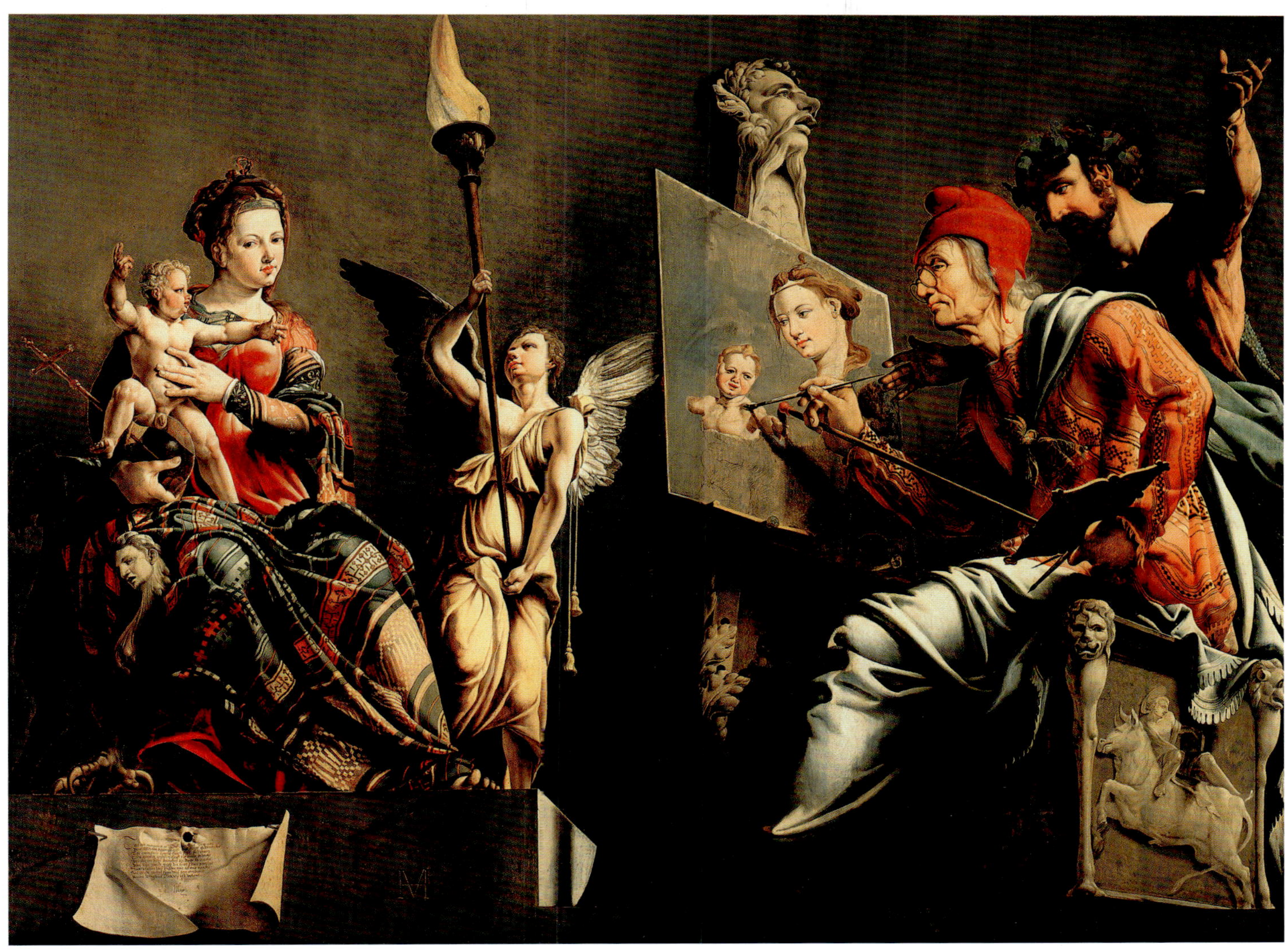

FIGURE 2 Maerten van Heemskerck, *Saint Luke Painting the Virgin*, 1532. Oil on panel, 168 × 235 cm (66 × 92½ in.). Haarlem, Frans Hals Museum

Heemskerck presented the Haarlem Guild of Saint Luke with a large panel, *Saint Luke Painting the Virgin* (fig. 2),[6] in which the saint and his subject are seen from a startlingly low perspective.

In the early summer of 1532, Heemskerck traveled to Rome, which, despite the devastating consequences of the 1527 Sack by Emperor Charles V, still offered a stimulating environment for young artists. Lodging with the art collector and patron Cardinal Willem van Enckenvoirt of Utrecht (1464–1534),[7] he joined several prominent Netherlandish painters, including Michiel Coxcie (1499–1592), who immersed themselves in the Roman classicism of Raphael and his pupils as well as new developments by post-Sack arrivals such as Francesco Salviati (1510–1563). In addition to Raphael's frescoes for the Villa Farnesina, which offered a variety of elegant poses and pictorial solutions to be studied, the frescoes in the papal apartments at the Vatican known as the Stanze, and the late monumental altarpiece *The Transfiguration*, Heemskerck experienced firsthand the artificial and expressive style emerging from the brushes of Salviati and Giorgio Vasari (1511–1574) during the mid-1530s. While Raphael's classicism was an important part of Heemskerck's education, it was Michelangelo's radiant palette and figural dynamism, most evident in the Sistine ceiling, that impressed him deeply. Heemskerck's nearly four years in Rome fundamentally altered his practice. His encounter with high-style Roman classicism and its almost abstract use of luminous color collided with the traditions of his native Netherlands. He resolved this confrontation between disparate approaches to painting in his mature style, seen in the *Ecce Homo* altarpiece, in which eloquent Michelangelesque physicality and brilliant color and the technical precision and descriptive surfaces of Northern practice are held in uneasy tension.

The Eternal City had still more to offer Heemskerck. As it had for the previous generation of artists from the North, notably Gossaert, the legacy of antiquity proved utterly captivating. Heemskerck evidently enjoyed access to the leading collections of ancient sculpture, such as the reliefs and statues tastefully arranged in the courtyards of the venerable della Valle and Sassi families (fig. 3), and he recorded numerous architectural monuments and fragments, some still partially buried, with unprecedented attention to detail and scale (fig. 4).[8] "[H]e neither slept away his time nor neglected it in the company of Netherlanders with boozing or whatever, but instead he copied many things, as much after antiquities as after the works of Michelangelo—also many ruins, ornaments, and all kind of subtleties of the ancients which are to be seen in abundance in this city, the painters' academy," noted Van Mander.[9] While in Rome, Heemskerck painted a fantastic landscape of the ancient world, *Panorama with the Abduction of Helen amidst the Wonders of the Ancient World* (fig. 5), as a compendium of the most famous works of antiquity known to the Renaissance. He also contributed to the designs for a triumphal arch erected for the entry of Emperor Charles V into Rome in 1536, an experience that would prove relevant for the Drenckwaerdt altarpiece.[10]

Armed with his drawings,[11] Heemskerck returned to Haarlem, probably via Mantua and Dordrecht, in late 1536. He quickly established himself as one of the leading painters in the Netherlands with large-scale altarpiece commissions across the region, including wings for Van Scorel's *Crucifixion* altarpiece in Amsterdam (1538–41; now lost) and the *Passion* triptych for the Sint-Laurenskerk in Alkmaar (fig. 6), as well as a large *Crucifixion* (1543; Ghent, Museum voor Schone

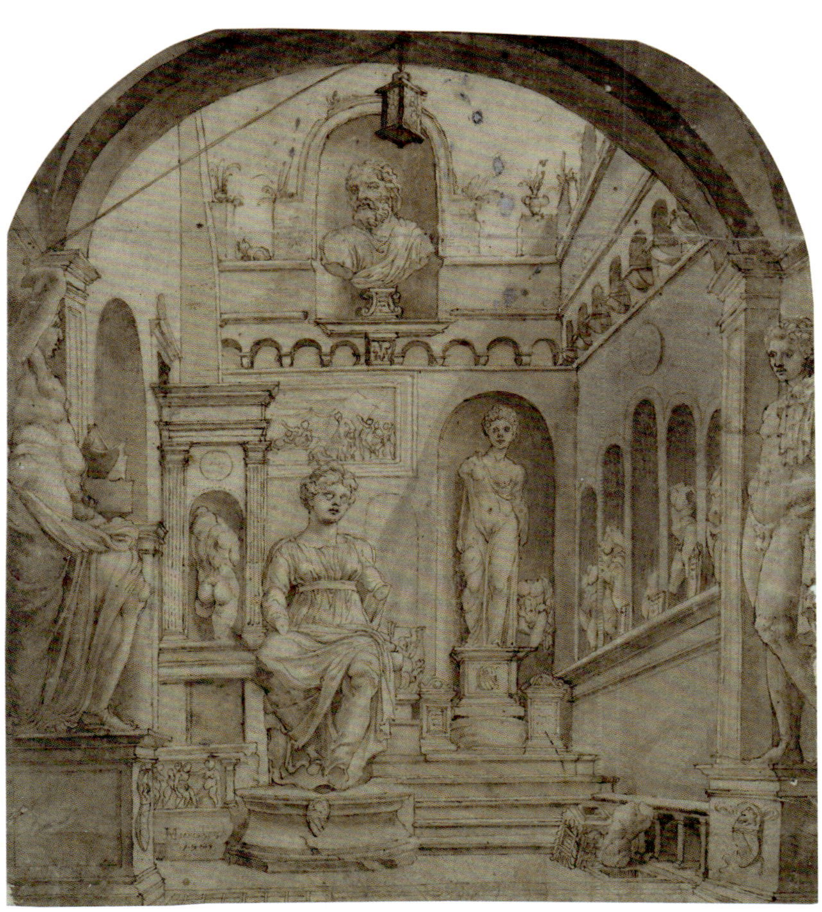

FIGURE 3 Maerten van Heemskerck, *The Statue Court of the Casa Sassi at Rome*, ca. 1535. Pen and ink, 23 × 21.5 cm (9 × 8½ in.). Berlin, Kupferstichkabinett, Staatliche Museen

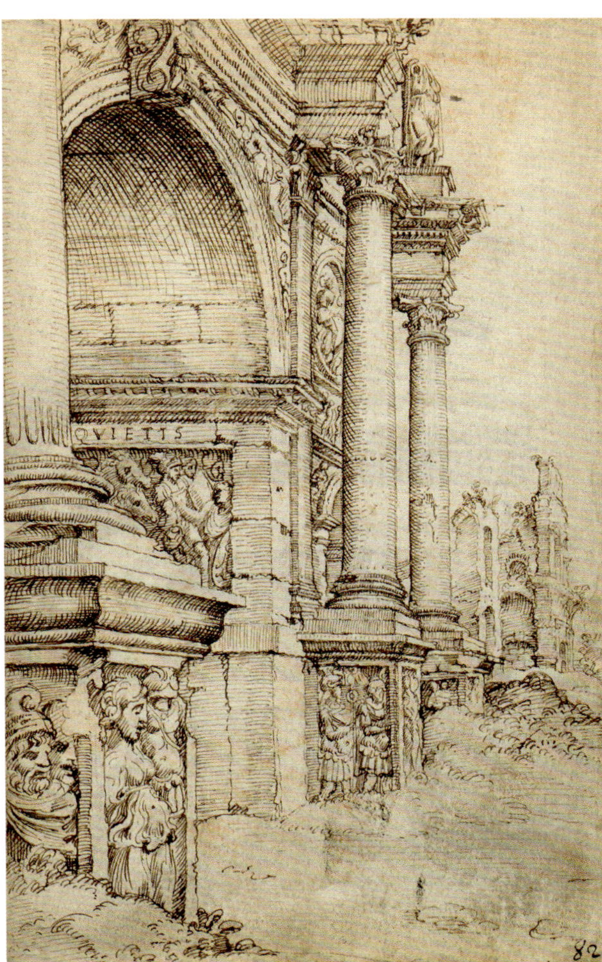

FIGURE 4 Maerten van Heemskerck, *The Arch of Constantine*, ca. 1535. Pen and brown ink, 20.9 × 13.3 cm (8¼ × 5¼ in.). Berlin, Kupferstichkabinett, Staatliche Museen

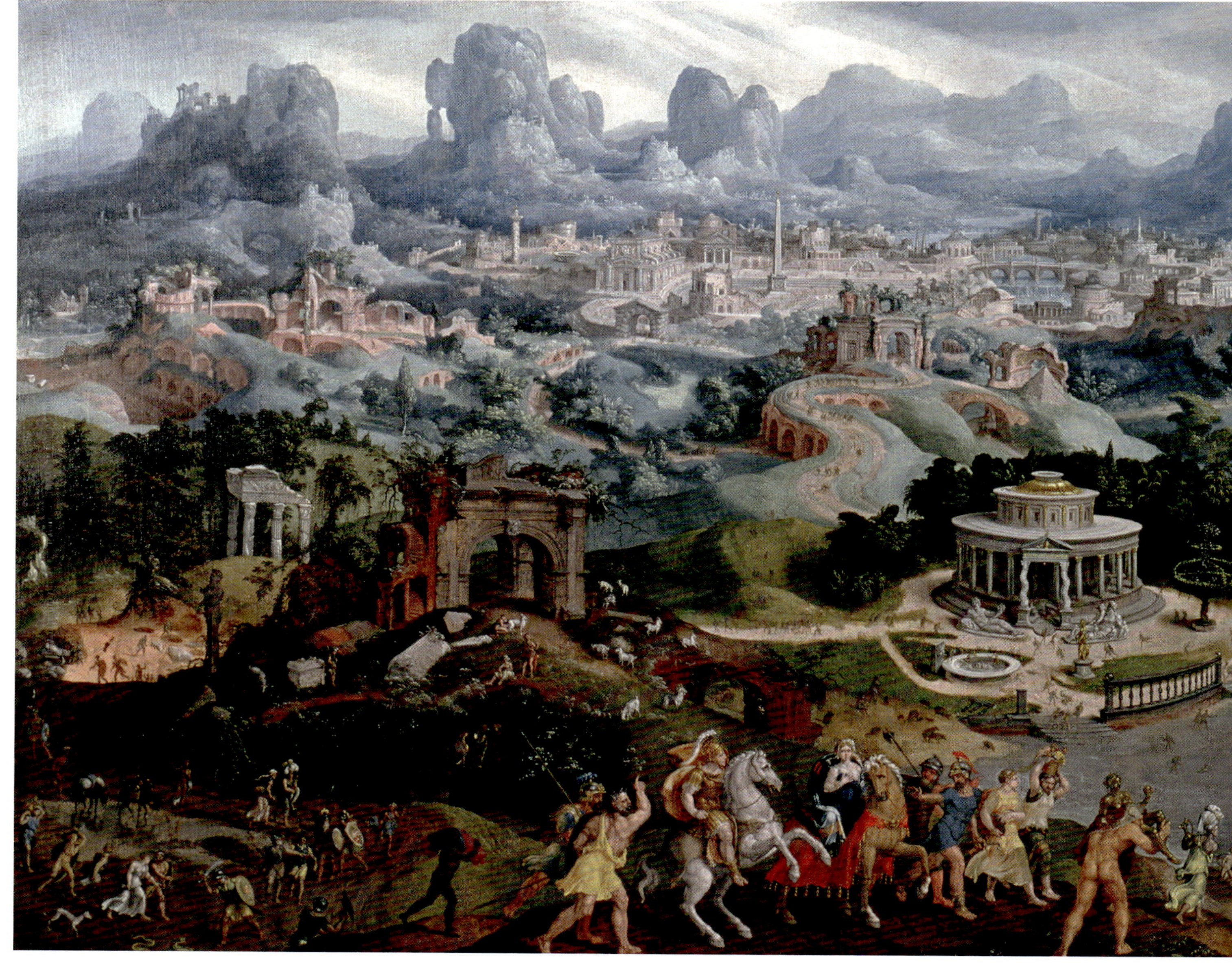

FIGURE 5 Maerten van Heemskerck, *Panorama with the Abduction of Helen amidst the Wonders of the Ancient World*, 1535. Oil on canvas, 147.3 × 383.5 cm (58 × 151 in.). Baltimore, Walters Art Museum

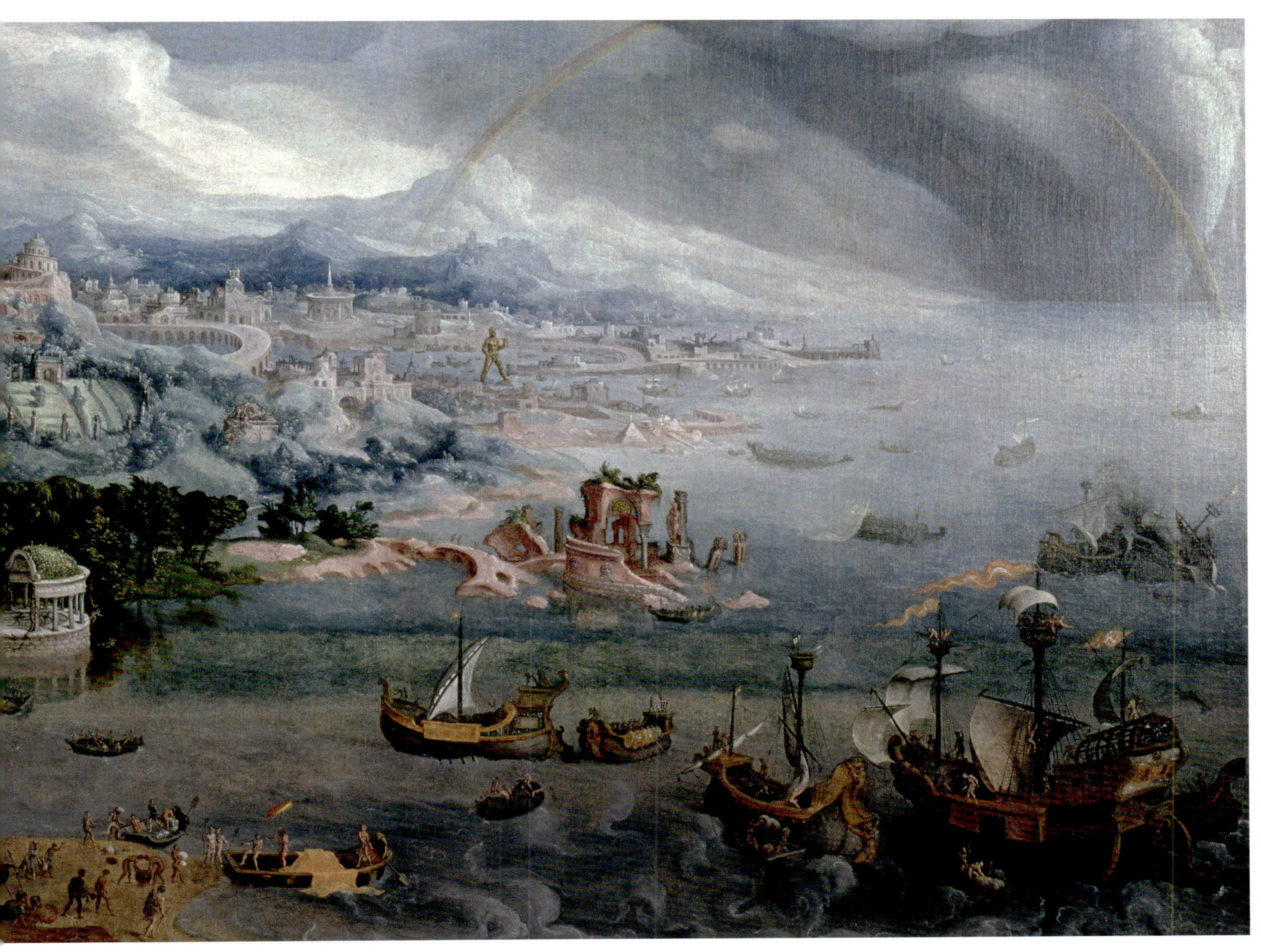

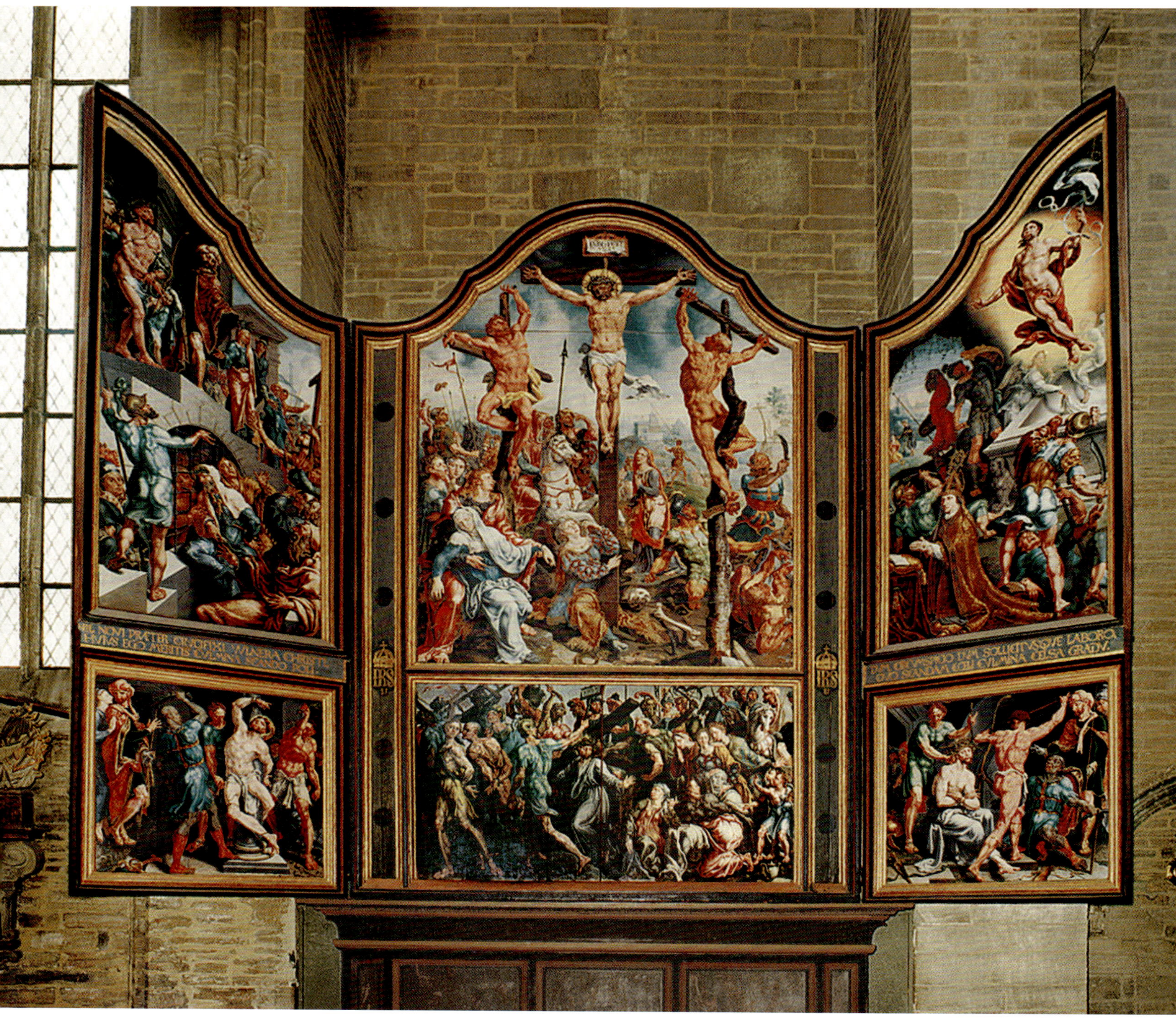

FIGURE 6 Maerten van Heemskerck, *Passion* triptych with scenes from the life of Saint Lawrence, 1538–42. Oil on panel; with frame: 405 × 790 cm (159 × 311 in.). Linköping Cathedral, Sweden

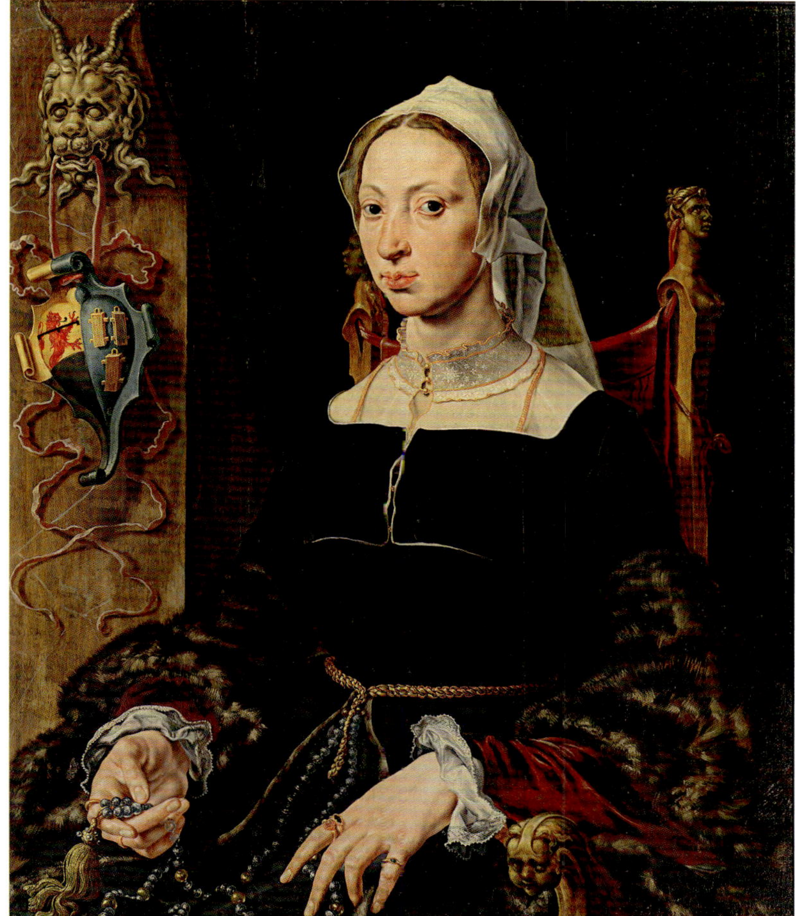

FIGURE 7 Maerten van Heemskerck, *Portrait of Machtelt Suijs*, ca. 1540–45. Oil on panel, 85 × 74 cm (33 7/16 × 29 1/8 in.). The Cleveland Museum of Art

Kunsten) and an altarpiece for the Haarlem Drapers' Guild (1546; center panel, now lost; Frans Hals Museum), among many others for churches and cloisters. The wave of riotous attacks on churches that swept across the Netherlands in 1566, accompanied by the violent destruction of paintings, sculptures, and other works of art associated with Catholic worship by Protestant iconoclasts, destroyed several of his paintings and all but ended such commissions.[12]

In both large-scale as well as private devotional paintings, Heemskerck created vivid compositions of dynamic figures, intensified by strong modeling and sophisticated use of vibrant color. Recent studies suggest that he worked in an efficient technique outside the norm of regional practice (see Szafran and Phenix). While the extreme poses and often-exaggerated features of his historical subjects intensify the narrative, his best portraits of the 1540s are equally forceful as elegant and monumental presences. They are often executed with swift, sure brushwork that is attentive to both likeness and the precise rendering of costume and jewelry. In his *Portrait of Machtelt Suijs*, strong light emphasizes both the inscrutable demeanor of the sitter and the undulating forms of her fingers, costume, and rosary (fig. 7).[13] Described admiringly by Van Mander as an artist who was "by nature diligent" (*van natueren vlijtigh wesende*) and who "worked steadily and was

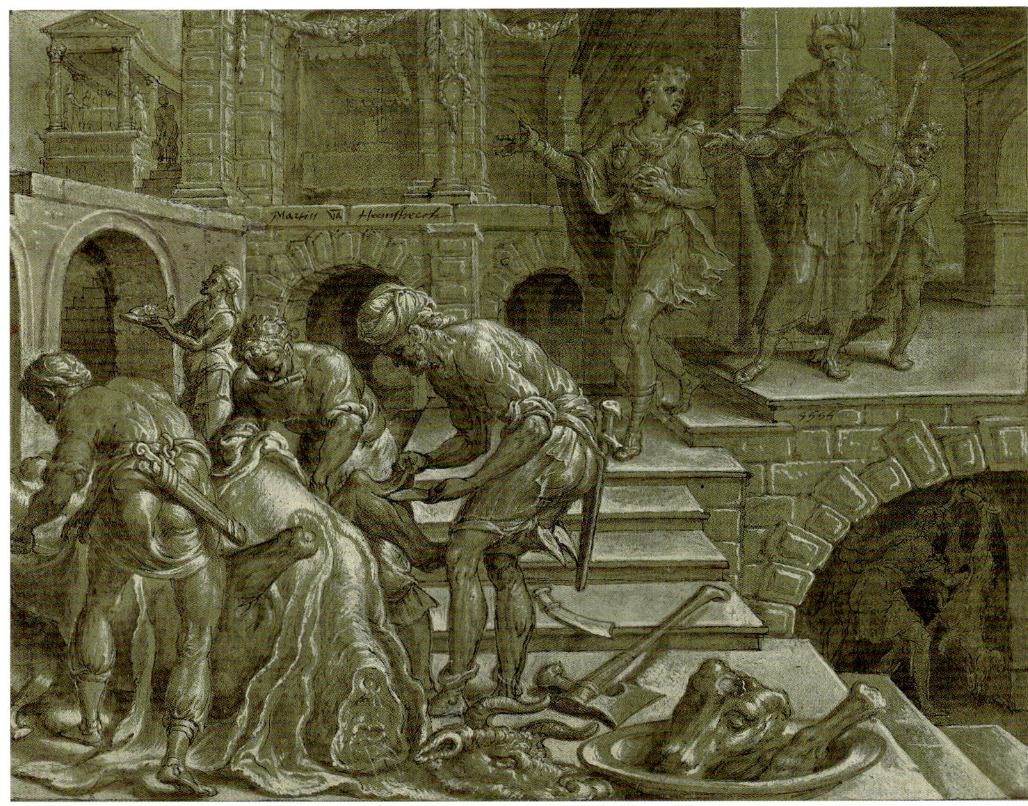

FIGURE 8 Maerten van Heemskerck, *The Parable of the King Who Prepared a Wedding*, 1555. Pen and brown ink, brush and wash over black chalk, heightened with white gouache on green prepared paper; incised; 20.3 × 26.4 cm (8 × 10 3/8 in.). Los Angeles, J. Paul Getty Museum

very quick in execution" (*al stadich wrocht, en seer veerdich van handelingh was*), Heemskerck was undoubtedly assisted by a studio, about which little is known.[14]

Intensely busy as a print designer from the late 1530s onward, Heemskerck produced several hundred drawings for professional printmakers that disseminated his reworking of antique sources and showcased his skill in devising complex figural compositions.[15] *The Parable of the King Who Prepared a Wedding* (fig. 8), for example, demonstrates his interest in color and architectural settings, while the detailed handling of *Judith* (fig. 9) reveals the refined technique of his draftsmanship.[16] Heemskerck drew continuously upon his intimate knowledge of ancient architecture and sculpture. He asserted the centrality of his Roman training anew in 1553 with his *Self-Portrait, with the Colosseum, Rome* (see fig. 1), in which he stands before a landscape with an artist (perhaps the youthful Heemskerck himself) intently drawing the Colosseum. A leading citizen of Haarlem, he held several civic posts and served as dean of the Haarlem Guild of Painters. Married twice with no children, Heemskerck became prosperous over the course of his career, and he even lent a large sum to Haarlem so that the city could ransom goods looted by Spanish forces during the 1572 siege.[17] Heemskerck died in 1574 at age seventy-six, a "special light for art in his time,"[18] and was buried in Saint Bavo's Cathedral in Haarlem. The impact of his inventions, particularly the rich iconography of his prints, influenced Rembrandt Harmensz van Rijn (1606–1669), among many others,[19] and reverberated well into the eighteenth century.

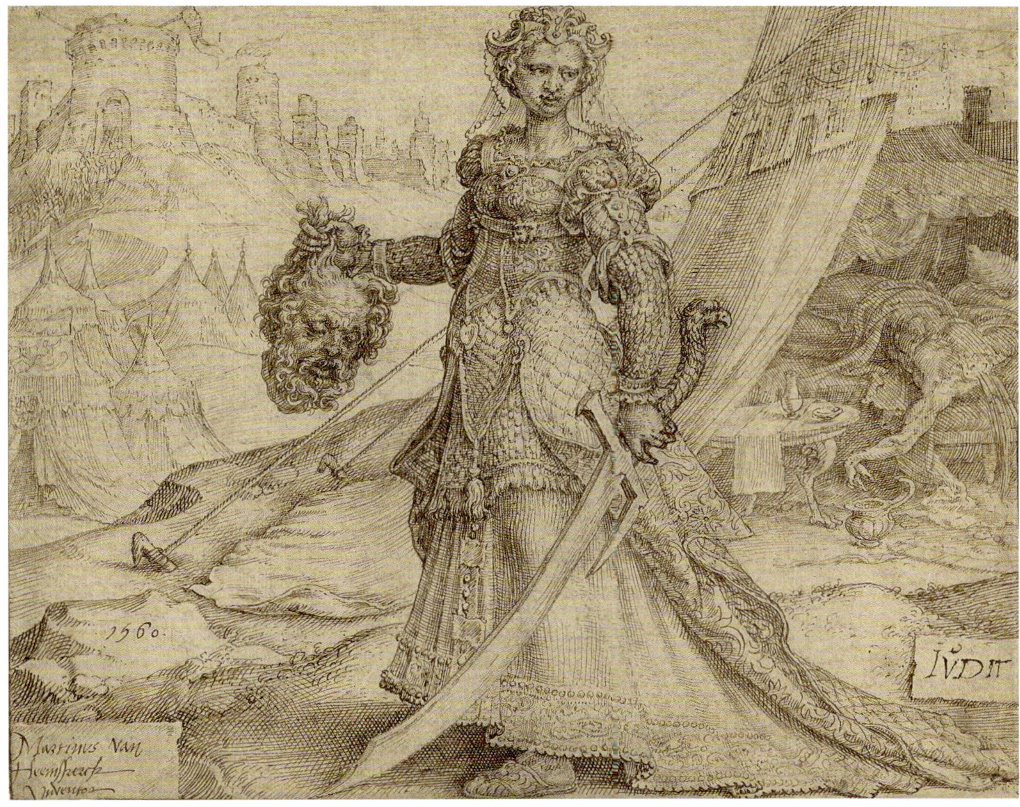

FIGURE 9 Maerten van Heemskerck, *Judith*, 1560. Pen and dark brown and light brown ink over black chalk; incised for transfer; 19.8 × 25.2 cm (7 13/16 × 9 15/16 in.). Los Angeles, J. Paul Getty Museum

THE *ECCE HOMO* TRIPTYCH

Heemskerck was sought by patrons throughout the northern Netherlands eager to possess his beautiful and memorable compositions. Although initially the enormous *Passion* triptych and individual portraits of many of the leading Alkmaar citizens involved in its commission and financing kept the artist busy through at least 1542, he was drawn to Dordrecht shortly thereafter to execute at least two altarpieces. The oldest city in the Netherlands, Dordrecht enjoyed considerable importance as a port strategically located at the confluence of several rivers and was the seat of significant government operations, such as the Mint of Holland (Munt van Holland), which had produced most of the coinage for Holland since 1366. Heemskerck's first Dordrecht altarpiece, the *Ecce Homo* triptych (now in Warsaw), was commissioned in about 1544 by one of its leading citizens, the wealthy and powerful Jan van Drenckwaerdt (d. 1549), for his chapel in the Augustinian church. It portrays Jan and his second wife, Margaretha de Jonge van Baertwyck (d. 1542).[20] A member of one of the city's most influential families, Jan was the eldest son of the mayor (*burgomeester*), Willem van Drenckwaerdt (d. 1488), and one of twenty-two children. Jan served as sheriff (*schout*) of Dordrecht from 1516 until his death in 1549.[21] An office traditionally held by members of Dordrecht's circumscribed patriciate, such as the Drenckwaerdts, the sheriff was appointed by Charles V in his capacity as the Count of Holland and carried authority apart from the city government. As the highest officer of the law in the city, the sheriff enforced the Right of Staple (the central privileges granted Dordrecht by the Counts of Holland in the late thirteenth and early fourteenth centuries to control and tax goods transported through its port), upheld city laws, and arrested and prosecuted offenders.[22] Jan could have met Heemskerck in connection with the artist's brief passage through the city on his way home from Rome or, more likely, through familial connections to Haarlem and the *Passion* triptych in Alkmaar.[23] The second commission, a smaller altarpiece completed in about 1545 (the central panel of which is now lost), portrays members of the De Vriese–Van Meerdervoort families, who also held important government offices and were related to the Drenckwaerdts.[24]

Heemskerck, renowned as a leading painter of the day, was ideally suited to execute the specific program of the Drenckwaerdt altarpiece. His modern imagery had already met the desires of patrons for powerful aids to devotion. He addressed the values of his Dordrecht patron by combining two compelling visual modes in the altarpiece: the potent language of devotional imagery articulating Christ's suffering and the learned, elite idioms influenced by ancient and modern Rome that were associated at the time with Emperor Charles V and Habsburg authority in the Netherlands. The altarpiece, comprising a central panel and two double-sided wings, attests to the devoutness of Jan and Margaretha. In the central panel, the viewer confronts the hunched and bound figure of Christ, wearing the crown of thorns and holding a makeshift reed scepter, emblems of kingship. The purple robe in which the soldiers dressed him has fallen from his shoulders, and he stands humbly, eyes downcast, at the edge of the stone *praetorium*. On the right, Pontius Pilate, taller and vividly attired, believing in Christ's innocence, presents him to the crowd with the words *Ecce Homo* ("Behold the Man!"), eliciting riotous derision and vociferous calls for Christ's crucifixion from the tight circle of spectators.[25] In keeping with tradition, Christ's tormentors are portrayed as savage and bestial. The startling intensity of their exaggerated physical attributes, such as bulging neck muscles, splayed fingers, gaping mouths, and bared, rotting teeth, draws attention to the quiet suffering of Christ. With the arched stone interior of the palace only dimly suggested and the number of onlookers reduced to a handful who serve as antitheses of response, the theatricality of the spectacle is brought into sharp focus. Recent cleaning permits a clearer view of several shadowy figures behind and to the side of Pilate (see figs. 51, 52, and 53) whose dim presence casts the foreground figures into strong relief. The man in the red cloak in the left foreground registers restrained shock in a manner strongly reminiscent of Raphael's expressive apostles in the foreground of *The Transfiguration*. In contrast, the sneering soldier behind Christ and Pilate who holds the switch used to flagellate Christ (partially obscured by the frame, but visible in fig. 31) and the rope binding Christ's wrists, along with the soldier dressed in green scale armor in the foreground, are familiar types from the *Saint Lawrence* altarpiece. Repulsive and grotesque, they personify the baseness of humanity. Artists often included youthful participants emulating the disrespectful behavior of their elders in scenes of Christ's degradation; perhaps the young man portrayed with such immediacy on the far left was an assistant in Heemskerck's studio.[26]

The Mocking of Christ and *Ecce Homo* themes preoccupied Heemskerck throughout his career in both paintings and prints. Central to his treatments of the presentation of the scourged Christ by Pilate to the crowd (ca. 1540–50), including the print series The Fall and Salvation of

Mankind through the Life and Passion of Christ (fig. 10) and paintings such as those for the *Saint Lawrence* altarpiece, is the juxtaposition of the collapsed yet magisterial Christ with the tensile figure of Pilate, whose authority is articulated by the elegant *contrapposto* of the ancient and modern marble sculptures upon which the figure is based.[27] Sixteenth-century patrons, who valued brilliant color and an admirable technique in their paintings, would not have been concerned by the repetition of popular subjects. In the Drenckwaerdt altarpiece, Heemskerck condensed the spectacle into a scene of great intensity. The robust figures fill the confines of the narrow panel to the foreground, confronting viewers with Christ's suffering and engaging them in the drama as witnesses. The tight circle of tormentors crowding the meek figure of Christ recalls Hieronymus Bosch's *Christ Mocked* (fig. 11), while the Antwerp master Jan Sanders van Hemessen's rowdy

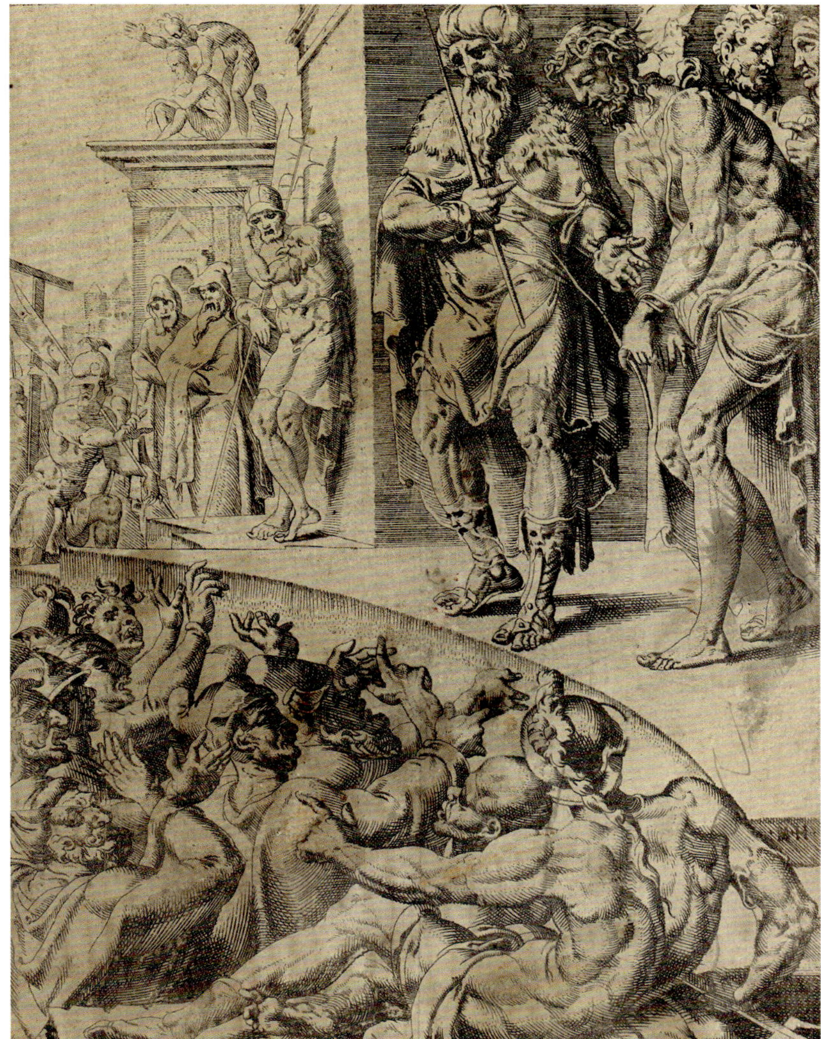

FIGURE 10 Dirck Volkertsz Coornhert (Dutch, 1522–1590) after Maerten van Heemskerck, *Ecce Homo*, 1544, from the series The Fall and Salvation of Mankind through the Life and Passion of Christ, 1548. Etching, 24.5 × 19.2 cm (9 2/3 × 7 1/2 in.). London, British Museum

Mocking of Christ (fig. 12) of the same year (1544) continues the traditional placement of Christ at the center but expands the figures to three-quarter length. Heemskerck's innovative full-length composition permits a wide range of expression, particularly since Christ stands to one side of the commanding Roman governor of Judaea. Pilate, whose gesture also eloquently directs our attention to the left wing, perhaps represented a cautionary example for Drenckwaerdt in the exercise of his office as sheriff. In combining seemingly disparate elements of forms derived from antique sculptural sources and expressive high style, Heemskerck embraced the essential duality of Roman high-style painting. The emotional impact of the scene, generated by the agitated contours, powerful modeling, and contorted poses of the figures, was accentuated by the artist's vibrant palette, though the intensity of the color and the chromatic juxtapositions between hues have changed significantly over time. In particular, the evidence of Christ's torture was originally far more dramatic, with bright red blood dripping copiously from wounds in his face and torso across his left shoulder and landing at his feet (see fig. 50).[28]

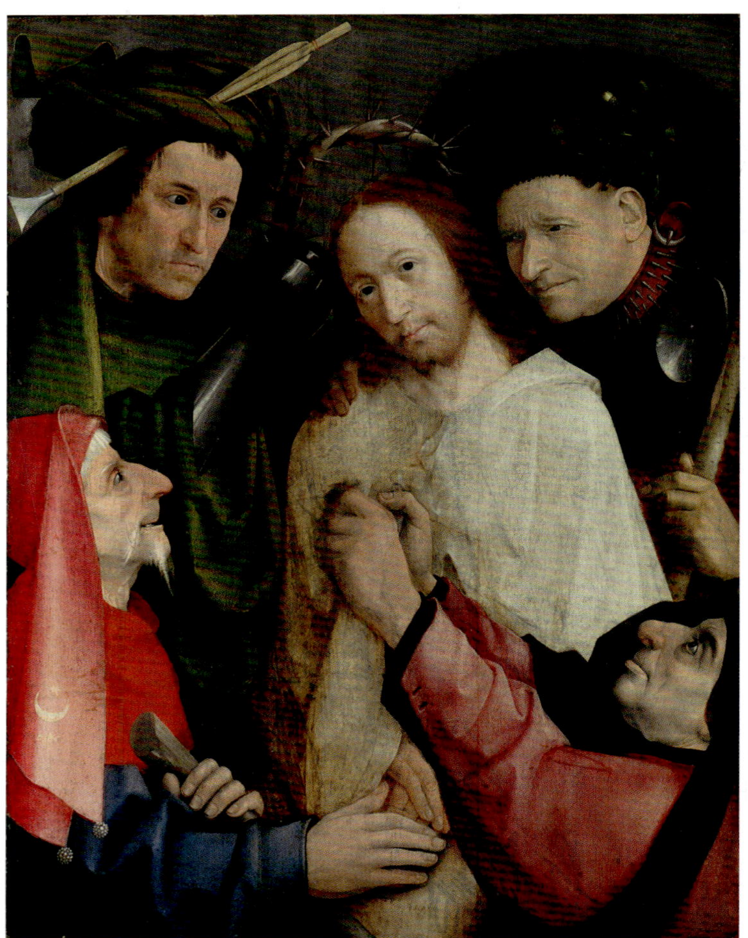

FIGURE 11 Hieronymus Bosch (Netherlandish, ca. 1450–1516), *Christ Mocked*, ca. 1490–1500. Oil on panel, 73.5 × 59.1 cm (29 × 23¼ in.). London, National Gallery

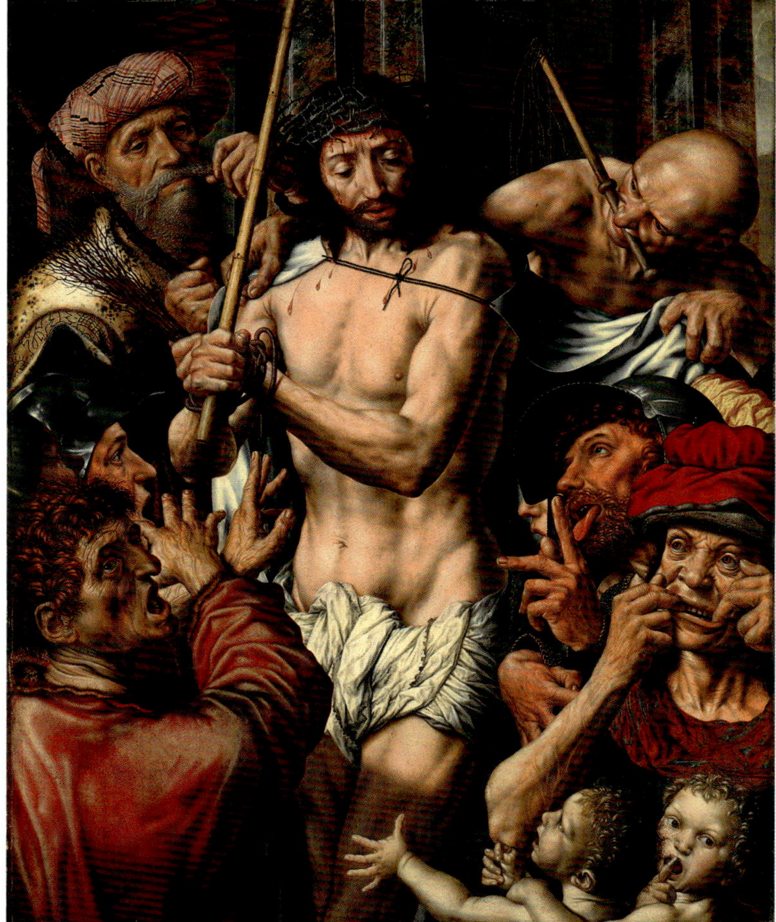

FIGURE 12 Jan Sanders van Hemessen (Flemish, active 1519–1556), *Mocking of Christ*, 1544. Oil on panel, 123 × 102.5 cm (48½ × 40⅓ in.). Munich, Alte Pinakothek

From their respective positions in the side panels, Jan van Drenckwaerdt (left) and Margaretha (right) kneel in prayer and gaze steadfastly at the *Ecce Homo* (see frontispiece). The prie-dieux draped in green velvet are decorated with their coats of arms. In the left wing Jan's red shield is quartered with a swan and a rampant lion with a label of three points, signifying Jan's descent from the Counts of Holland, and in the right wing the arms of Margaretha's distinguished family are halved with those of her husband.[29] The couple married after 1519 (it was the second marriage for both) and had no children.[30] In the left wing Jan's namesake, Saint John the Evangelist, holds his attribute of the chalice with the dragon in his left hand, a reference to the attempt to poison him as a test of his faith, and blesses the sheriff with his right.[31] Over a red garment Jan wears a magnificent long black *tabbaard* lined with lynx fur (virtually the uniform of distinguished men of the period) that reveals deep red sleeves. His arms protrude from the upper opening of the *tabbaard* sleeve, allowing the long remainder, clearly lined in the same fur, to hang below. A gold chain falls between the folds of his collar, and the large gold signet ring is decorated with his coat of arms. Margaretha's patron saint, Margaret of Antioch, presents and protects her in the traditional manner. Elegantly composed, her head covered by a diaphanous veil held in place by a gilt circlet ornamented with a lion's head (see fig. 59), the saint holds the cross—with which she was said to have escaped Satan in the form of a dragon that had consumed her (the dragon rears up beside Margaretha's left shoulder)—and an open Bible.[32] The page on the right bears the date of the triptych, 1544, and text beginning "Margarieta s . . . ," which is otherwise indecipherable. The appearance of the date of the altarpiece above her underscores the likelihood that the altarpiece served primarily as an epitaph (*memorietafel*) for Margaretha, who died in 1542, and then for her husband, who died in 1549. The couple was buried in the chapel and also portrayed in a stained-glass window (now lost) in the exterior wall.[33] Befitting her privileged status and wealth, Margaretha is richly dressed in a white linen cap and blouse tied at the neck and a black gown with a velvet bodice lined in fur that cascades, in the height of fashion, in palpably soft folds above red velvet sleeves.[34] A jeweled rosary of gold and coral beads hangs from her gold girdle chain and rests on the prie-dieu, while four gold rings set with precious stones adorn her fingers.

While the central panel exemplifies Heemskerck's forceful physical style of the early 1540s and would have been considered a modern articulation of Christ's suffering and humanity by contemporaries, he combined traditional Netherlandish features with his Italianate style in the wings. The mixture of old and new, classical and Northern elements strongly appealed to learned patrons. Jan and Margaretha are portrayed with Heemskerck's characteristic elegance and sensitivity as well as close attention to detail. Seen in three-quarter view, the sitters appear aloof and dignified, in keeping with the solemn commemorative purpose of their likenesses in the chapel. The heads have been executed somewhat more freely than in independent portraits of this period, such as *Portrait of Machtelt Suijs* (see fig. 7). The brushwork is complemented by the animated folds and textures of velvets and furs. It is intriguing to consider when Heemskerck might have recorded Margaretha's likeness, given her death in 1542, two years before the date on the wing in which she appears. The artist may have made a drawing very early in the planning stages of the triptych, or he may have relied on an extant portrait of Margaretha in rendering her likeness posthumously. Heemskerck also imparted monumentality to his patrons, presenting Jan and Margaretha as substantial, forceful presences within the crowded fields afforded by the side panels.

Saint Margaret of Antioch, clad in a clinging chemise belted under the bust in the manner of the ancient sculpture Heemskerck sketched in Rome (see fig. 3), contrasts with the mature Margaretha de Jonge van Baertwyck. In the juxtaposition of these female figures, Heemskerck indulged his fascination with analogous qualities of skin and stone, moving from Margaretha's fashionably pale complexion to the statuesque saint and finally to the marble decoration of the interior itself. Two small statuettes in a niche, a woman holding a snake and another wearing a crown of flowers and cradling a dove, offer a further commentary on Margaretha's Christian virtues. Heemskerck's allegorical language was specific and fairly consistent, and the two figures may represent Prudence and Sincerity.[35] Panels of antique trophies in low relief decorate the back wall. As a result of the recent cleaning, the corresponding ornamentation in the left wing behind Saint John is now more clearly visible. A dark stone relief of a mounted soldier trampling a barbarian woman appears on the wall behind the chalice, and bands of reliefs with nude soldiers cover the back wall.[36] Two statuettes, a man (at left) and possibly a woman holding an orb, occupy a niche over the saint's left shoulder. The relief decorations in the wings of the altarpiece are free variations on the sculpted friezes Heemskerck had drawn in Rome, particularly those on the Arch of Constantine, while the niche figures recall other Roman monuments and Renaissance displays of antiquities. A testament to the thoughtfulness with which Heemskerck undertook the commission, the antique ornamentation underscores Jan's erudition and humanist taste as well as serving as a reference to his authority.

By contrast, the exterior of the altarpieces is simpler, with both patron saints repeated in grisaille. Part of a long tradition, with origins in the oeuvre of Jan van Eyck (ca. 1395–1441), the heavy, fictive stone figures of Saint John and Saint Margaret are draped in the manner of antique sculpture. Saint Margaret's straight-angled features resemble other visages in Heemskerck's paintings and prints from the period. While the sturdiness of the proportions and a certain bluntness of the figures suggest that they are largely the product of the workshop, they were nonetheless carefully conceived to create the illusion of stone sculptures standing in niches and particularly to take advantage of the diagonal viewing angle from the entrance to the chapel. Strong light from the left, from the windows in the far wall of the nave and through the entrance to the chapel, would highlight the projecting joints of their legs and shoulders, cast shadows on the marble wall behind, and illuminate cracks in the lobate vaults above them. Saint John the Evangelist holds the chalice by the stem, with Satan taking the form of a serpent. Impervious to the roar of the dragon at her feet, Saint Margaret gestures emphatically with the cross while marking her place in the open Bible. With the attributes of the cross and Bible held in balance, the saint recalls Heemskerck's representation of Faith (fig. 13), and she surely bears this additional meaning here and in the inside wing.[37] Since the doors of the triptych were opened to reveal the colorful interior scenes only on Sundays and important church feast days, the grisaille saints were the most visible aspect of the *Ecce Homo* altarpiece.

The activated triptych disclosed another surprise when the doors were drawn aside: the elaborately carved, painted, and gilded frame around the central panel. This extraordinary feature evokes the magnificent celebratory architecture of a triumphal arch: a shallow, coffered vault spans the central field, ending in pilasters decorated with plaques bearing the motto ESPOIR / CONFORT / DRENCKWAIRT (Hope brings comfort [to the] Drenckwaerdt[s]).[38] This dictum refers to the solace to be taken by the Drenckwaerdts as they meditate on Christ's sacrifice and their hope for salvation.[39] Beneath the inscriptions, a hand emerges from a cloud holding a pierced ewer from which dew spills forth to form a hanging garland composed of fruit, flowers, and two placards with the date 1544.[40] The ewer motif may be both a play on the family name—*drinkwaart* / worth drinking—and a reference to the Song of Salvation: "Thy dead men shall live, together with my dead body shall they arise. Awake and sing, ye that dwell in dust: for thy dew is as the dew of herbs, and the earth shall cast out the dead."[41] Scrolling foliate decoration reminiscent of Roman

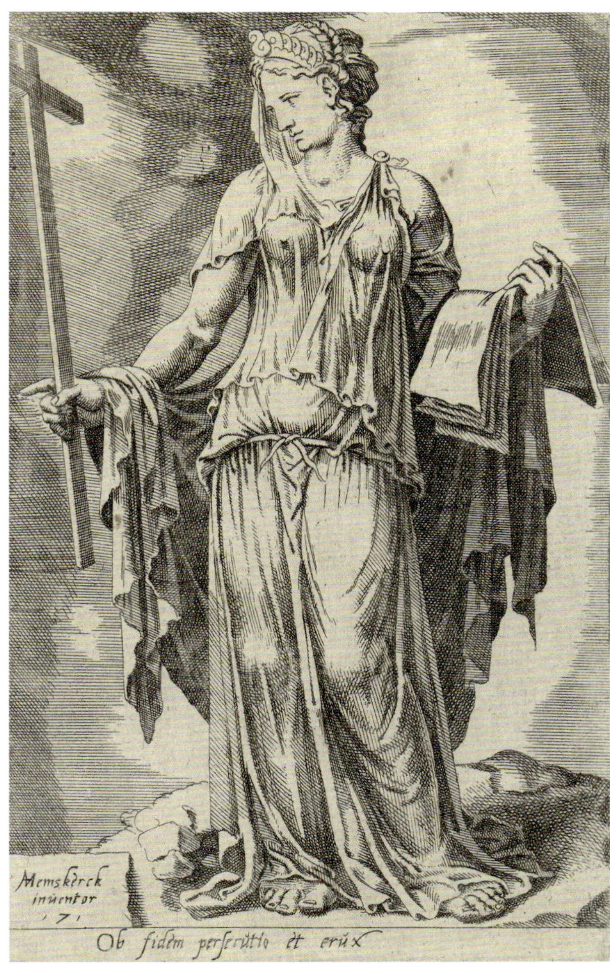

FIGURE 13 Dirck Volkertsz Coornhert (Dutch, 1522–1590) after Maerten van Heemskerck, *Faith Engendering Persecution*, 1550, from the series The Road to Eternal Bliss, 1550. Etching, 21.9 × 14.2 cm (8½ × 5½ in.). Amsterdam, Rijksmuseum

architectural ornament adorns narrow panels on either side. The pilasters, set at a slight angle, together with the vaulted arch, suggest a receding corridor through which the *Ecce Homo* is visible. The forced perspectival framework is closely related to the popular *inkijkgens* (squint views) that decorated pulpits, choir screens, and other architectural features in the Netherlands, and that were themselves often indebted to the fantastic architecture of Heemskerck's prints.[42]

While tabernacle frames with perspective arches had been common in Italy since the late fifteenth century, classicizing architectural vocabulary became more available in the Netherlands following the 1539 publication of Sebastiano Serlio's treatise on architecture.[43] Both of these accessible sources could have provided models for the frame. However, the combination of the coffered perspectival arch and allegorical decoration suggests that Heemskerck himself was closely involved with the design of the Drenckwaerdt altarpiece frame. It was not uncommon for painters to be responsible for providing frames for altarpieces, due perhaps to the practicalities of painting on a prepared panel with an engaged frame.[44] Here the fundamentally propagandistic mode of the triumphal arch form alluded to Jan's humanist interests, but it was also a powerful statement of his eminent status and allegiance to Charles V. Dordrecht had recently affirmed its loyalty to the emperor, receiving him with splendid ceremony in September 1540. The extensive carved decoration of the choir stalls in the Grote Kerk, created between 1538 and 1542, celebrated Charles V with scenes of ancient Roman and religious triumphs and extensive use of "antique" decoration (fig. 14).[45] On September 25, 1549, the year of Jan van Drenckwaerdt's death, Charles V, together with his son and heir, the future Philip II, made an even more spectacular entry into Dordrecht with an illustrious retinue, and the two were honored with many "displays, gates, paintings and triumphal arches."[46] The monumental arched form of the ephemeral event was repeated in the carved-stone entrance to the mint, located close to the Augustinian church and rebuilt by the emperor in 1555 (fig. 15). Heemskerck's Roman drawings, such as *The Arch of Constantine* (see fig. 4), reveal his interest in the impressive surviving arches in Rome, and in his biography, Van Mander remarked on Heemskerck's skill as an architect.[47] He may therefore have designed the frame for the Drenckwaerdt altarpiece himself, or more likely, his ideas were executed by the atelier of one of the sculptors active in imperial service, such as Jean Mone (ca. 1485/90–ca. 1549), according to Heemskerck's specifications. Dordrecht was an active center of creative wood carving in the mid-sixteenth century, and the relief work on the decorated frame is compatible with that on the Grote Kerk choir stalls and other civic commissions, such as the large oak chimneypiece for the Kloveniers Guild hall (ca. 1560; Dordrecht, Simon van Gijn Museum), which includes fruit tendrils with plaques.[48] Although impressive, the Drenckwaerdt frame lacks rigor in the combination of architectural elements. For example, the angles of the vault and pilasters are not coordinated, and the archway lacks the usual interior side walls. These eccentricities suggest that the narrow format of the central panel and the dimensions of the chapel imposed constraints on its design, and more important, that the frame was created by local Dordrecht craftsmen charged with carrying out sophisticated ideas for a specific location.[49]

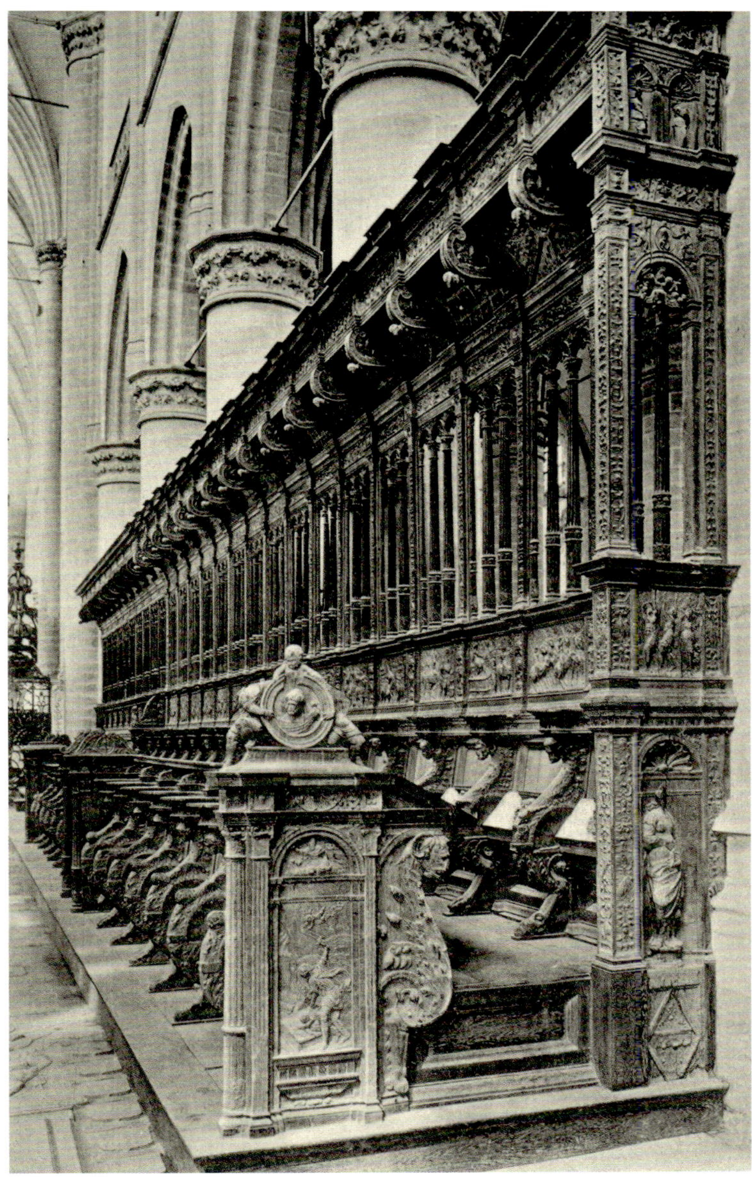

FIGURE 14 North choir stalls, 1538–39, Grote Kerk, Dordrecht

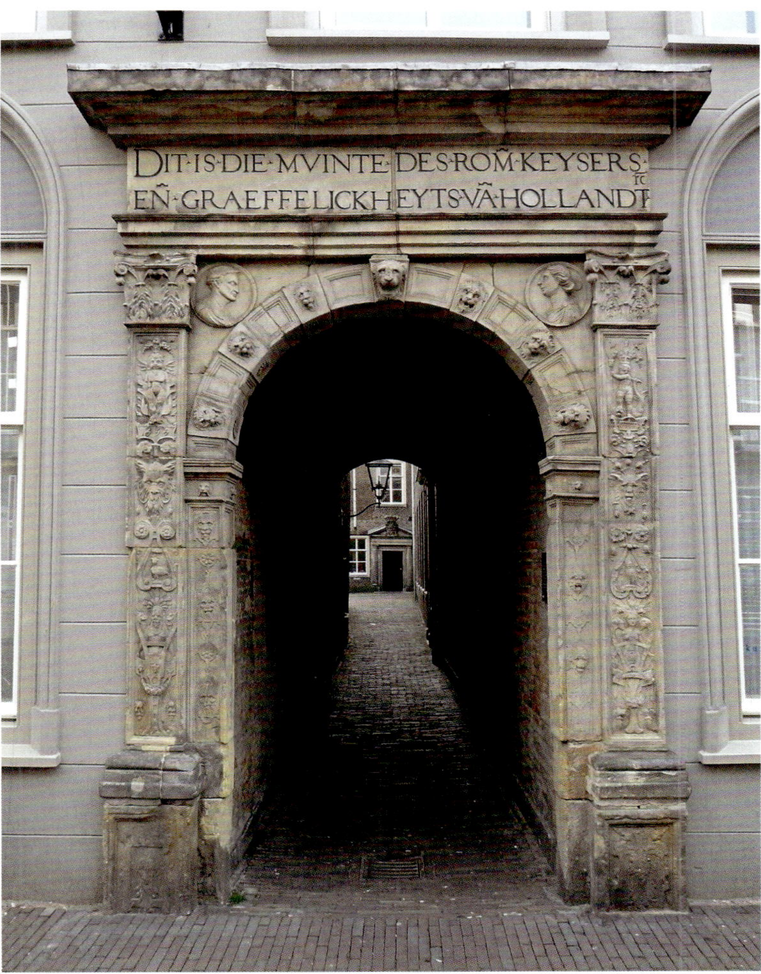

FIGURE 15 Entrance to the Mint of Holland, 1555, Dordrecht

THE DRENCKWAERDT CHAPEL The *Ecce Homo* altarpiece almost certainly decorated the altar in Jan van Drenckwaerdt's chapel, which had a privileged location in the church that belonged to Dordrecht's Augustinian cloister (fig. 16).[50] Founded in 1275, the monastery was one of the city's oldest and most prestigious foundations as well as the biggest and most important Augustinian cloister in the Netherlands. A center of learning and teaching, it attracted multitudes of laymen to its church, who flocked to hear sermons held in the vernacular. In about 1450 the old single-aisle monastery church was replaced with a new choir and nave. Additional space was needed to accommodate the almost overwhelming number of people who wished to be buried in the church, where masses for the dead were said regularly.[51] An aisle was added on the southwest side of the nave, along with four separate private chapels.[52] The two center chapels (fig. 17) were erected by the Drenckwaerdt family and used by Jan himself and his father, Willem.[53] Rectangular in shape, the chapels were lit from both sides, notably by the bank of windows that lined the nave of the church on the left (fig. 18).

The church of the Augustinians served as an important spiritual and communal center. Guilds held their meetings in its large dining room, and the church itself hosted confraternities dedicated to Saint Catherine and Saint Nicholas. Jan belonged to the venerable Brotherhood of Saint Anthony Abbot, whose membership was drawn from Dordrecht's most prestigious families.[54] Pieter Bruegel the Elder's church interior depicts five sacraments, with an emphasis on the instruction of faith, and vividly evokes the busy atmosphere of the interior of the Augustinian church as

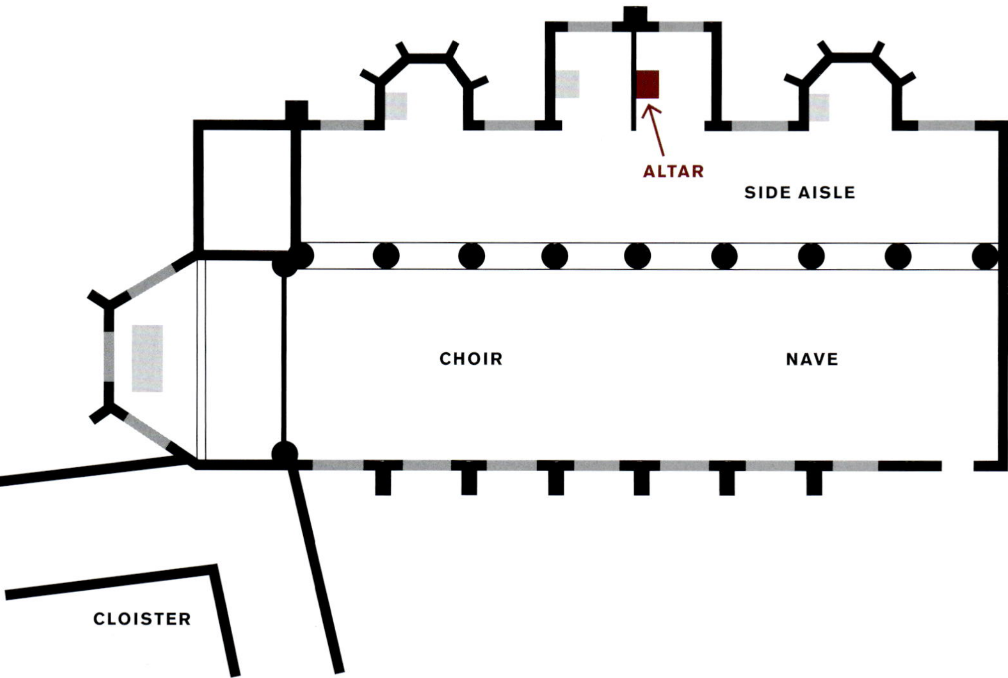

FIGURE 16 Schematic ground plan of the Augustinian church, Dordrecht, showing Jan van Drenckwaerdt's chapel and altar

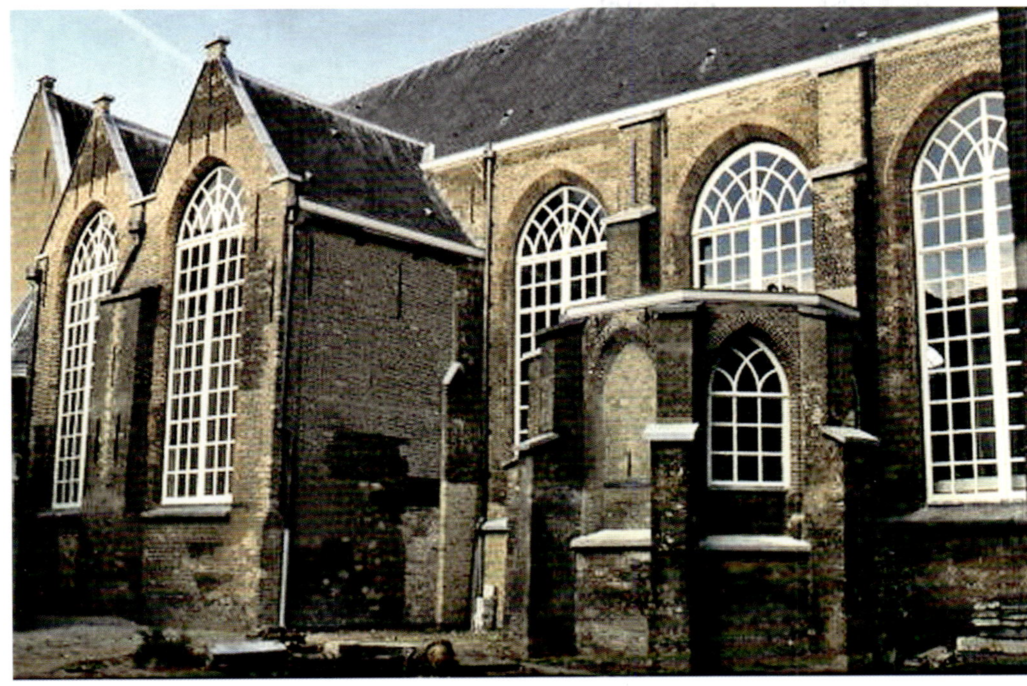

FIGURE 17 Exterior of the Augustinian church, Dordrecht, from the southeast, with the two Drenckwaerdt chapels on the left

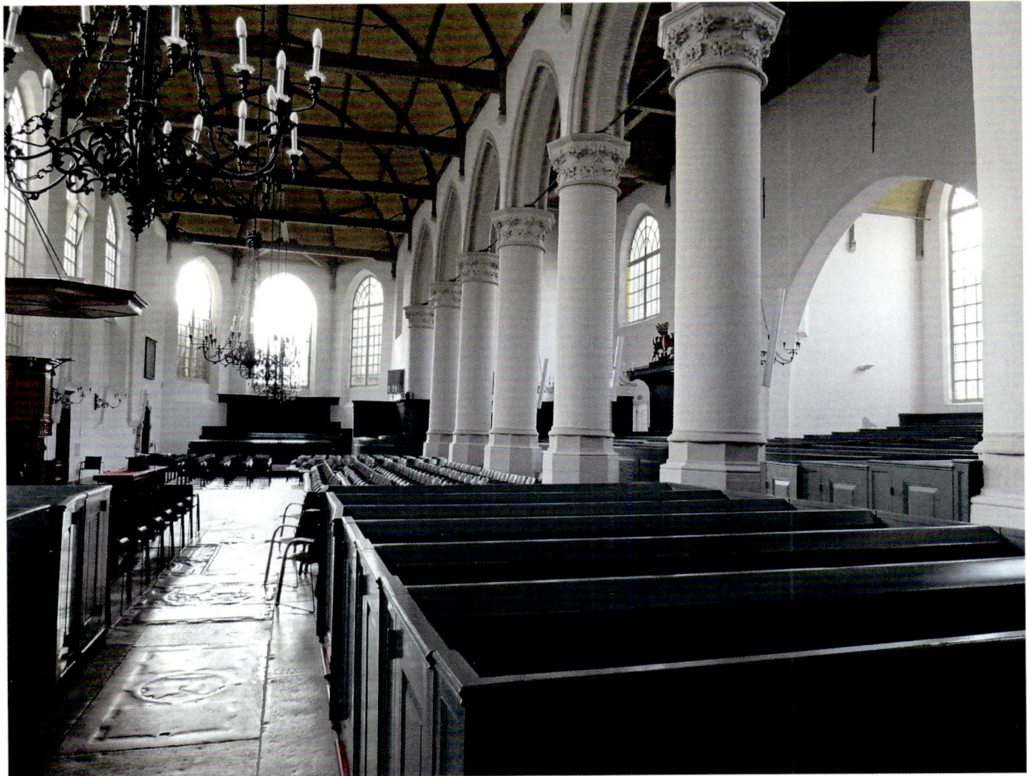

FIGURE 18 Interior of the Augustinian church, Dordrecht, with the former Drenckwaerdt chapels, now a single bay, on the right

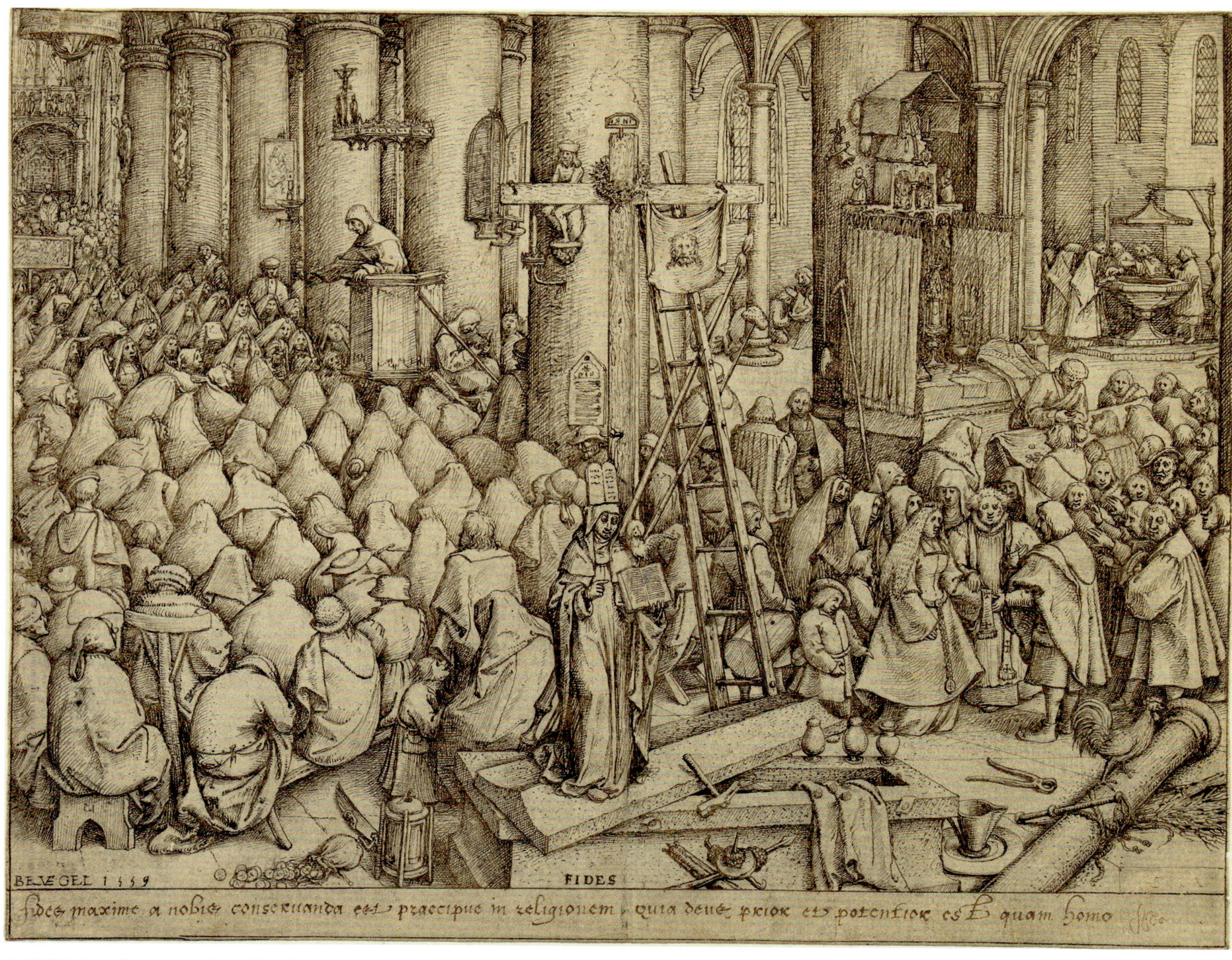

FIGURE 19 Pieter Bruegel the Elder (Flemish, ca. 1525/30–1569), *Faith*, 1559. Pen and brown ink; contours indented for transfer; 22.5 × 29.5 cm (8 7/8 × 11 5/8 in.). Amsterdam, Rijksmuseum

many activities take place simultaneously (fig. 19). In Dordrecht the vast quantity of graves discovered during recent renovation indicates that there must have been an almost unceasing cycle of burials, with the concomitant flow of attendees to mass and the pungent combination of incense and deteriorating bodies.[55] The whitewashed interior of the church today reflects its use by the Reformed faith since 1572. Earlier in the sixteenth century, during the period of Catholic worship, it would have presented a more ornamented appearance, though probably not lavish, given the Augustinian order's commitment to poverty. The lower parts of the walls, themselves quite possibly colored deep red or some other rich hue, were enlivened by painted decoration, notably around the organ in the side aisle, and polychromed statues of Saint Augustine and other saints might have stood on altars and against pillars. Elaborately carved gravestones covered the floor. Painted and/or sculpted altarpieces probably stood on the altars of all four private chapels and the high altar, although the appearance and construction of these altars remain a mystery. Stained-glass windows at the side would have transmitted dancing colored light through those confined spaces. Remarkably, the *Ecce Homo* triptych is the sole surviving altarpiece from the church. Liturgical music was integral to services in the church, where the monks sang, and confraternities and individual patrons hired minstrels as part of masses celebrating the name days of their patron saints.[56]

POSTSCRIPT

While the first stirrings of Martin Luther's ideas reached Dordrecht in 1519 and affected the cloister in the early 1520s, the monastery remained relatively calm from the 1530s onward. Decades later the *Ecce Homo* triptych itself was caught up in, and indeed saved by, the turmoil of political and religious change in the Netherlands that would eventually lead to the establishment of the independent Dutch Republic. Jan's nephew Willem van Drenckwaerdt held the post of sheriff after Jan's death. Like his uncle, Willem was a staunch Catholic and was known for his uncompromising pursuit of Anabaptists. In 1572, the fourth year of the Dutch Revolt, when the so-called Watergeuzen (the Protestant rebel forces known as "sea beggars"), led by the Calvinist William de Lumey, baron de la Marck, blocked the port on June 25 and demanded Dordrecht's submission, Willem's orders to the city's militia to hold firm were countermanded. Dordrecht became the first city to formally side with the Revolt, an act of rebellion against Philip II. The Watergeuzen and representatives from cities across the northern provinces met in secret in the great dining room of the Augustinian church. During the First Assembly of the Free States (Eerste Vrije Statenvergadering), July 19–23, also known as the Union of Dordrecht (Unie van Dordrecht), William of Orange was formally elected stadtholder and leader of the Revolt.[57] Willem van Drenckwaerdt was forced to flee, finally taking up residence in Brussels, where he died in 1606. The prior of the monastery, Jan Crabbe, was captured, and the monks fled the city. The first openly Reformed services of the rebellious provinces were held in the former Augustinian church on July 25, 1572. By that time, its decorations, including altarpieces, had been removed.[58] According to the Dordrecht historian Jan van Beverwijck, the painting in which "they [Jan van Drenckwaerdt and Margaretha de Jonge van

Baertwyck] were both artfully painted" was taken to the nearby house, called the Berkenpoort, of the city government's lawyer (*pensionaris*), Matthijs Berck (d. 1586).[59] A wealthy wine merchant and collector, Berck lived only a few hundred yards from the chapel, and the painting probably left through the door used by the congregation for burial services in the Van Beveren chapel. Like many other religious paintings of significance during the Dutch Revolt, the *Ecce Homo* triptych was swiftly redefined as a secular prized example of artistic mastery by one of the region's most famous painters. Berck was close to William of Orange, who stayed in the house in 1575–76, followed by other illustrious guests. Many works of art from Dordrecht's churches were sold and transferred during that period.[60] The triptych, including its "old, richly carved" frame, next reappeared at the Stuttgart auction of the Faber collection in 1870,[61] and subsequently entered the collection of the book publisher and municipal politician Heinrich von Korn of Breslau (1829–1907), joining contemporary works by Arnold Böcklin (1827–1901) and Adolf Menzel (1815–1905).[62] Von Korn presented the altarpiece to the Schlesische Museum von bildenden Künste Breslau, where he had been chairman of the consistory. The *Ecce Homo* triptych was later given by the museum to the National Museum in Warsaw; it has been part of the collection since 1946.[63]

NOTES

1. Karel van Mander, *Het Schilder-boeck* (Haarlem, 1604), fol. 244v. Hadrianus Junius, *Batavia: In qua praeter gentis et insulae antiquitatem originem* (Leiden, 1588). Unless otherwise noted, all translations are mine.

2. For the destruction of Heemskerck's works during the iconoclasm, see David Freedberg, "Art and Iconoclasm, 1525–1580: The Case of the North Netherlands," in *Kunst voor de Beeldenstorm: Noord-Nederlandse Kunst, 1525–1580; Catalogus,* exh. cat., edited by Jan Piet Filedt Kok, Willy Halsema-Kubes, and Wouter Th. Kloek (Amsterdam: Rijksmuseum, 1986), p. 77.

3. Reinhold Grosshans, *Maerten van Heemskerck: Die Gemälde* (Berlin: Horst Boettcher Verlag, 1980), pp. 159–62, 158, cat. 46; Hanna Benesz in *Transalpinum: From Giorgone and Dürer to Titian and Rubens; Painting from the Collections of the Kunsthistorisches Museum in Vienna, the National Museum in Warsaw, and the National Museum in Gdansk*, edited by Dorota Folga-Januszewska and Antoni Ziemba (Lesko: Bosz, 2004), p. 158, cat. 37.

4. The *Ecce Homo* triptych was included in the seminal exhibition organized by the Rijksmuseum, Amsterdam, *Kunst voor de Beeldenstorm: Noord-Nederlandse Kunst, 1525–1580,* exh. cat., edited by Jan Piet Filedt Kok, Willy Halsema-Kubes, and Wouter Th. Kloek (Amsterdam: Rijksmuseum, 1986), addendum (unpaginated), cat. 135 (entry by Jefferson C. Harrison).

5. For Heemskerck's training, see Junius, *Batavia*, p. 238; Van Mander, *Schilder-boeck,* fols. 244v–245r.

6. The painting was completed May 23, 1532; see Pieter Biesboer et al., *Painting in Haarlem, 1500–1850: The Collection of the Frans Hals Museum*, edited by Neeltje Köhler, translated by Jennifer Killian and Katy Kist (Ghent: Ludion, 2006), pp. 497–500, cat. 203 (entry by Epco Runia).

7. Although Van Mander says only that Heemskerck "boarded with or stayed with a cardinal through one or other recommendation" (*daer commend hadde zijn onderhoudt oft onthouden hy een Cardinael door eenighe recommendatie*), it is likely that Van Scorel introduced him to Enckenvoirdt; Van Mander, *Schilder-boeck*, fol. 245v; translation from Hessel Miedema, ed., *Karel van Mander: The Lives of the Illustrious Netherlandish and German Painters from the First Edition of the Schilder-boeck (1603–1604): Preceded by the Lineage, Circumstances, and Place of Birth, Life, and Works of Karel van Mander, Painter and Poet, and Likewise His Death and Burial, from the Second Edition of the Schilder-boeck (1616–1618)*, introduction and translation by Hessel Miedema (Doornspijk: Davaco, 1994–99), vol. 1, p. 241. The painter and biographer Giorgio Vasari met Heemskerck shortly after his arrival in Rome in early July 1532. Giorgio Vasari, *Le vite de' piu eccellenti pittori, scultori e architecttori*..., edited by Gaetano Milanesi, 7th ed., vol. 7 (Florence: G.C. Sansoni, 1906), p. 582.

8. Christian Hülsen and Hermann Egger, *Die römischen Skizzenbücher von Marten van Heemskerck im Königlichen Kupferstichkabinett zu Berlin*, 2 vols. (Berlin: Julius Bard, 1913–16); Ilja M. Veldman, "Heemskerck's Romeinse tekeningen en 'Anonymous B,'" *Nederlands Kunsthistorisch Jaarboek* 38 (1987), pp. 369–82.

9. "*Hy oock zijnen tijt niet verstapen noch versuymt by den Nederlanders met suypen oft andersmae heel veel dinghen geconterfeyt so nae d'Antijcken als nae Michel Angnolen wercken: Oock veel Ruywynen bywercken alderley*

aerdicheden der Antijcken die in deser Schilder-Academisch Stadt overvloedisch te sien zijn," Van Mander, *Schilder-boeck*, fol. 245v; translation from Miedema, ed., *Karel van Mander*, vol. 1, p. 241.

10. "*Un Martino, ed altri giovani tedeschi*" (A Martin, and other young Germans), Vasari, *Le vite*, vol. 6, p. 586; Miedema, ed., *Karel van Mander*, vol. 4, translated by Derry Cook-Radmore (1997), p. 80.

11. Two albums of drawings survive in the Kupferstichkabinett, Berlin; see Hülsen and Egger, *Die römischen Skizzenbücher*. For the influence of Giulio Romano's frescoes in the Palazzo del Te, Mantua, on Heemskerck, see Ilja M. Veldman, *Maarten van Heemskerck and Dutch Humanism in the Sixteenth Century*, edited by Michael Hoyle (Maarssen: Gary Schwartz, 1977), p. 12.

12. Van Mander, *Schilder-boeck*, fol. 246r–v; Grosshans, *Maerten van Heemskerck*, pp. 23–24, 133–48, cat. 29; pp. 171–76, cat. 55; pp. 45, 148–49, cat. 45; David Freedberg, *Iconoclasm and Painting in the Revolt in the Netherlands, 1566–1609* (Ph.D. diss., Oxford, 1972), *Outstanding Theses in the Fine Arts from British Universities* (New York: Garland, 1988).

13. Jan van Drenckwaerdt was related to Machtelt Suijs through his second marriage, to Margaretha de Jonge van Baertwyck. Machtelt's husband, Dirick van Teijlingen, *kerkmeester* (church warden) of the Sint-Laurenskerk in Alkmaar, was one of the donors who financed the *Passion* triptych. Jan and Margaretha attended their wedding, and Jan's brother Boudewijn van Drenckwaerdt married Machtelt's younger sister; see Ann Tzeutschler Lurie, "Heemskerck's *Portrait of Machtelt Suijs* at the Cleveland Museum of Art," *Burlington* 134 (November 1992), p. 700.

14. Van Mander, *Schilder-boeck*, fol. 246v; Miedema, *Karel van Mander*, vol. 1, p. 245. Van Mander identified only three pupils: Jacob van Gouda, Symon Jansz Kies, and Jacob Rauert; Van Mander, *Schilder-boeck*, fols. 227v, 242r, 246v; Borritt Willemsz was registered in the Guild of Saint Luke as a pupil in 1547; Irene van Thiel-Stromen, "Maerten Jacobsz van Heemskerck," in Biesboer et al., *Painting in Haarlem*, p. 197.

15. Several engravers executed his designs for prints—including Cornelis Bos, Dirck Volkertsz Coornhert, Philips Galle, and Cornelis Cort—which were published by Hieronymus Cock in Antwerp and Jan van Zueren in Haarlem. *Maarten van Heemskerck: The New Hollstein; Dutch and Flemish Etchings, Engravings, and Woodcuts, 1450–1700*, part 2, compiled by Ilja M. Veldman, edited by Ger Luijten (Roosendaal: Koninklijk van Poll, in cooperation with the Rijksprentenkabinet, 1993–94).

16. Veldman, *New Hollstein*, vol. 1, part 2, p. 50, under no. 343 (*The Parable of the King Who Prepared a Wedding*), from the series A Parable of the King Who Prepared a Wedding, engraved and etched by Dirck Volkertsz Coornhert; Veldman, *New Hollstein*, vol. 1, part 1, p. 222, under no. 268 (*Judith*), from the series Exemplary Women from the Old and New Testament, engraved by Philips Galle; see Nicholas Turner, Lee Hendrix, and Carol Plazzotta, *European Drawings 3: Catalogue of the Collections* (Los Angeles: J. Paul Getty Museum, 1997), pp. 208–9, no. 84.

17. Adriaan van der Willigen, *Geschiedkundige aanteekeningen over Haarlemsche schilders, en andere beoefenaren van de beeldende kunsten: Voorafgegaan door eene korte geschiedenis van het schilders- of Saint Lucas Gild Aldaar* (Haarlem: De Erven F. Bohn, 1866), p. 131.

18. "*In zynen tÿt der Const een byzonder licht is gheweest*" Van Mander, *Schilder-boeck*, fol. 247r; translation from Miedema, ed., *Karel van Mander*, vol. 1, p. 246.

19. The plates were printed in large editions and continued to be produced through the seventeenth century. Heemskerck's series The Story of Daniel, Bel and the Dragon, particularly the engraving *Daniel Refusing to Worship Bel*, published by Hieronymus Cock (1565), provided Rembrandt with the unusual subject for his painting *Daniel and Cyrus before the Idol Bel* (1633). Oil on panel, 23.5 × 30.2 cm (9¼ × 11⅞ in.), Los Angeles, J. Paul Getty Museum, 95.PB.15. Veldman, *New Hollstein*, vol. 1, part 1, p. 191, no. 226; J. G. van Gelder, "Een Rembrandt van 1633," *Oud Holland* 75 (1960), pp. 73–78.

20. Jan's first wife, Josijne van Bekesteyn of Haarlem, died in 1519. Jan van Beverwijck, *'t Begin van Hollant in Dordrecht: Mistgaders der eerster Stede beschrijvinge, regeringe, ende regeerders: Als oock de gedenckvaerdighste geschiedenissen aldaer gevallen* (Dordrecht, 1640), p. 19.

21. Van Beverwijck, *'t Begin van Hollant*, pp. 18–19.

22. John Paul Elliott, "Protestantization in the Northern Netherlands: A Case Study; The Classis of Dordrecht, 1572–1640," 2 vols. (Ph.D. diss., Columbia University, 1990), p. 609; Henk F. K. van Nierop, *The Nobility of Holland: From Knights to Regents, 1500–1650*, translated by Martin Ultee (Cambridge and New York: Cambridge University Press, 1993), pp. 157–58.

23. Van Mander recounts a bizarre tale of how Heemskerck narrowly avoided becoming the victim of a robbery and murder scheme run by the Smidt family in their Dordrecht inn on his return journey from Italy; Van Mander, *Schilder-boeck*, fol. 245v. The Smidt family was prosecuted in 1538 by Jan van Drenckwaerdt. The episode is also recounted by Van Beverwijck, *'t Begin van Hollant*, pp. 339–45, and Matthys Balen, *Beschryvinge der stad Dordrecht: Vervatende haar begin, opkomst, toeneming, en verdere stant... Als mede een verzamelinge van eenige geslachtboomen, der adelijke, aal-oude, en aanzienlijke heeren-geslachten, van, en in, Dordrecht, enz....* (Dordrecht, 1677), pp. 819–27.

24. *Two Altar Wings with Donors: Jacob de Vriese and Machteld van Meerdervoort and Their Children*, ca. 1545. Oil on panel, 68 × 27 cm (26¾ × 10⅝ in.), Strasbourg, Musée des Beaux-Arts, inv. 90 a/b. The identification of the donors was made by Nico Plomp and Truus van Bueren, "Luiken met gebedsportretten van Maarten van Heemskerck," *Genealogie* 5 (1999), pp. 88–91, and was unknown to Grosshans, *Maerten van Heemskerck*, pp. 166–67, cat. 50. Machteld van Meerdervoort's grandmother was Cunera van Drenckwaerdt, Jan's sister.

25. "Pilate therefore went forth again, and saith unto them, Behold, I bring him forth to you, that ye may know that I find no fault in him. Then came Jesus forth, wearing the crown of thorns, and the purple robe. And Pilate saith unto them,

Behold the man! When the chief priests therefore and officers saw him, they cried out, saying, Crucify him, crucify him. Pilate saith unto them, Take ye him, and crucify him: for I find no fault in him" (John 19:4–60).

26. In his biography of the artist, Van Mander asserts that Heemskerck painted some figures in his mythological and religious paintings from life, particularly in his early career, an unusual practice at the time. Van Mander, *Schilder-boeck*, fol. 245r.

27. While not based on a particular work, the figure resembles the Apollo *Citharoedos*, which Heemskerck had drawn in the Casa Sassi Collection in Rome (fig. 3), where the sculpture is located in the niche in the right foreground; Benesz, *Transalpinum*, p. 158, cat. 37.

28. See Szafran and Phenix, p. 61. A similar loss of color was observed in the figure of Christ in the central panel of Heemskerck's *Ecce Homo* (1559–60; Haarlem, Frans Hals Museum); see Biesboer et al., *Painting in Haarlem*, p. 508.

29. For the coats of arms, see J.-B. Rietstap, V. Rolland, and H. V. Rolland's *Armorial Général Illustrations* (Baltimore: Genealogical Publishing Company, 1967), vol.1, pl. 215 (Drenckwaerdt); vol. 3, pl. 280 (Jonge). Apparently from the village of Westenrijk, Jan's forebears took the name of their estate, Drenkwaart, in the early fifteenth century (Aart de Boon, correspondence to the author, July 29, 2011). Margaretha's family had occupied prominent positions in Dordrecht since at least the mid-fifteenth century.

30. Margaretha's first husband was Jacob van der Duyn; Balen, *Beschryvinge*, p. 1098.

31. Jacobus de Voragine, *The Golden Legend: Readings on the Saints*, translated by William Grainger Ryan (Princeton, NJ: Princeton University Press, 1993), vol. 1, p. 53.

32. De Voragine, *Golden Legend*, vol. 1, pp. 368–70.

33. Van Beverwijck, *'t Begin van Hollant*, p. 19.

34. Margaretha's contemporaries wear similar attire: *Portrait of Sophia van Amerongen* (ca. 1550; Philadelphia Museum of Art), *Portrait of Machtelt Suijs* (fig. 7), and *Machteld van Meerdervoort* (ca. 1545–50; Strasbourg, Musée des Beaux-Arts).

35. Grosshans notes the same combination of serpent and dove in a female figure attributed to Heemskerck, *Allegory of Prudent Sincerity* (*Allegorie der Klugen Einfalt*), *Maerten van Heemskerck*, pp. 202–3, cat. 77. The reference may be to Matthew 10:16: "Behold, I send you forth as sheep in the midst of wolves: be ye therefore wise as serpents, and harmless as doves." The statuette resembles Prudence in Heemskerck's *Prudence and Justice*, ca. 1537 (Vienna, Kunsthistorisches Museum); Grosshans, *Maerten van Heemskerck*, pp. 124–25, cat. 22; and in the engraving by Cornelis Bos after Heemskerck, *Prudence and Justice*, 1537; Veldman, *New Hollstein*, part 2, p. 141, no. 453.

36. They are similar in effect to the trophy reliefs on pillars visible in Rome during the first part of the sixteenth century (now Florence, Galleria degli Uffizi); see Phyllis Pray Bober and Ruth Rubinstein, *Renaissance Artists and Antique Sculpture: A Handbook of Sources* (London: Harvey Millar, 1986), p. 206, no. 175.

37. Veldman, *New Hollstein*, part 2, p. 120, no. 424.

38. See Szafran and Phenix for a discussion of the structure and finish of the frame.

39. The inscription may also be interpreted as "Hope is the consolation of the Drenckwaerdts." See Benesz, *Transalpinum*, p. 158, cat. 37. The sentiment "Hope comforts" had a long usage in medieval poetry and music. It was not the motto of the Drenckwaerdts; their motto was *Argent Fait Tout* (Money Does All); Van Beverwijck, *'t Begin van Hollant*, p. 23.

40. The dates probably reinforce earlier inscriptions. See Szafran and Phenix.

41. Isaiah 26:19.

42. See, for example, the low-relief scenes of the Four Evangelists in vaulted temple interiors on the pulpit of Oude Kerk, Delft (1548); D. Bierens de Haan, *Het Houtsnijwerk in Nederlanden Tijdens de Gothiek en de Renaissance* (The Hague: Martinus Nijhoff, 1921), pp. 135–36, pl. 118.

43. Sebastiano Serlio, *Generale reglen der architectvren op de vyve manieren van edificien: Te vveten Thvscana, Dorica, Ionica, Corinthia, ende composita, metden exemplen der antiqviteiten die int meeste deel concorderen metde leeringhe van Vitrvvio* (Antwerp, 1539).

44. For example, the contract for the wings of the Haarlem Drapers' altarpiece (1546–47) required Heemskerck to provide the frame. See Biesboer, *Painting in Haarlem*, p. 503, cat. 206. For the contract, see Liesbeth M. Helmus, *Schilderen in Opdracht: Noord-Nederlandse contracten voor altaarstukken, 1485–1570* (Utrecht: Centraal Museum, 2010), pp. 389–90, no. 54. "*De lijst van het altaarstuk moet worden gemaakt en beschilderd in opdracht en op kosten van de schilder*" (The frame of the altarpiece must be made and painted at the commission and at the expense of the painter).

45. See Herman A. van Duinen, *De Koorbanken van de Grote- of Onze Lieve Vrouwekerk te Dordrecht* (Leiden: Primavera Pers, 1997).

46. "*Veel Vertooningen, Schilderyen, Poorten, ende Triumphael-Boogen*," Van Beverwijk, *'t Begin van Hollant*, p. 346.

47. "*Hy was een seer goet ordineerder, jae een Man die de heele Weerelt schier vervult heeft met zijn inventien, wesende oock een goet Architecht, ghelyck in al zijn dinghen overvloedich te sien is*" (He was a very good designer, yes: a man who, in a manner of speaking, filled the world with his inventions, added to which he was also a good architect as all his works make abundantly clear); Van Mander, *Schilder-boeck*, fol. 246v, translation from Miedema, ed., *Karel van Mander*, vol. 1, p. 245.

48. Jan Piet Filedt Kok, Willy Halsema-Kubes, and Wouter Th. Kloek, "Kunst voor de Beeldenstorm 1986: Aanvullingen en correcties op de catalogus," *Bulletin van het Rijksmuseum* 35 (1987), p. 258.

49. Lynn Roberts independently proposed that the frame had been made in Dordrecht (e-mail correspondence to Gene Karraker, Paintings Conservation, J. Paul Getty Museum, August 4, 2011).

50. Van Beverwijck, *'t Begin van Hollant*, p. 19; Grosshans, *Maerten van Heemskerck*, p.159

51. Herman A. van Duinen, "Een Augustijnenklooster van Aanzien: Conventus Sancti Augustini Dordracencis, 1275–1572," in *Jaarboek Historische Vereniging Oud-Dordrecht,* edited by Herman A. van Duinen and C. Esseboom (Dordrecht: Oud-Dordrecht, 2010), pp. 49–50, 61.

52. Van Duinen, *Augustijnenklooster*, pp. 61, 63.

53. The two Drenckwaerdt chapels were joined into a single bay in 1647; Van Duinen, *Augustijnenklooster*, p. 63.

54. Van Duinen, *Augustijnenklooster*, p. 184.

55. Aart de Boon, verbal communication with the author, March 2011; A. Nelemans and K. Blokland, *Sepulture Augustijnenkerk Dordrecht* (Sliedrecht: Oudheidkundige Vereniging "Sliedrecht," Werkgroep Genealogie, 1998).

56. Van Duinen, *Augustijnenklooster*, pp. 73–76.

57. Van Beverwijck, *'t Begin van Hollant*, p. 349ff.

58. Dordrecht's churches were not violently assaulted by iconoclasts in 1572, as Grosshans erroneously suggests. Grosshans, *Maerten van Heemskerck*, p. 159.

59. "*Het taffereel daer sy beyde konstigh ingeschildert zijn, is uyt de kerck-roovingh verlost, ende in't naeste huyse van de pensionaris Berck gebracht*"; Van Beverwijk, *'t Begin van Hollant*, p. 19.

60. John Loughman, "Een stad en haar kunstconsumptie: Openbare en privé-vezamelingen in Dordrecht, 1620–1719," in *De Zichtbaere Werelt: Schilderkunst uit de Gouden Eeuw in Hollands Oudste Stad,* exh. cat., edited by Peter Marijnissen et al. (Zwolle: Waanders and Dordrechts Museum, 1992), p. 56.

61. *Catalogue der von dem verstorbenen Herrn Commerzienrath Faber in Stuttgart hinterlassenen Sammlung von Oelgemälden alter und neuer Meister*, April 26–27, 1870, p. 5, lot 16.

62. "Heinrich von Korn, 1829–1907," *Silesian Art Collections*, http://www.silesiancollections.eu/Kolekcje/Korn-Heinrich-von-1829–1907-Breslau (accessed January 4, 2011).

63. Benesz, *Transalpinum*, p. 158, cat. 37.

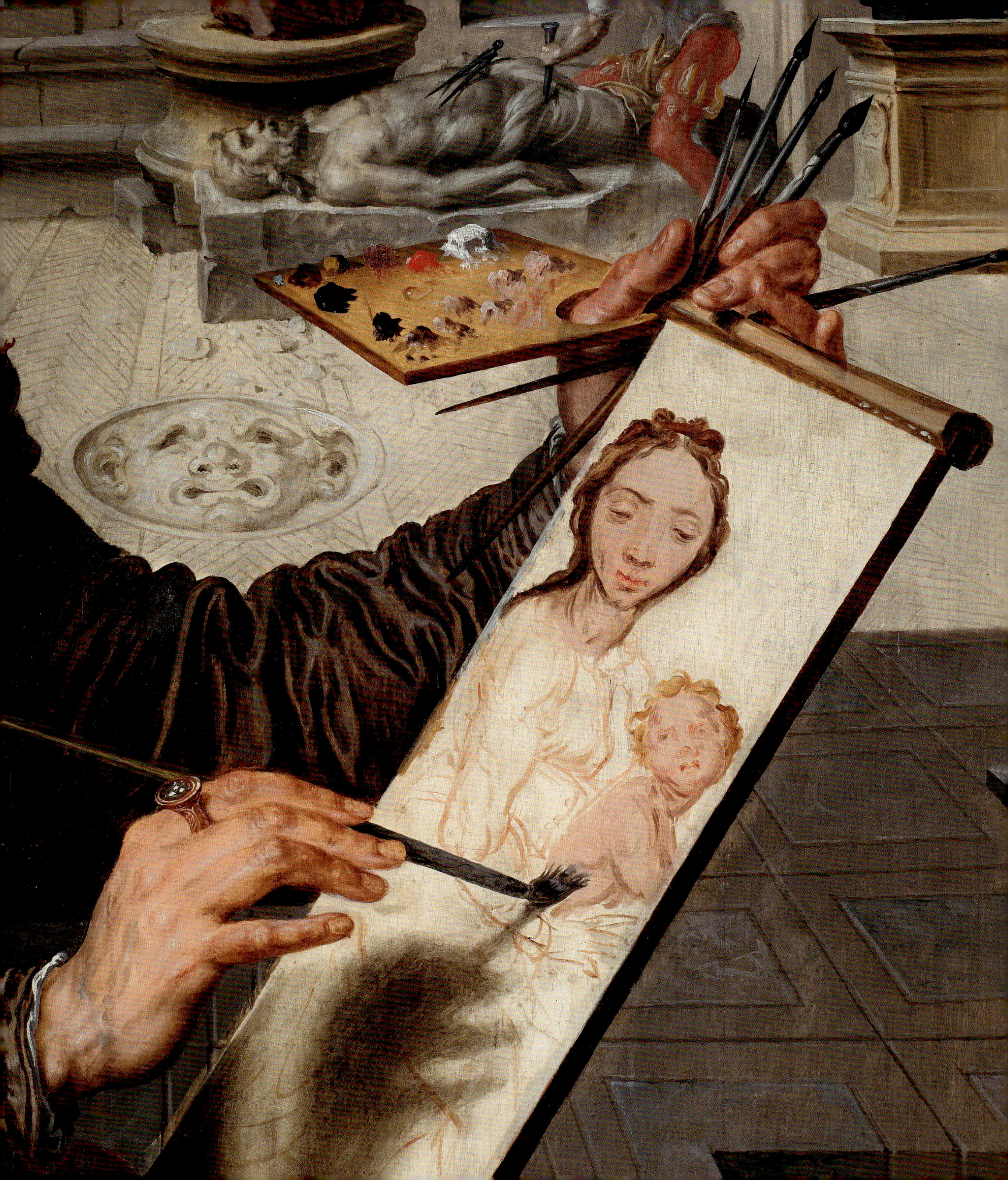

THE *ECCE HOMO* TRIPTYCH: HEEMSKERCK'S MATERIALS AND METHODS

YVONNE SZAFRAN
ALAN PHENIX

As one of the leading Netherlandish artists of his time and among the second generation of Northern European artists to have traveled to Italy, Maerten van Heemskerck incorporated techniques and ideas that he encountered there into his practice, expanding on some of what he had already learned in the studio of his master, Jan van Scorel. By 1544, the year the *Ecce Homo* triptych was painted, Heemskerck had successfully formulated a working method that was firmly based on traditional Northern techniques but also incorporated certain materials and methods adopted from Italy that facilitated his prolific creativity. The *Ecce Homo* triptych exemplifies this wonderfully expressive, expedient, and colorful style, and it has survived in an unusually intact state, an important example of a private devotional altarpiece by Heemskerck. The work's extremely good condition makes it an ideal candidate for exploring in-depth his materials and working methods.

Much is known about the methods and materials of painting in the Netherlands in the sixteenth century. A variety of sources, including guild rules,[1] contemporary commentary, contracts with patrons, and treatises that describe in detail the process of painting,[2] provide a basis for understanding how painters such as Heemskerck worked. One of the best-known books about this period is fellow Haarlem painter and biographer Karel van Mander's *Schilder-boeck* (1604), which includes insightful commentary about Heemskerck's working methods based on conversations with the artist's contemporaries.[3] In addition, two paintings by Heemskerck titled *Saint Luke Painting the Virgin*, one made early in his career (see fig. 2) and one later (fig. 20), both depict fascinating details of a painter at work, including a palette, brushes, and works in progress. The changes evident in *The Erythraean Sibyl* (fig. 21) provide further visual substantiation of his process and methods, contributing to a preliminary understanding of the methods and techniques that Heemskerck may have used in the *Ecce Homo* triptych.

While the altarpiece is in remarkable condition, from the beginning of this study it was evident that layers of dirt, discolored varnish, and past restorations obscured the brilliance of the original colors (fig. 22), although the painting's appearance has also changed due to Heemskerck's choice of materials. Dirt, discolored, nonoriginal coatings, and past restorations were removed,[4] revealing very few losses (fig. 23) and providing a valuable opportunity to closely examine the original structure and materials of an intact altarpiece. The layered structure of the painting was examined and analyzed, from wooden support to ground, to preparatory drawing and underpaintings (intermediate layers of paint), up to the finished painting. Scholars have similarly studied a number of Heemskerck works in recent years, and the investigation of the *Ecce Homo* triptych adds to a growing body of knowledge regarding his technique, which had both traditional and innovative aspects for a Dutch painter of the time.[5]

Delving into the intricacies of his technique and materials unveiled a master working with great agility and assurance. Heemskerck painted the altarpiece as a mature artist, several years after he had returned home from Italy, and it is exciting to see his fully established and confident technique, which facilitated his development of a particularly popular and powerful devotional

Detail, figure 20

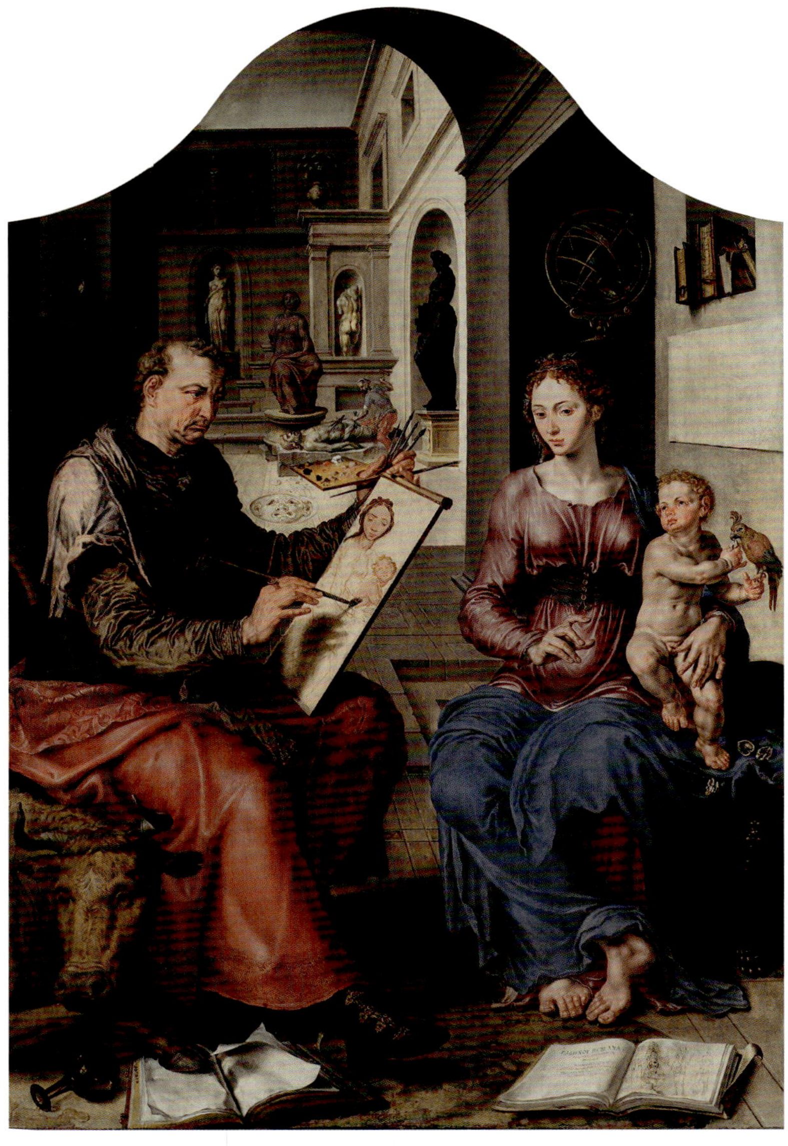

FIGURE 20 Maerten van Heemskerck, *Saint Luke Painting the Virgin*, ca. 1545. Oil on panel, 205.5 × 143.5 cm (81 × 56½ in.). Rennes, Musée des Beaux-Arts

theme—*Ecce Homo* ("Behold the Man!")—for a specific commission from the Drenckwaerdt family. The technical analysis performed as part of the conservation treatment generally corroborates contemporary views about his economical and versatile approach and complements existing studies of other works. This inquiry also revealed additional distinctive features of his rapid and confident painting technique, including his use of some unusual paint additives and binding media. It is apparent that certain aspects of his technique contributed to the changed appearance of the painting today, and it is these aspects that are perhaps the most compelling findings that emerged from the technical examination of the triptych.

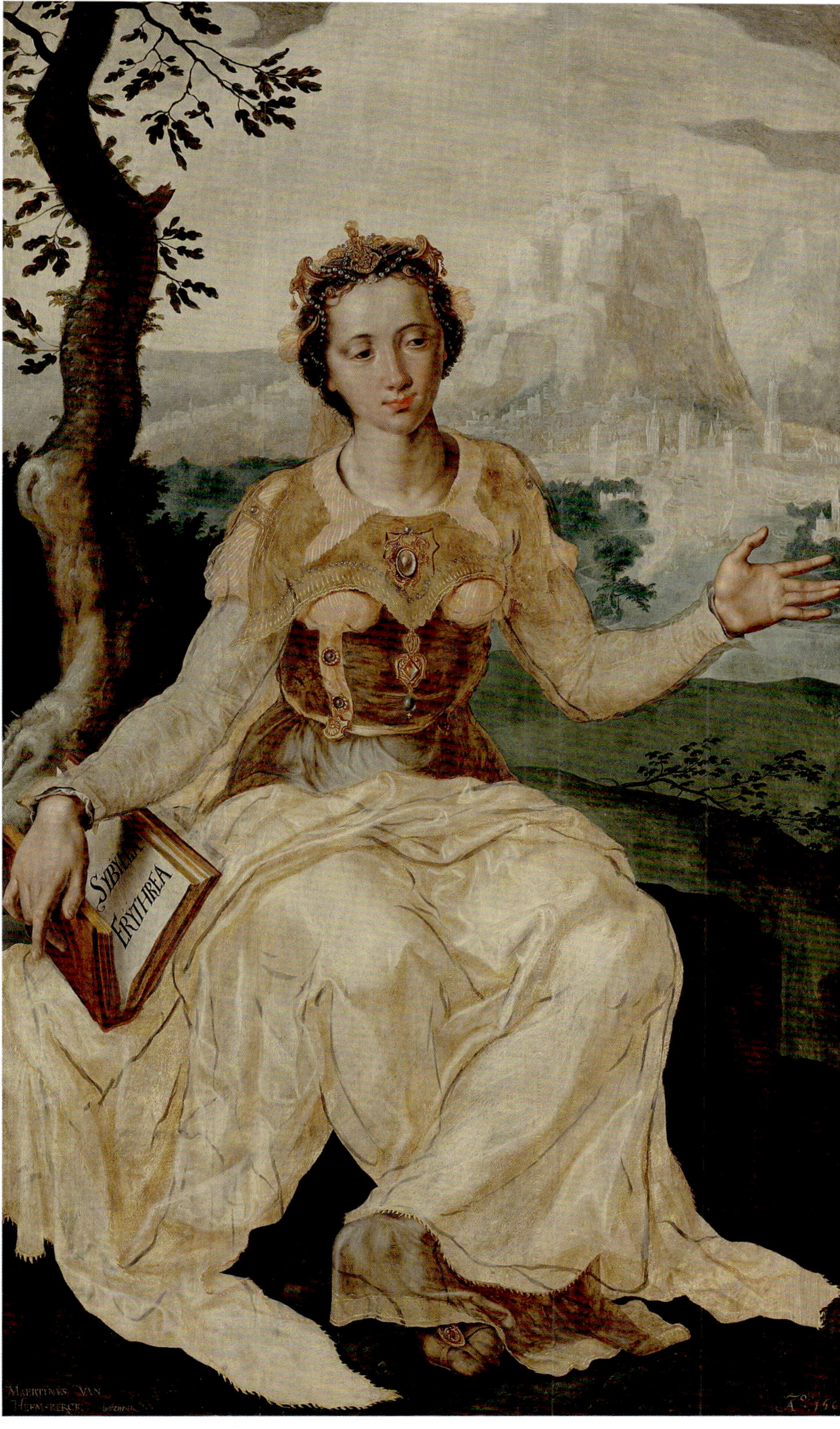

FIGURE 21 Maerten van Heemskerck, *The Erythraean Sibyl*, 1564. Oil on panel, 126 × 76.2 cm (50 × 30 in.). Amsterdam, Rijksmuseum

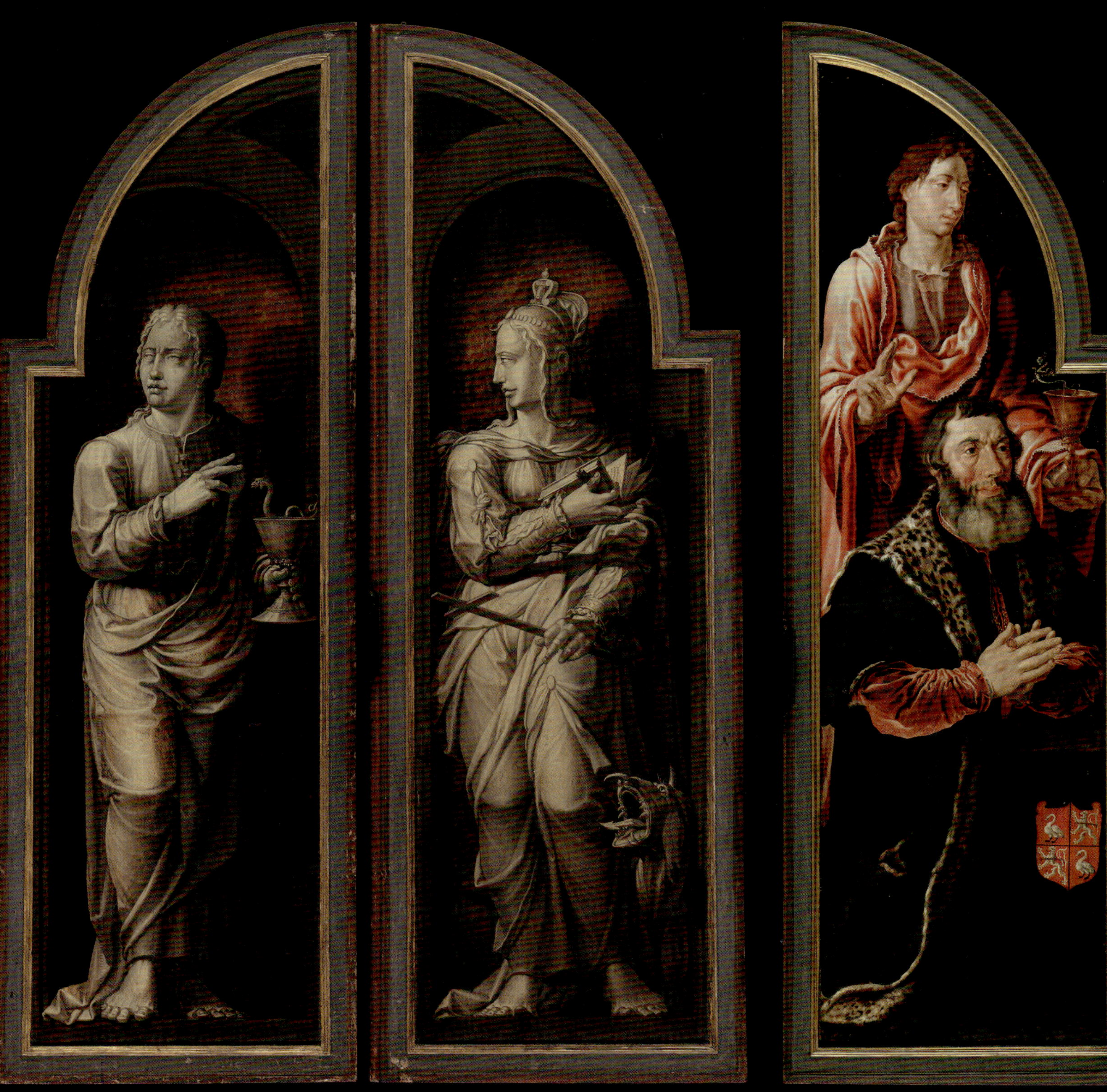

FIGURE 22 **BEFORE CLEANING**
Pretreatment photographs document Heemskerck's *Ecce Homo* triptych before the removal of dirt, nonorginal coatings, and past restorations.

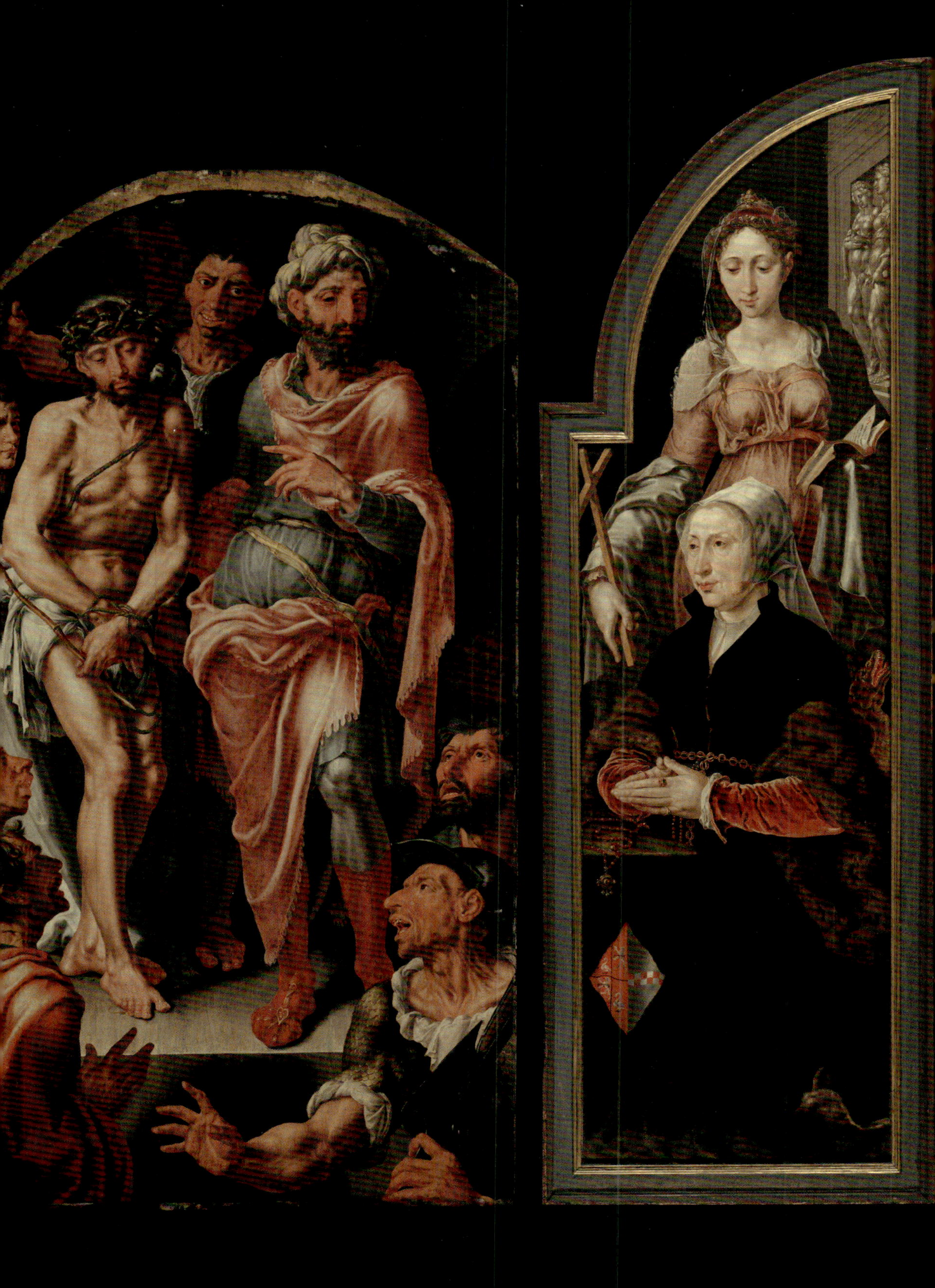

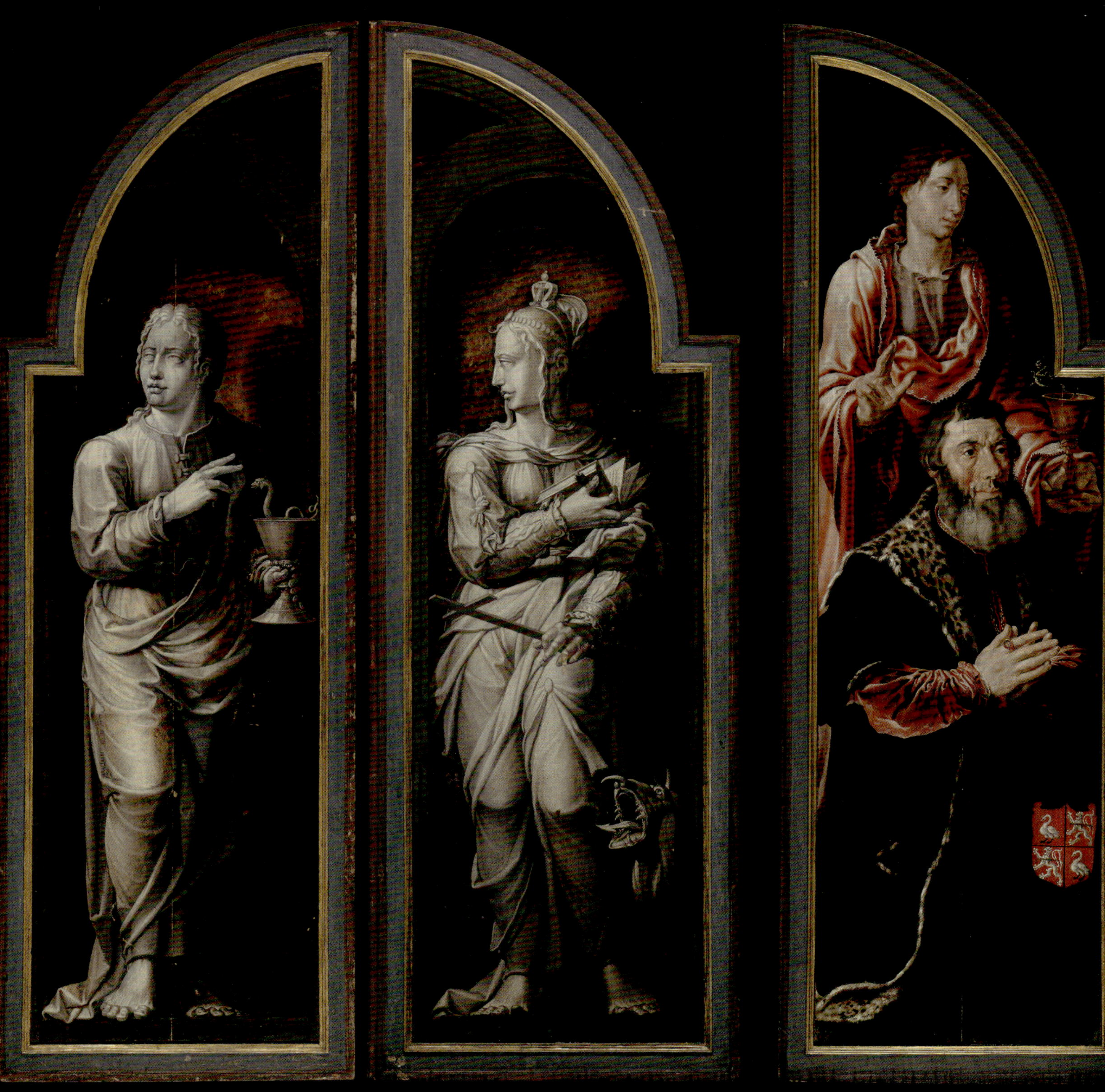

FIGURE 23 **AFTER CLEANING**

Cleaning revealed the very good condition of the painting, despite some losses of original paint along the panel joins.

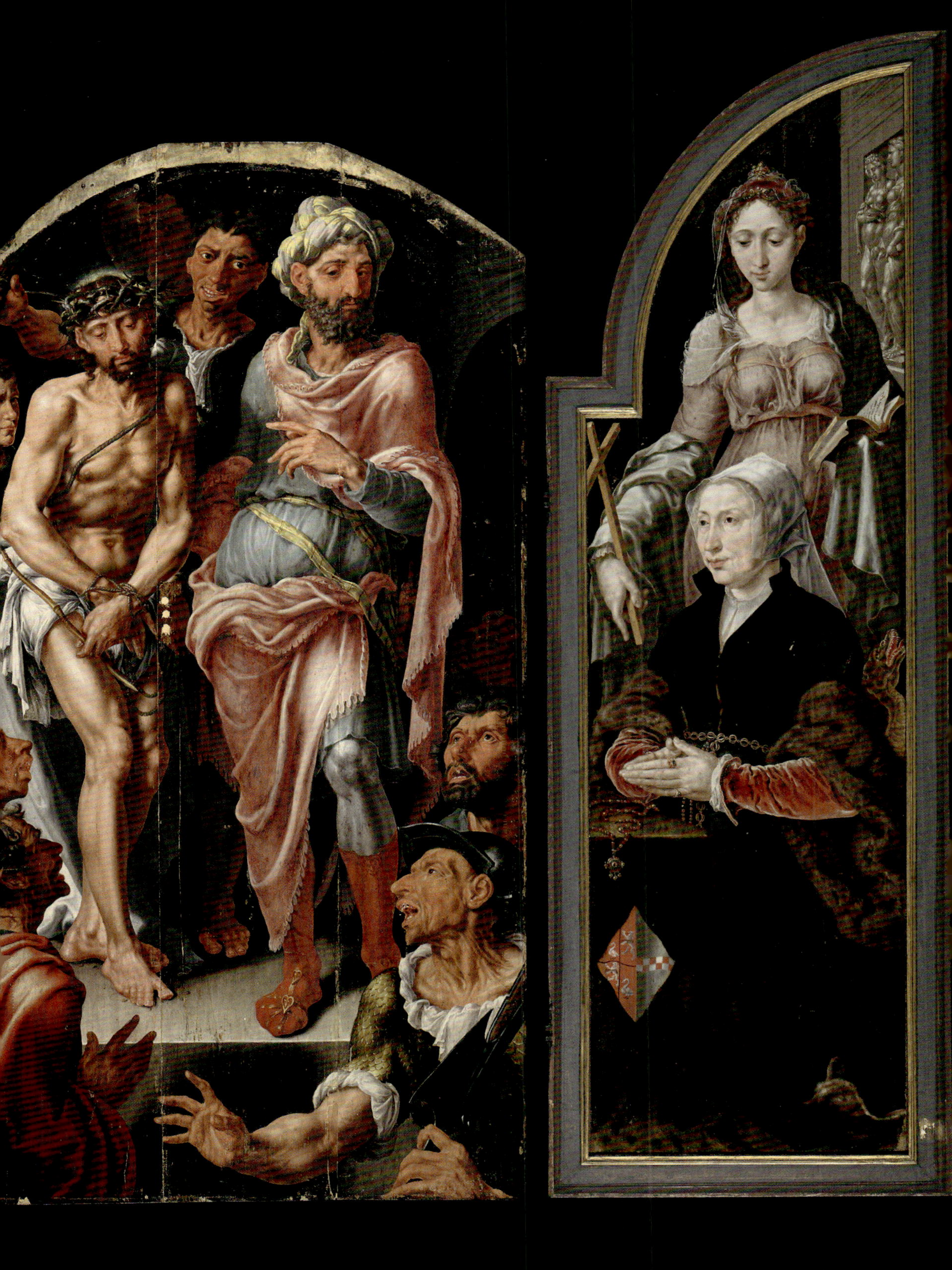

TECHNICAL EXAMINATION AND CHEMICAL ANALYSIS

A fuller perspective of the artist's methods and materials was achieved with close visual inspection and documentation of the painting's surface with the aid of a stereo microscope, and by examining the painting with an assortment of noninvasive imaging techniques, including X-radiography (fig. 24), ultraviolet photography (fig. 25), and infrared reflectography (fig. 26).[6] Another noninvasive analytical technique, X-ray fluorescence (XRF) spectroscopy,[7] was used to provide initial indications of the presence of inorganic pigments on the basis of the presence of particular elements, but the bulk of the scientific evidence on the artist's working method and materials came from microscopical examination and various forms of instrumental chemical analysis on tiny samples of paint. Following the usual approach, samples were taken from the edges of preexisting damages or from the extreme edges of the panels and examined in a variety of ways. The principal method involved preparing the samples as cross sections, which revealed the sequence of application of layers and the types of pigment that make up the various strata. Microscopical examination of the cross sections alone brought to light much about the various materials of the painting, providing visual evidence of pigment mixtures and of how the artist achieved particular color and optical effects.[8] The prepared cross sections were also examined by the analytical technique of environmental scanning electron microscopy with energy-dispersive X-ray spectroscopy (ESEM-EDS),[9] which allows high magnification and spatially resolved identification of the elements in individual layers, down to the level of an individual pigment particle; the identity of a pigment can often be reliably inferred from the elemental composition, which can be more or less characteristic. In order to answer some specific questions regarding pigment composition that could not be addressed solely by ESEM-EDS and to confirm some findings from that technique, Raman microspectroscopy was also performed on selected samples, both unmounted paint fragments and prepared cross sections.[10] The organic binding media in selected samples were analyzed by gas chromatography–mass spectroscopy (GC-MS).[11] In combination, these methods of examination and chemical analysis revealed much about Heemskerck's practice and added new insights into his working methods and materials.

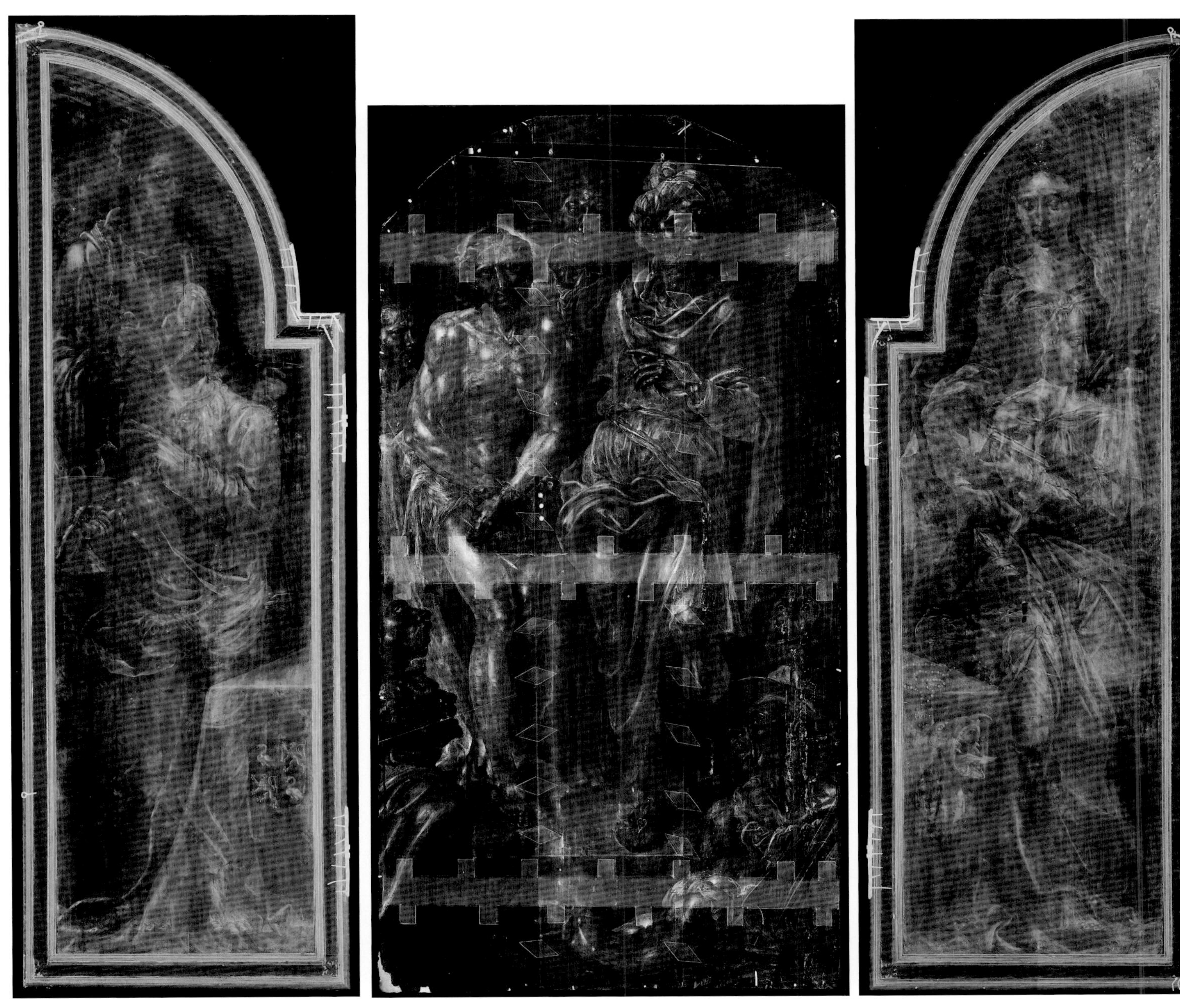

FIGURE 24 **X-RADIOGRAPHS**

The X-radiographs show the physical structure of the panels as well as the compositions on both sides of the double-sided wings.

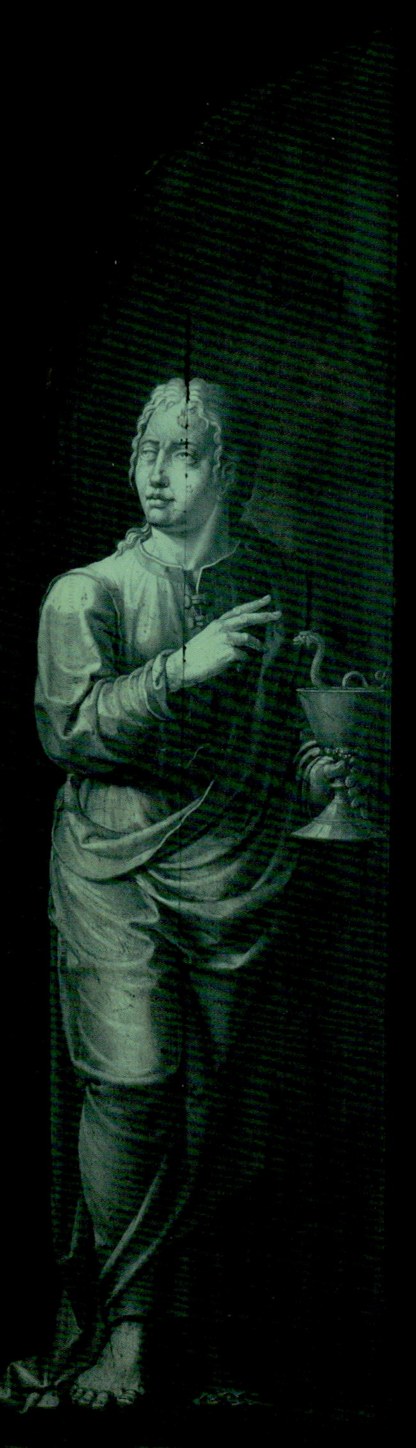

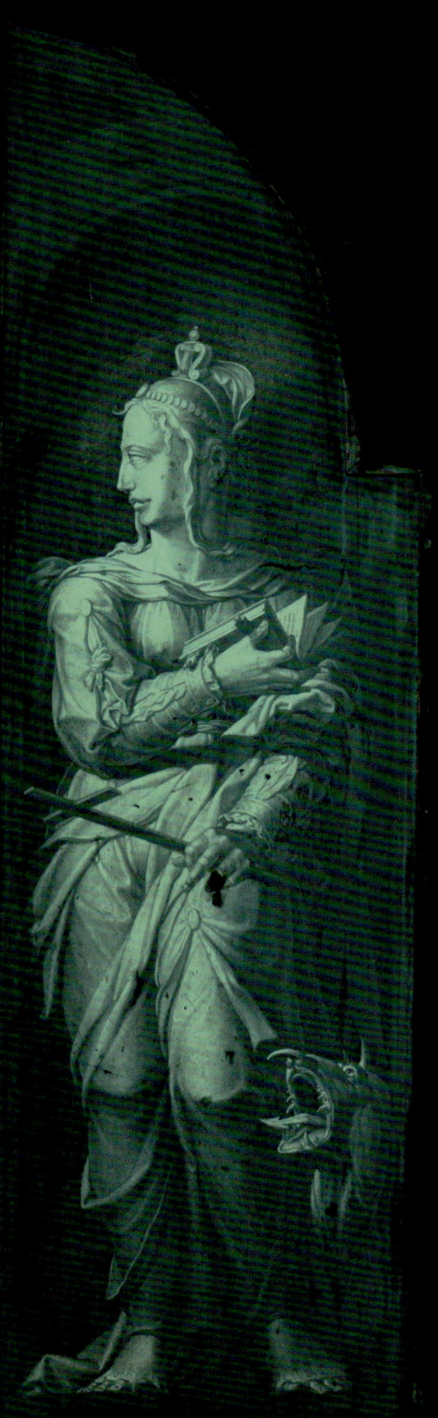

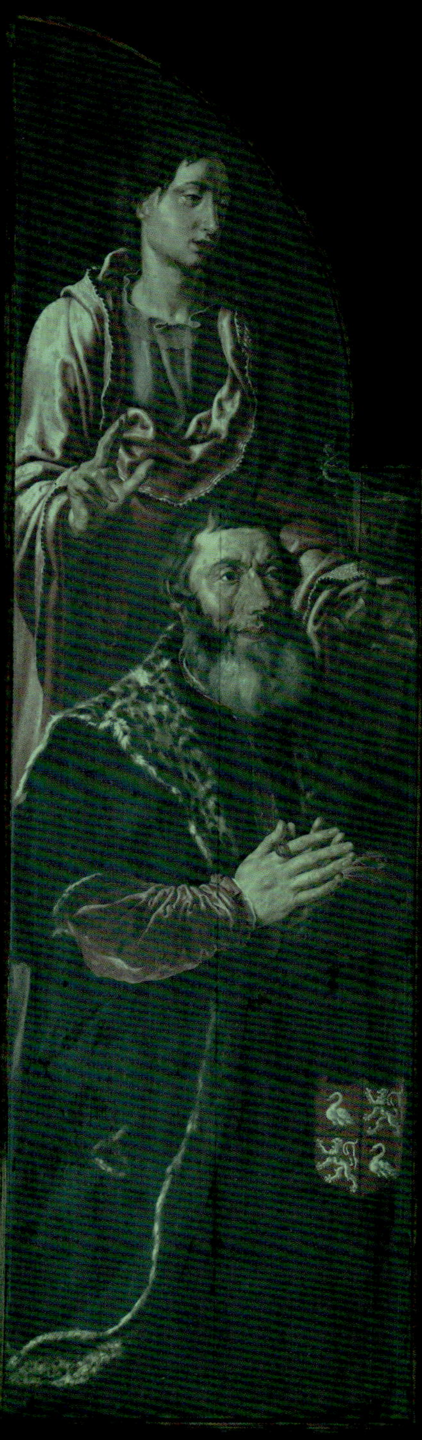

FIGURE 25 **ULTRAVIOLET PHOTOGRAPHS BEFORE CLEANING**

Examination under ultraviolet light before cleaning revealed highly fluorescent varnish layers as well as old restorations that show as dark areas.

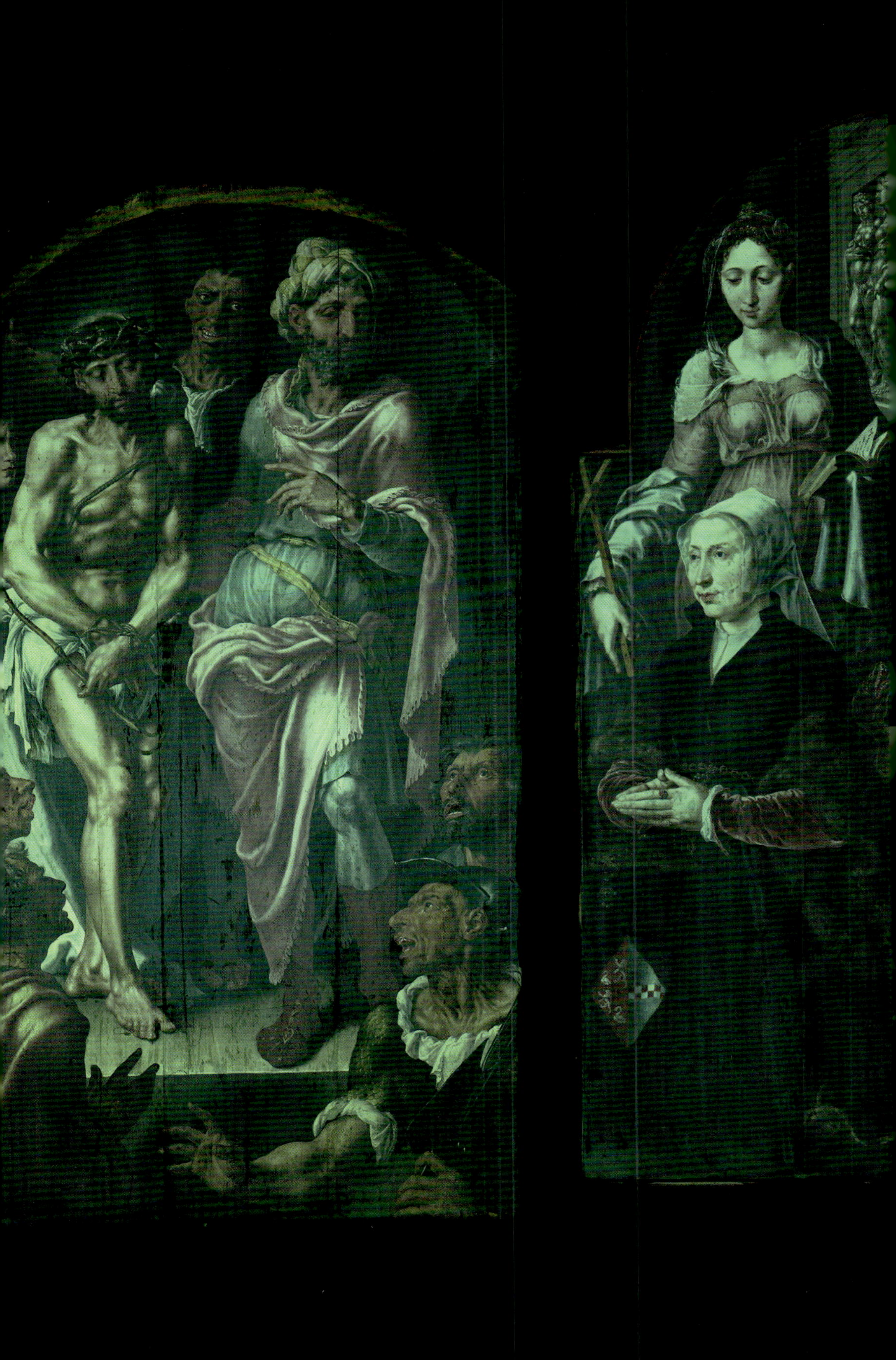

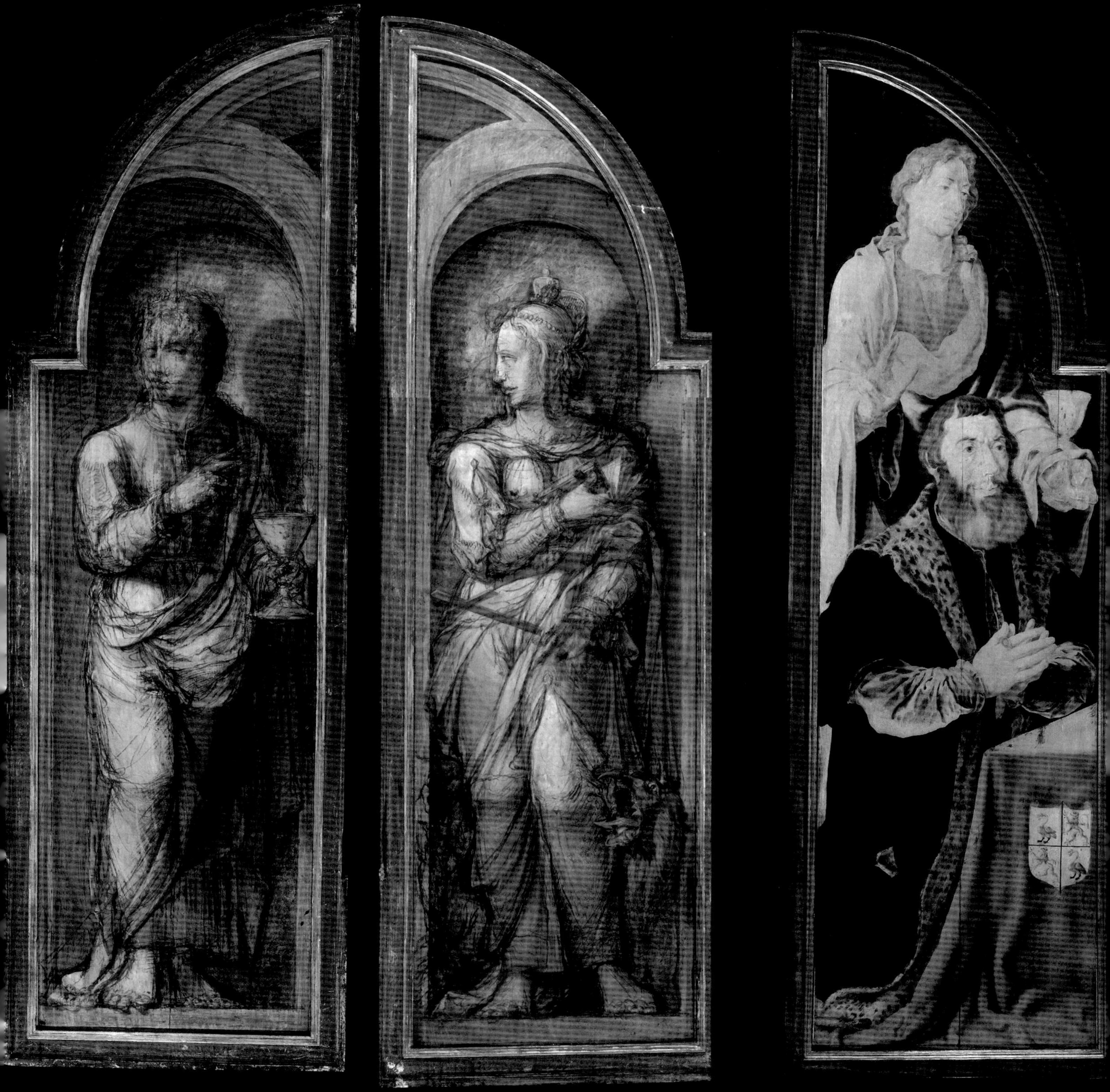

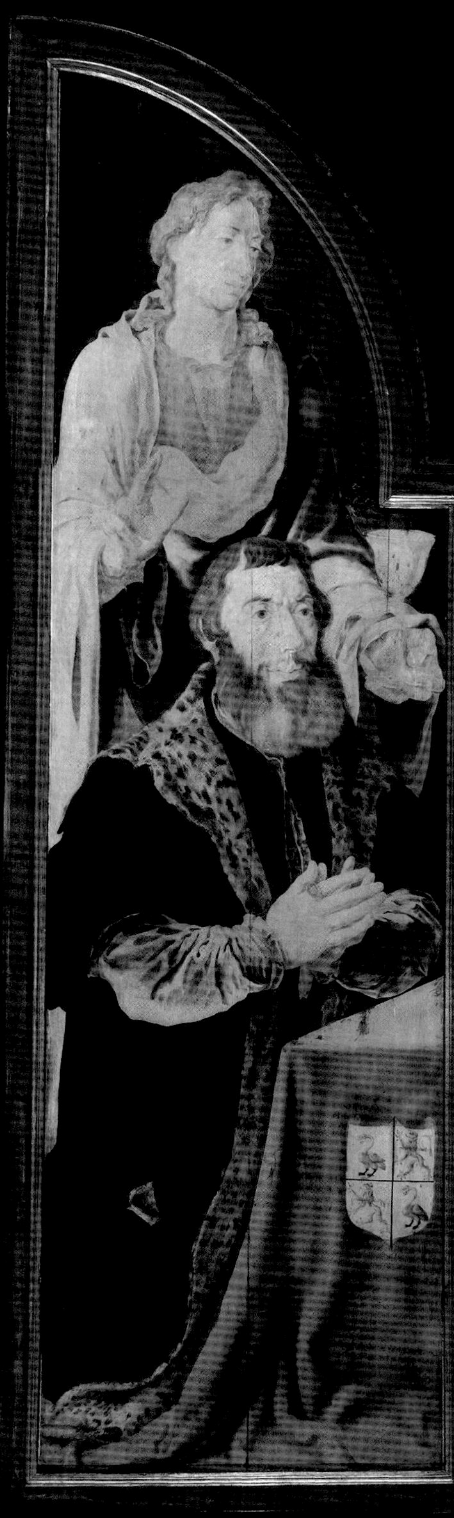

FIGURE 26 **INFRARED REFLECTOGRAMS**

The infrared images show the easily visible underdrawing on the exterior wings.

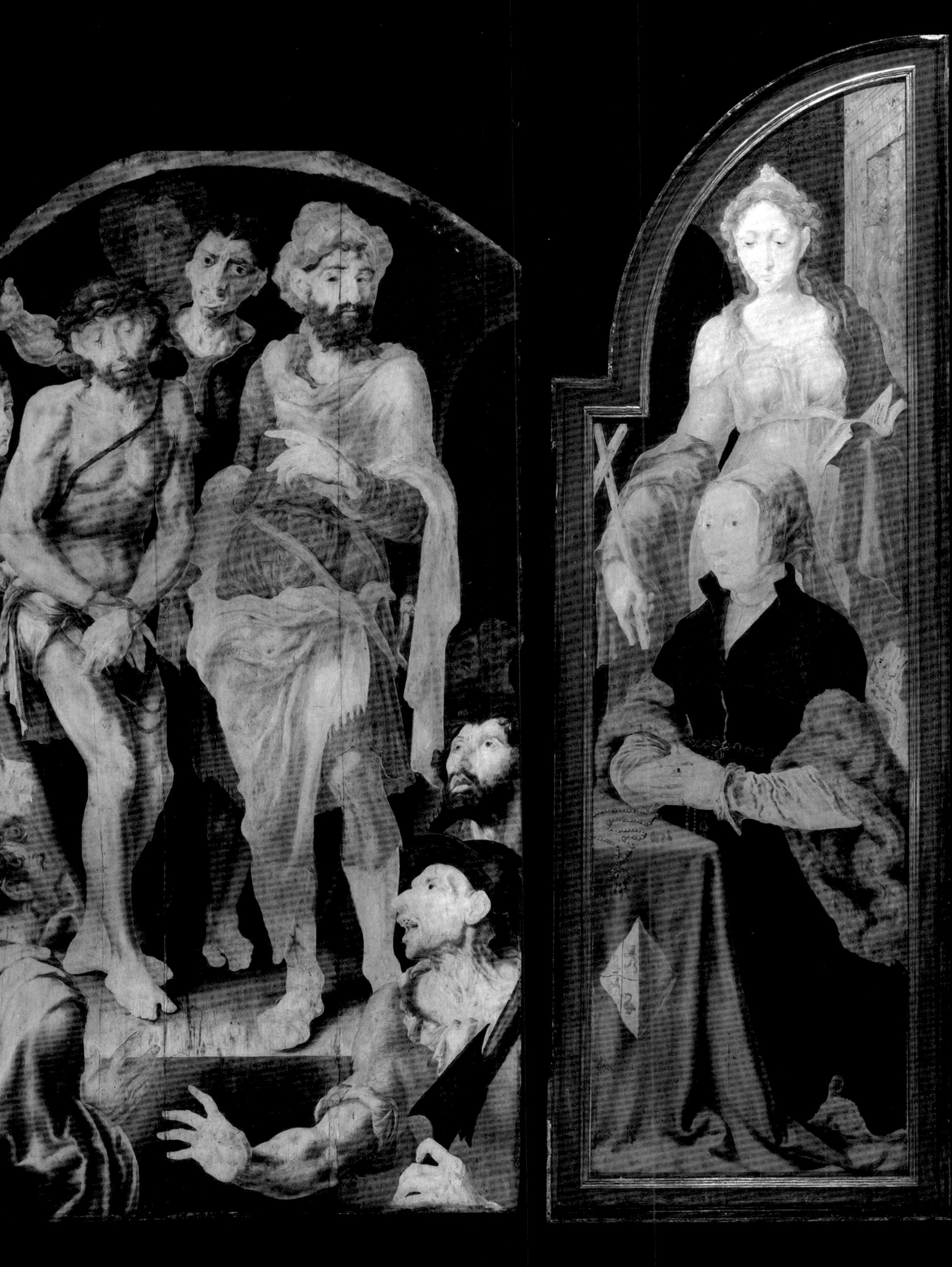

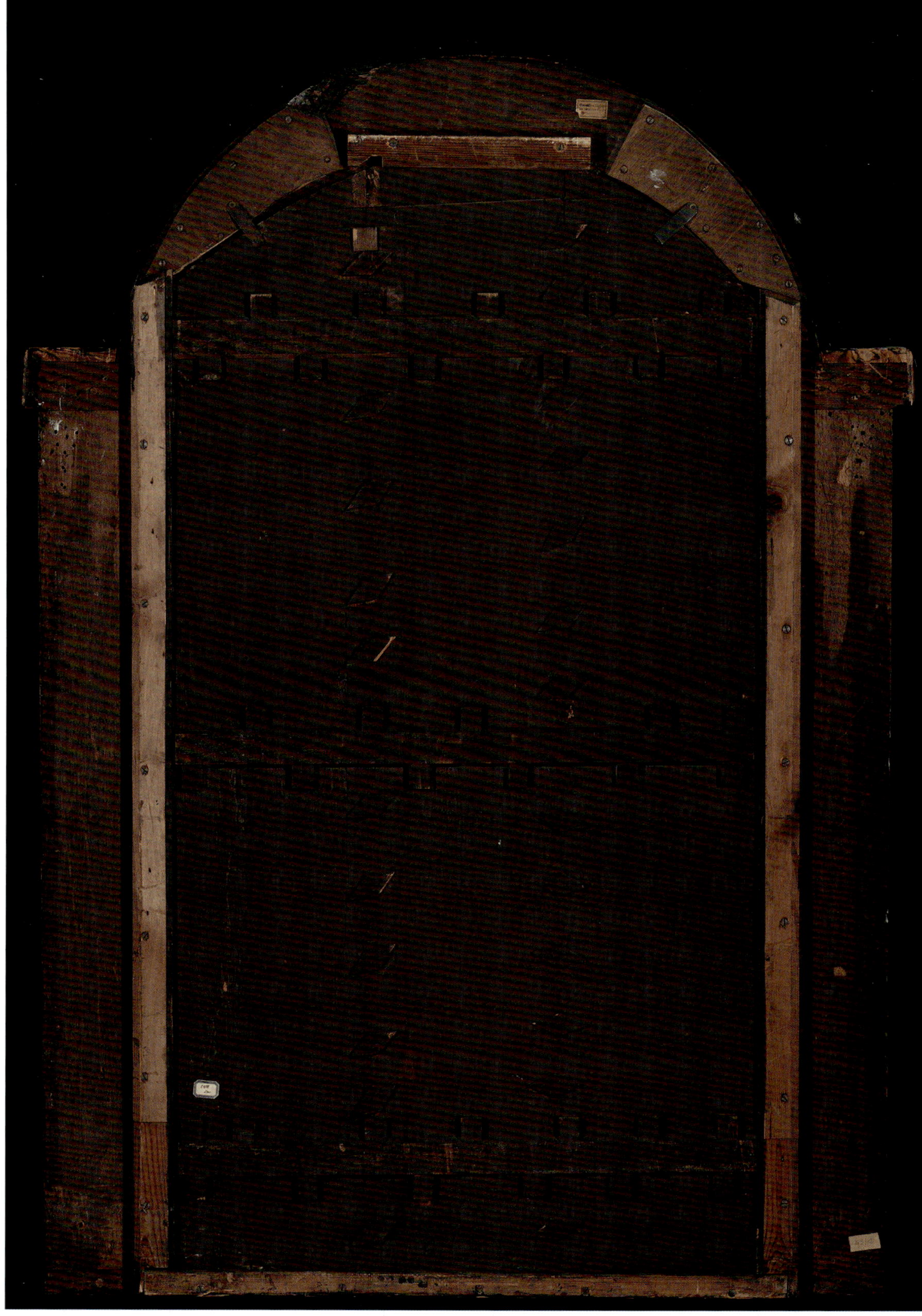

FIGURE 27 Back of the central panel in its frame

THE SUPPORT

Most Netherlandish altarpieces of this period were painted on wooden supports, and Heemskerck met patron demand for such commissions with hinged-panel triptychs. The *Ecce Homo* triptych's intact structure is characteristic of many of his works, consisting of three oak panels hinged together at their frames. The side wings are painted on both sides, the reverse of which provided the most-often-seen view, as the wings were only opened to reveal the entire altarpiece on specific days (see Anne T. Woollett's essay in this volume).

The central panel is made of three vertically grained oak planks approximately 29 cm wide and approximately 1.5 cm thick, glued together along the vertical edge with an arched form along the top (fig. 27). The two side panels are similarly composed of two vertically grained planks approximately 25.5 cm wide, also glued along the vertical edge, their tops echoing the arch of the central panel, allowing them to be closed when needed. The plank joins of all three panels were originally aligned and reinforced with wooden dowels (fig. 28), a feature noted in other paintings

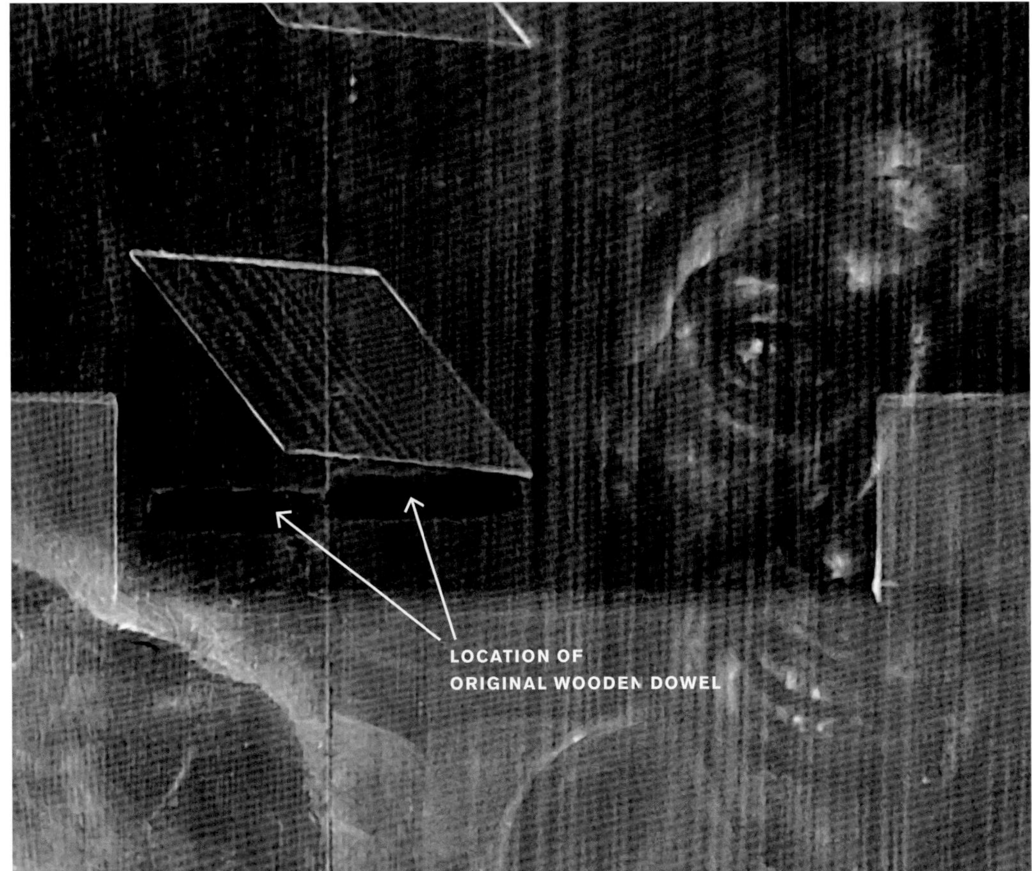

FIGURE 28 This detail of the X-radiograph of the central panel shows where a dowel originally aligned the planks that made up the panel.

by Heemskerck.[12] Examination of the back of the central panel indicates that there was a major restoration campaign in the past, resulting in butterfly inserts along the glue joins and cracks, and it must be assumed that the planks were separated at that time and possibly slightly reduced in their width, as certain compositional details on the front are no longer aligned. Three horizontal battens were also added to the central panel at some point, but the former location of older, probably original, battens can be observed on the back, where two shallow channels would have accommodated them. By contrast, the supports of the side panels appear to be completely intact, with only a few vertical splits.

Examination of the bottom edge of the central panel, along with close investigation of the back as well as the X-radiograph, suggests that certain areas of the panel had been altered at some point in the past, with additions to the original support in a few areas using newer oak, in other areas a softer wood, possibly pine. The lower half has a veneer of this later wood as well, and the entire back appears to have then been coated with a brown paint after these additions were made. The support of the central panel has evidence of old worm infestation, probably the reason for such an intrusive treatment. Fortunately, these past interventions have only minimally affected the painted surface.

THE FRAME

As discussed in Anne T. Woollett's essay, the elaborate architectural frame is an important component of the triptych's presentation, adding to the grandeur and monumentality of Heemskerck's work. Its blue-and-gold decoration (figs. 29 and 30) is somewhat unusual in the North but not without precedent[13] (black and gold being more typical in the Netherlands at the time), and past restorations make it difficult to fully understand the frame's likely original appearance. Prior observations by scholars[14] have suggested that the paint on the frame is original; however, the blue in the recessed areas of the frame appears to be more recent,[15] and it is not clear when it was applied, whether it replicates an original finish, or whether there is any original finish underneath it. The engaged frames on the wings were part of the structure from the beginning; close examination of their edges reveals continuous original paint film straddling the inner edge of the frame and the painting's surface. The central panel, however, was painted before it was framed; one can clearly see the exposed ground on the top edge of the panel, where Heemskerck painted the right hand of the figure on the left into this unpainted area (fig. 31). Part of the hand is not visible when the painting is in its frame, suggesting that the frame for the central panel was not present or even designed in the early stages of painting. On the central panel, holes and remnants of nails can be seen on the edges, and it is presumed that these relate to the original framing process, perhaps involving direct placement of the panel in the chapel.[16] The structure of the frame, presumed to be original, has no rebate (indentation to accommodate the painting), as might be more typical for the period, further supporting the idea of direct installation in the chapel.

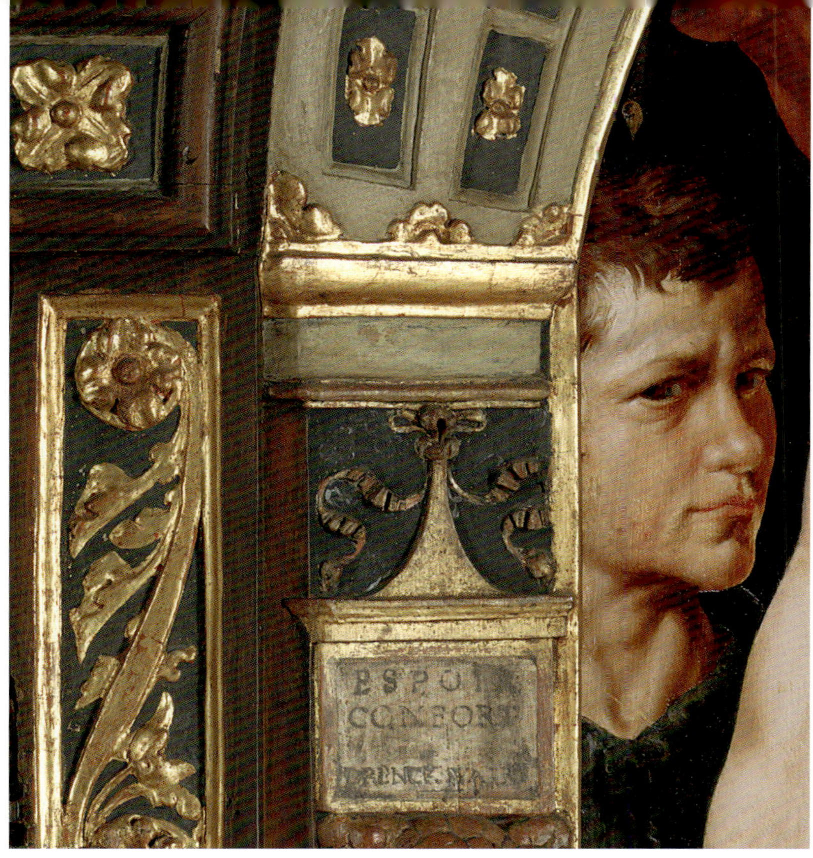

FIGURE 29 A fictive coffered vault rises above the plaque.

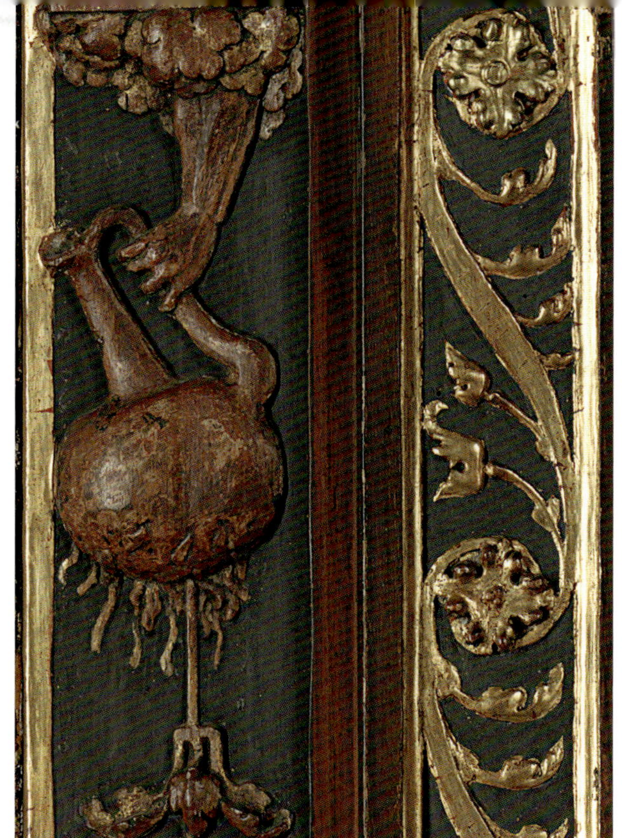

FIGURE 30 The allegorical decoration refers to the Drenckwaert family.

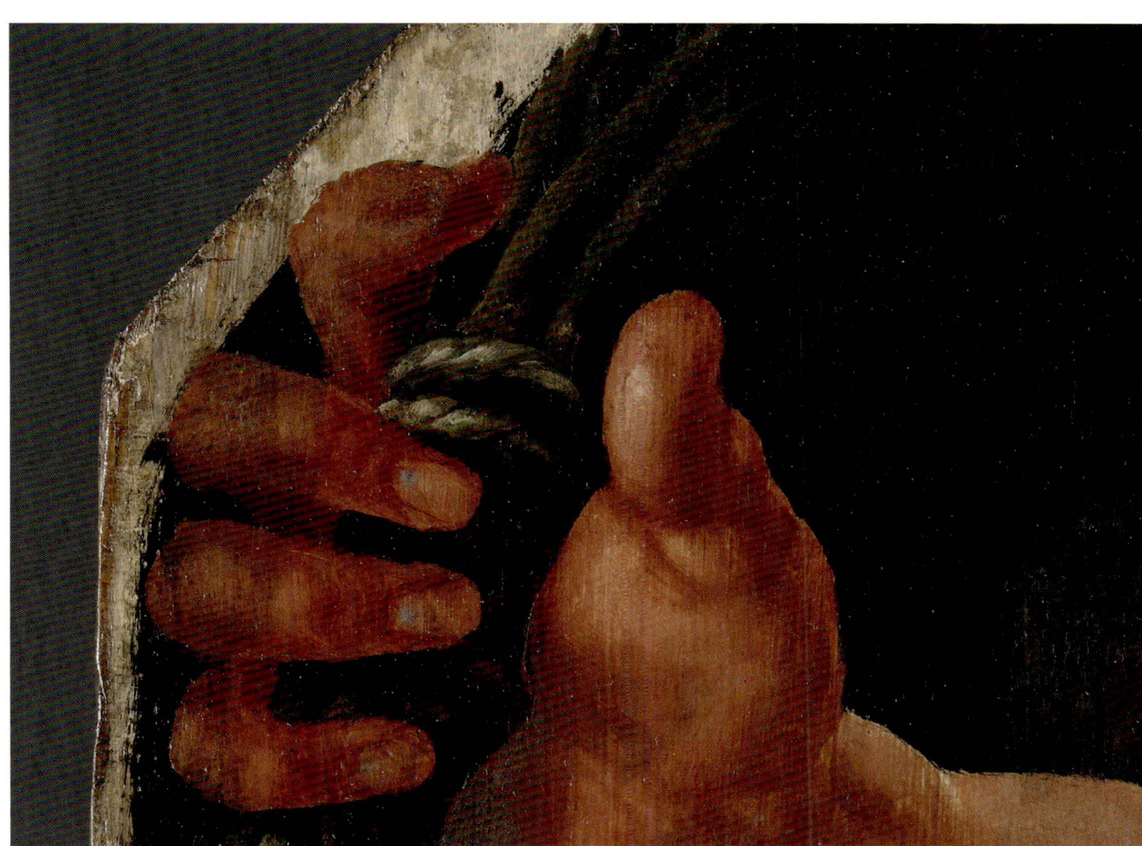

FIGURE 31 The entire hand was probably painted before the frame was designed; some of the hand is now obscured by the frame.

PREPARING THE PANEL FOR PAINTING

As was typical for the period, the panel was prepared before being painted, either in Heemskerck's own workshop or by the panelmaker who supplied the panel, with a preparatory white ground made of calcium carbonate (probably natural chalk) and animal glue, scraped down until it was smooth and level. The ground layer appears to be quite thin, allowing the wood grain to show through as a strong visual component due to the increased transparency of the paint layers over time.

As was common practice, Heemskerck applied a thin, rather streaky layer of additional priming on top of the white calcium carbonate ground. The brushstrokes of this layer can be seen on the surface of the painting in some areas, showing no relation to the forms painted on top. Composed of lead white, calcium carbonate, and a carbon black, the layer is visible at the top, unpainted edge of the central panel as a thin pale gray layer over the ground (see fig. 31). It is so thin in places that it is barely detectable in some of the cross sections though clearly visible in others (see figs. 45a and 46a). This layer can be seen as brushy strokes in the X-radiograph, due to its lead white content. X-radiography suggests that this layer was applied and then scraped away and possibly reapplied on the grisaille reverses of the wings, suggesting a possible reuse of materials or change in concept during the process of creating the altarpiece (fig. 32).

A thin, lead white–based priming layer applied over the ground is quite usual in Netherlandish painting of the later fifteenth and early sixteenth centuries. Such a priming possibly provided several simultaneous functions: fixing any initial drawing on the ground while leaving it partially visible, sealing the ground to prevent excessive absorption of oil from the paint, and providing an appropriate foundation to confer luminosity to the superimposed colored paints. Such lead white–based primings are typically bound in an oil medium, but in the case of the *Ecce Homo* triptych, the medium has been positively identified as collagen-based animal glue.[17] Heemskerck's modification of the more traditional oil priming meant that he could start painting immediately, as the glue medium would have dried quite quickly.[18]

PLANNING THE COMPOSITION

The directness of Heemskerck's painting process is evident even in the planning stages, when he modified and simplified what was at the time a somewhat complex and graphic process. Netherlandish painters usually made a preparatory drawing, or underdrawing, directly on the panel, most commonly in chalk, charcoal, or ink. It was generally drawn directly on the ground, although it is sometimes found on top of the priming layer.[19] This preparatory design, which the artist followed when painting, sometimes shows through thin paint layers that have become increasingly transparent over time. Furthermore, imaging techniques such as infrared photography and infrared reflectography can often reveal the underdrawing, depending on the material used. Black chalk, charcoal, and carbon black ink are all usually easily seen with these techniques; however, because of their material composition, iron gall ink and red chalk are generally not detected.

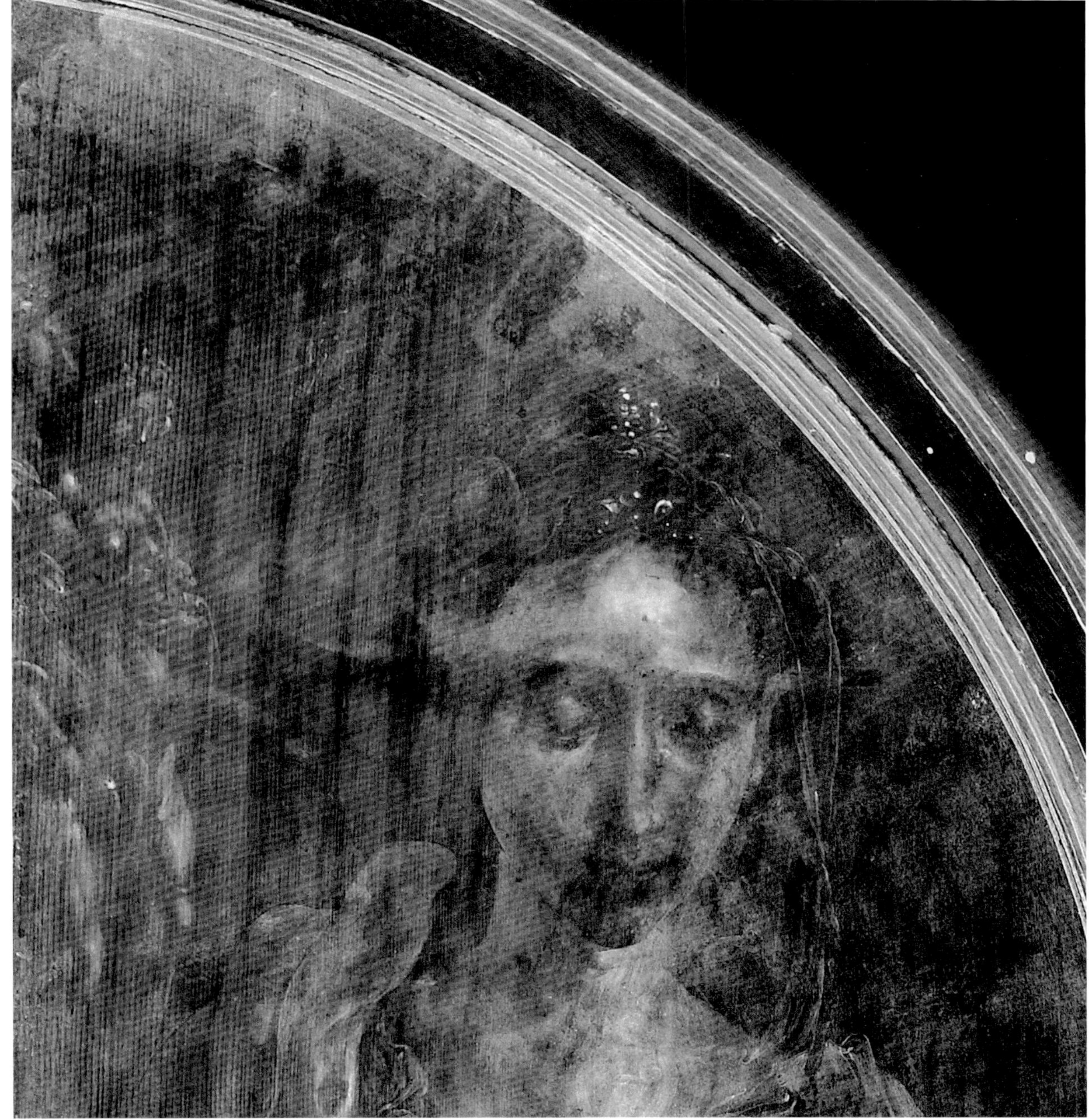

FIGURE 32 The scraping of the preparatory layers is visible in the X-radiograph of the wing panel.

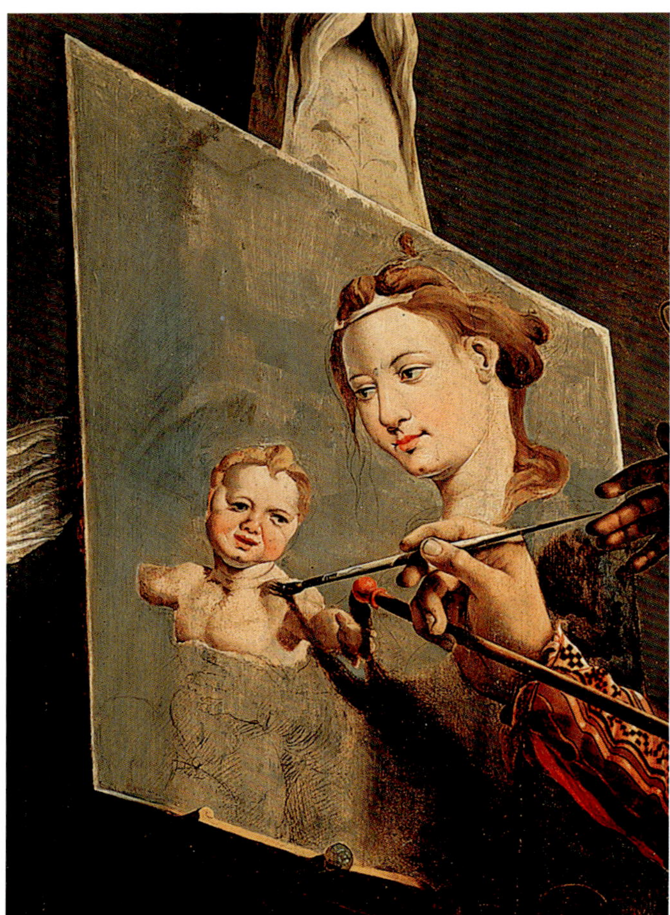

FIGURE 33 Maerten van Heemskerck, *Saint Luke Painting the Virgin* (detail of figure 2)

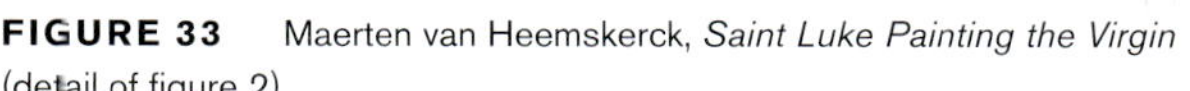

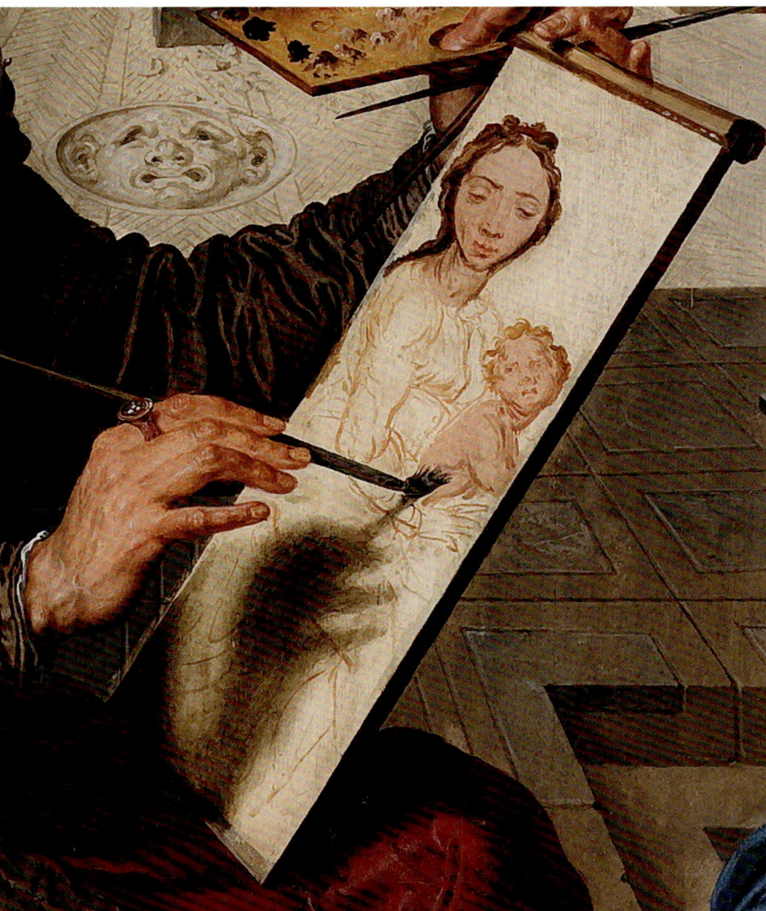

FIGURE 34 Maerten van Heemskerck, *Saint Luke Painting the Virgin* (detail of figure 20)

In Heemskerck's 1532 *Saint Luke Painting the Virgin*, Saint Luke's composition has been underdrawn in black (fig. 33); in his later painting of the same subject (fig. 34), Saint Luke has drawn on the panel with a red material. Given that Heemskerck's journey to Italy took place in the years between the making of the two paintings, it is tempting to speculate that he often chose red chalk as his preferred underdrawing medium after his observations of Italian technique while he was in Rome (which might then explain the lack of discernible underdrawing in many of his works).[20]

Perhaps because of this evolution in his drawing method, it is difficult to characterize Heemskerck's underdrawing on the main interior scenes of the *Ecce Homo* triptych, as virtually none can be seen through what are noticeably thin paint layers, nor can any be firmly identified in the infrared reflectograms (see fig. 26).[21] This may also be due in part to Heemskerck's fairly close adherence to his overall design, making identification of underdrawn lines (as opposed to final painted lines) in the infrared reflectogram particularly difficult.

For a panel of this size, it is presumed that the composition would have been worked out on paper, probably at a reduced scale, and the overall design enlarged and transferred to the panel by some means. There are at least two known instances of Heemskerck transferring his design by

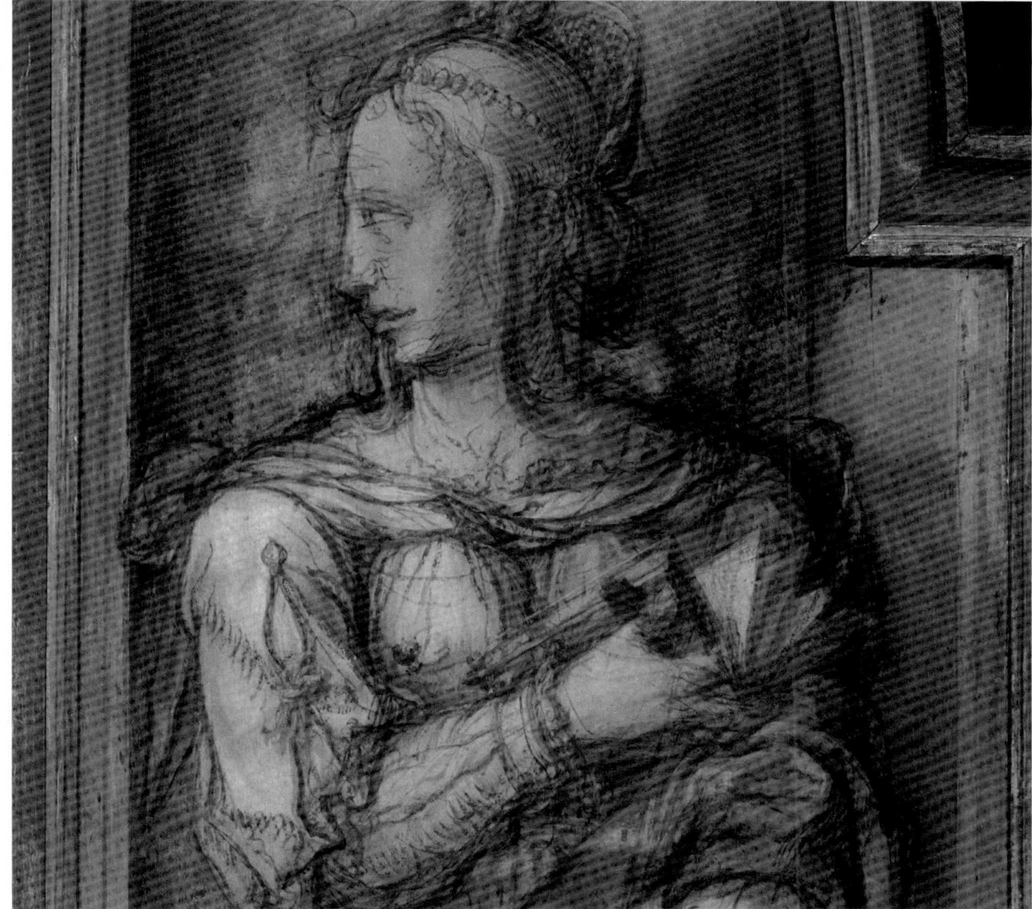

FIGURE 35 Preparatory drawing under the paint is clearly visible in the infrared reflectogram of the exterior wing.

squaring—that is, drawing a grid on the preparatory drawing on paper and on the panel prepared for painting—a method also used by Jan van Scorel as well as a number of contemporary Italian artists that allowed a scaled enlargement of the composition.[22] While there is no evidence of squaring on the triptych, such lines probably would have been made in charcoal and brushed away before painting, leaving little, if any, trace. Individual drawings might also have been used to create the complex composition, the final work a compilation and integration of a set of individual elements. It is possible that a smaller presentation drawing was made for the Drenckwaerdts, eliminating the need for detailed drawing on the panel, as this worked-out design could be used for reference during the painting process. A few shallow incisions in the ground layer can be found marking the main forms, suggesting that they were transferred to the panel by some means of tracing. There seem to be few changes or deviations in the final painting, and it is clear the composition must have been set in the early stages of work.

By contrast, extensive underdrawing is visible on the reverse of the side panels. It has a lively and energetic spontaneity loosely defining the forms of the final grisaille paintings, which are stylistically different and were probably executed by members of the workshop. The medium appears to be black chalk, and it is clearly visible in the infrared reflectogram (fig. 35).

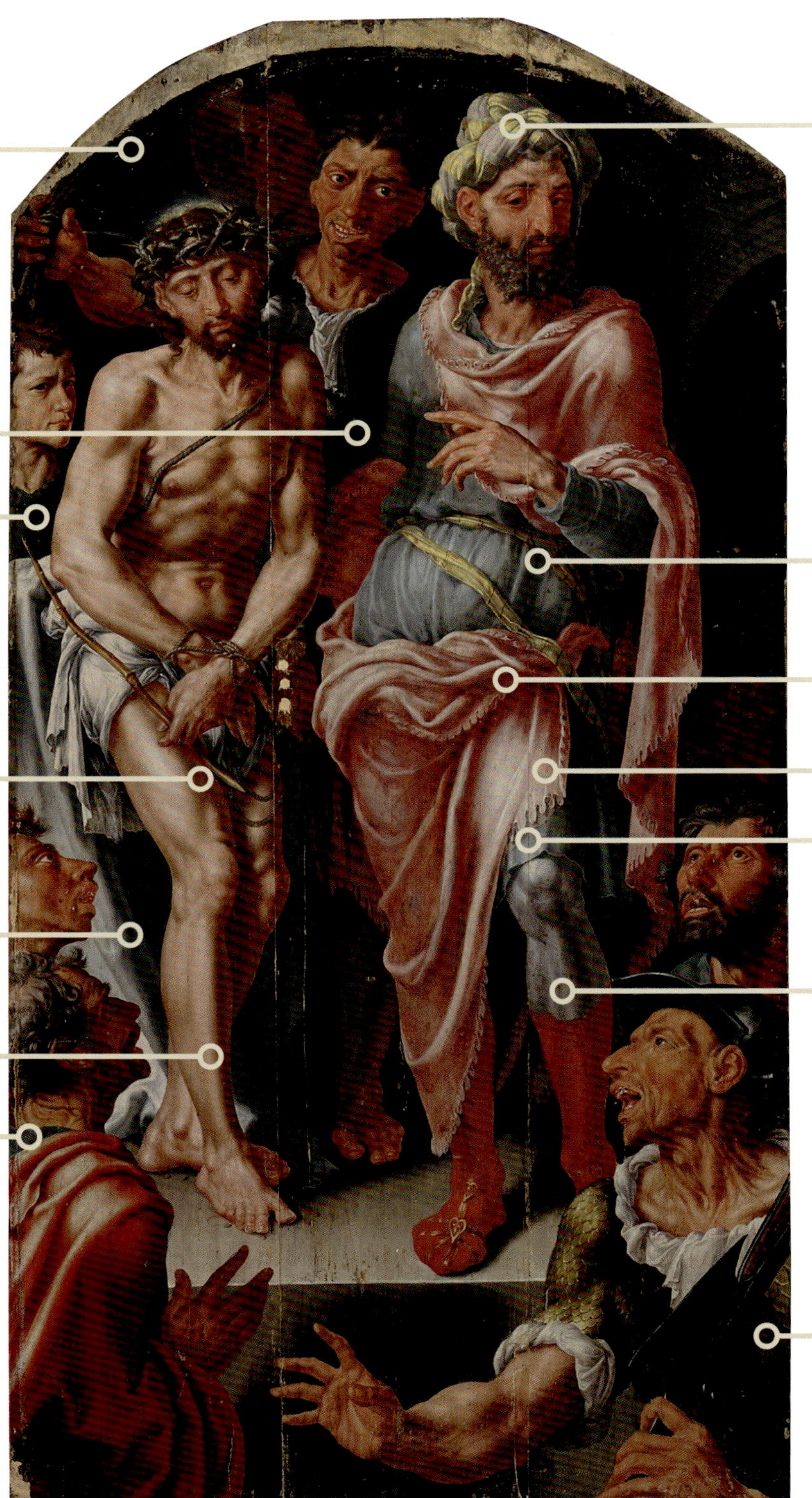

FIGURE 36 Summary of pigment occurrences indicated by chemical analysis of paint samples

PAINT: VARIATIONS ON A HUE Heemskerck's innovative approach to painting was reflected in his colors—both his pigment choices and the way in which he used them allowed him to paint with a broad range of tonal values, and his color juxtapositions add to a dramatic and heightened final appearance, albeit somewhat changed over the years due to fading and discoloration. His surprising use of orpiment and realgar in later paintings[23] suggests he was somewhat experimental in his choices, as these pigments were more commonly used in Italy and were somewhat rare for the Netherlands. Analysis of the *Ecce Homo* triptych points to his use of a fairly conventional but rather restricted palette that has been cleverly altered with a few fascinating additions. His technique is characterized by nuanced variations on particular color themes using subtly different combinations of certain pigments and underpaintings. Materials found in the triptych include most of the common pigment substances of the period: calcium carbonate (which features in some paints as well as in the priming and ground), lead white (basic lead carbonate), at least one carbon black (including wood charcoal), natural red and yellow iron oxide earth pigments, lead-tin yellow (lead-tin oxide), vermilion (mercuric sulfide), azurite (basic copper carbonate), smalt (a blue, cobalt-containing glass), a copper-based transparent green (probably verdigris, basic copper acetate), and at least one red lake pigment (an organic plant- or insect-derived dyestuff precipitated onto an inert substrate) (fig. 36).[24] Obvious omissions from the list of pigments identified in the triptych are ultramarine (from natural lapis lazuli),[25] yellow or orange arsenic sulfide pigments (orpiment and realgar), and any other green or yellow colors.

The pigments would have, no doubt, been bought from an apothecary or color supplier and would have varied in quality and price; given that Van Mander described Heemskerck as "thrifty" (*vergarigh*),[26] it is interesting to see how his choices might have affected the changed appearance of the triptych over time.

One of the distinctive features of Heemskerck's technique in the *Ecce Homo* triptych is his use of the blue pigments smalt and azurite. Smalt is ground-up blue potassium glass containing cobalt as colorant (fig. 37) that became more frequently used as a pigment in the sixteenth century as supplies of azurite and ultramarine dwindled. Its color, when first made, is very strong and slightly purplish blue; because of this, Heemskerck may have liked it as a substitute for ultramarine.[27] Smalt was used extensively throughout the interior paintings of the triptych, and in paints of a

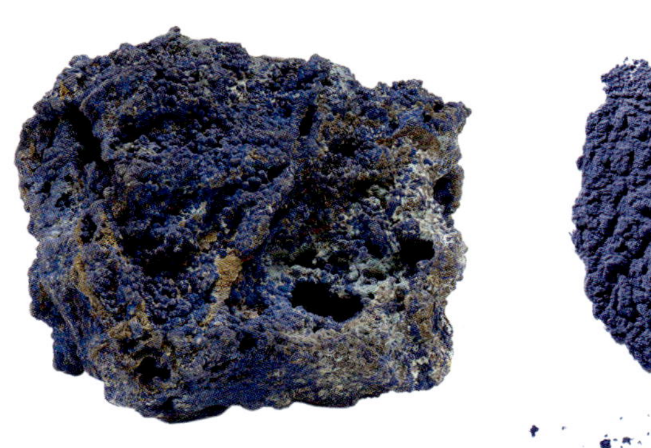
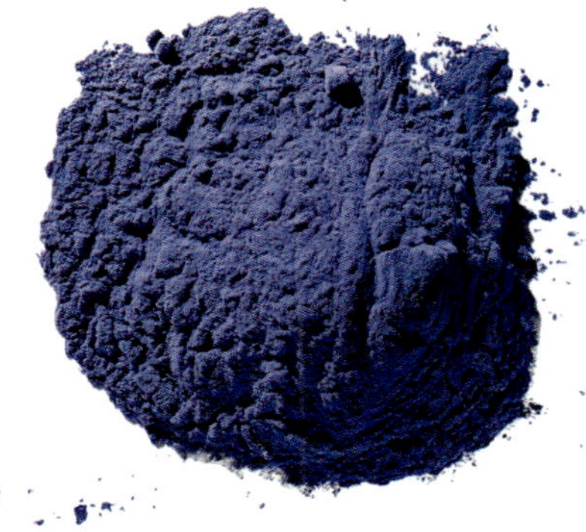

FIGURE 37 Two blue pigments used in the *Ecce Homo*: azurite in mineral form (left) and smalt, or ground blue potassium glass (right)

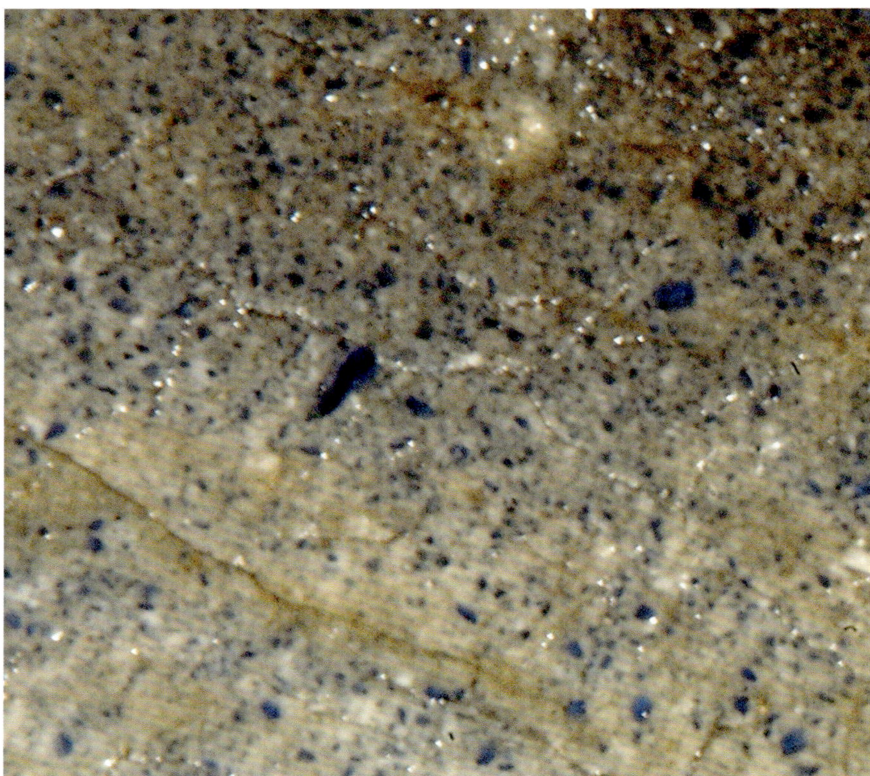

FIGURE 38 One of the larger particles of smalt retains its blue color.

variety of colors, to the extent that it is the dominant blue colorant within the work. The pigment—often now severely discolored—occurs, essentially alone, in what were probably originally pure (royal) blue passages, such as the inner garment of the figure at the lowest left of the central panel, the tunic of the young man in the upper left of the central panel, and the cloak of Saint Margaret in the interior of the right wing. In these paints, some larger particles of smalt retain a strong blue color (fig. 38), but the majority appears now as weak blue-gray; in each case, the binding medium appears degraded and discolored.[28] These passages of painting, all now a dull green-gray, must have been stunningly rich dark blues when first painted. Smalt's fading properties were probably not known at the time Heemskerck was using the material so extensively.[29]

In addition to being used in the pure blue draperies, smalt was also employed widely throughout the painting in shades of gray, purplish gray, and purple, often with varying proportions of a red lake pigment. Instances include the blue-gray of Pilate's tunic, the light blue-gray of the cloth behind Christ, and Saint John the Evangelist's purple tunic. In the first of these examples—the blue-gray of Pilate's tunic—a strong reddish color can be seen toward the base of the uppermost paint layer, but the red color disappears toward the surface, which strongly suggests severe fading of an organic red lake pigment (figs. 39a and 39b). If the differential red coloration evident in this sample does indeed derive from the fading of an organic red colorant, it may indicate that Pilate's tunic was originally quite different in color from how it now appears, as a rather greenish blue-gray;[30] a modulated purplish blue seems probable.

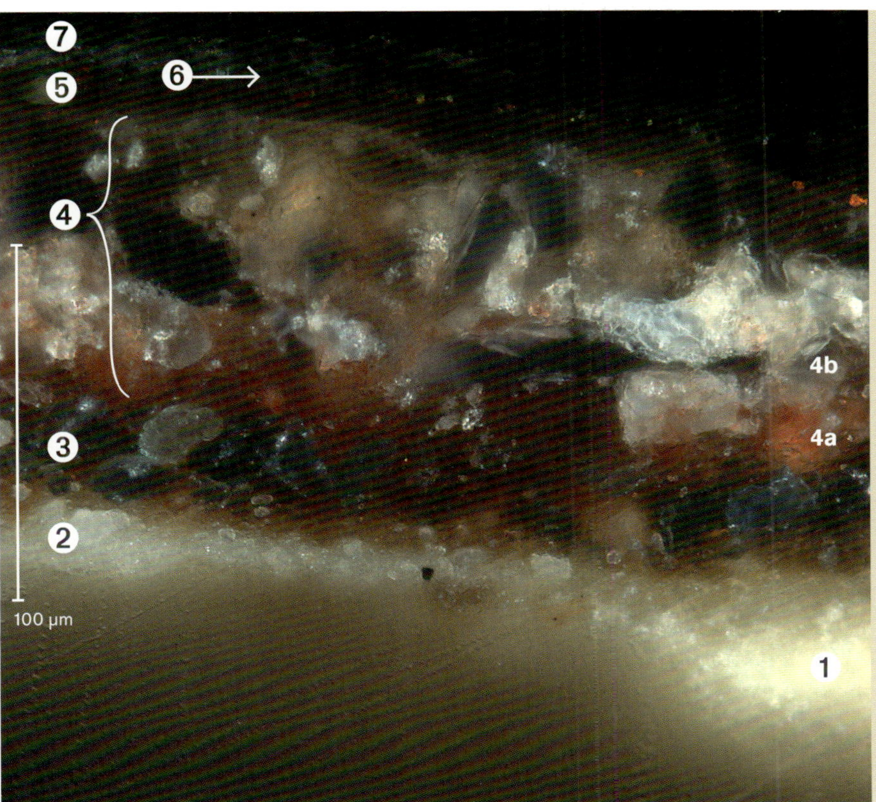

FIGURE 39A

Cross-section sample from the shadow of a fold in Pilate's blue-gray tunic, viewed with visible light

- **7** Varnish
- **6** Restoration/retouching
- **5** Varnish, probably not original
- **4** Thick, purple-blue paint, composed mostly of smalt and red lake, in which some internal stratification is evident; upper substratum (4b) appears severely depleted in red colorant, probably due to fading from exposure to light, and the paint appears degraded and porous; in lower substratum (4a), the red lake pigment is well preserved.
- **3** A now-brownish paint layer composed mostly of a copper-based blue (probably azurite), transparent red lake (difficult to discern), and a little lead white, all seemingly embedded in discolored medium
- **2** Near-white priming composed of lead white, calcium carbonate, and a little carbon black
- **1** Calcium carbonate ground

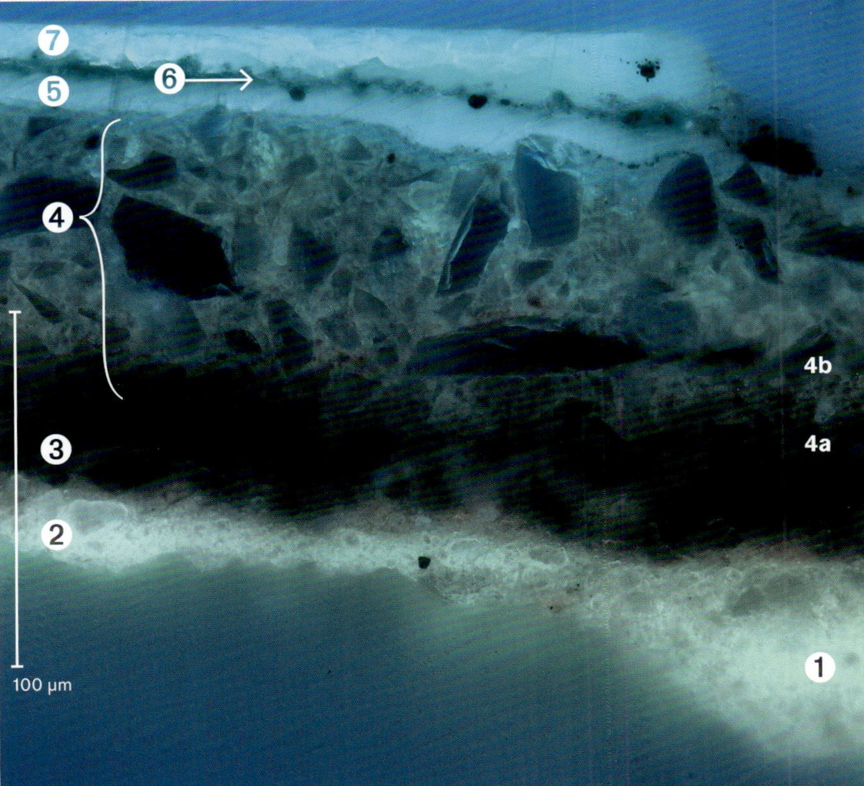

FIGURE 39B

The same sample as in fig. 39a, viewed by ultraviolet fluorescence. The glassy particles of smalt, some only weakly colored, can be seen much more distinctly, as can the layers of varnish and old restoration.

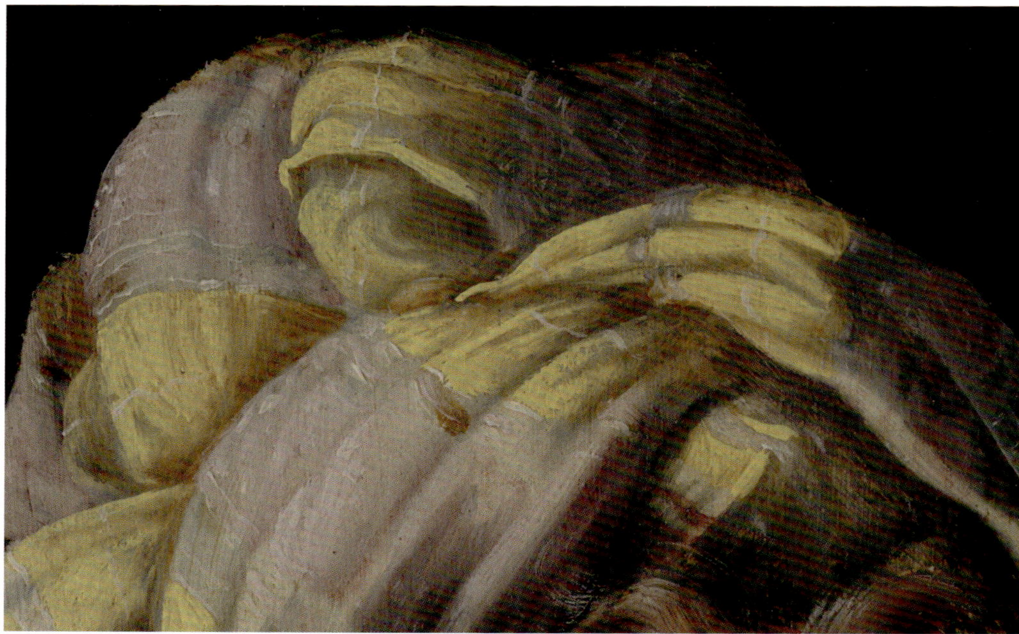

FIGURE 40 The azurite-based underpaint is detectable in Pilate's turban.

Two samples from the cloth held by the young man just behind Christ also show visual evidence of fading of an organic red colorant in the uppermost paint layer, where it also occurs with smalt. Again, it might be surmised that the cloth was originally more purplish in color than the cool, neutral gray it appears now.

While smalt is used widely through the painting, azurite is used comparatively sparingly. Azurite was an expensive material in the 1540s, with supply limited due to the occupation by the Turks of the area of Hungary in which a major source of the mineral was located.[31] In the majority of cases where azurite occurs in the *Ecce Homo* triptych, curiously and distinctively, it is mostly in layers of *underpainting* beneath paints containing smalt, rather than in the upper, final applications. Examples of smalt-containing paints underpainted with azurite include the blue-gray of Pilate's tunic, noted above, the garment of the young man holding the cloth behind Christ, and the inner garment of the figure at the lower left of the central panel. Only in a sample from the blue-gray of Pilate's stocking was azurite found in bluish paint at the uppermost level, where it occurs with lead white, red lake, and black. Given that Pilate's now-greenish-gray tunic was probably once purplish, the color contrast between the tunic and the stocking must originally have been very subtle indeed.

Azurite-based underpainting occurs as well under lead-tin yellow, in blue-gray underpainting to Pilate's turban (figs. 40 and 41), and in the now dark green-brown of the tunic of the central figure (holding a switch) behind Christ and Pilate in the central panel, where it was used in combination with lead white and charcoal to give a strong gray-blue foundation to the green glaze (now severely discolored) that provides the final rendering of the drapery (fig. 42). This combination of intense transparent green glaze over blue underpaint must originally have produced a saturated green that would have contrasted powerfully with Pilate's red and purple clothing.

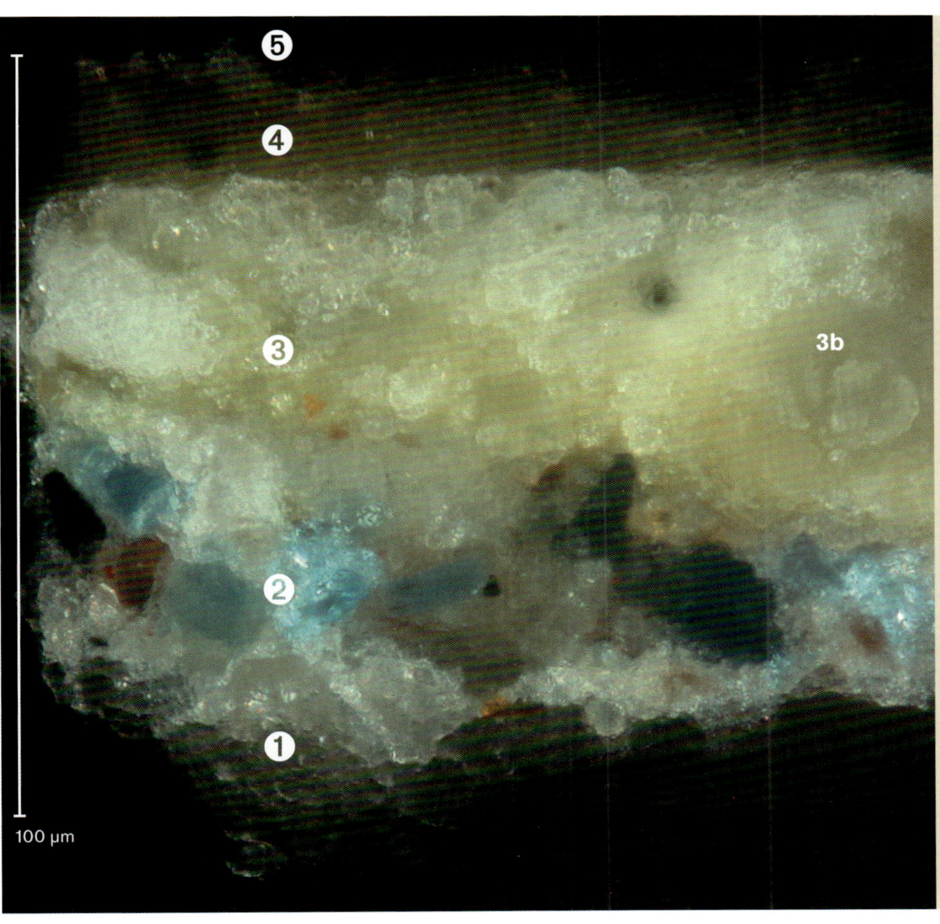

FIGURE 41

Cross-section sample from the yellow highlight on Pilate's turban

- **5** Nonoriginal varnish
- **4** Filler from an old restoration intervention
- **3b** The large transparent amorphous feature in the yellow paint at far right is probably a lead soap aggregate, an alteration phenomenon caused by a reaction of the pigment with the oil binding medium.
- **3** The opaque pale yellow highlight is mostly lead-tin yellow.
- **2** Purplish-gray underpainting composed of weakly colored azurite particles, lead white, carbon black, and a little red lake
- **1** Thin layer of ground (A layer corresponding to the priming cannot be discerned in this sample; if present, it is imperceptibly thin.)

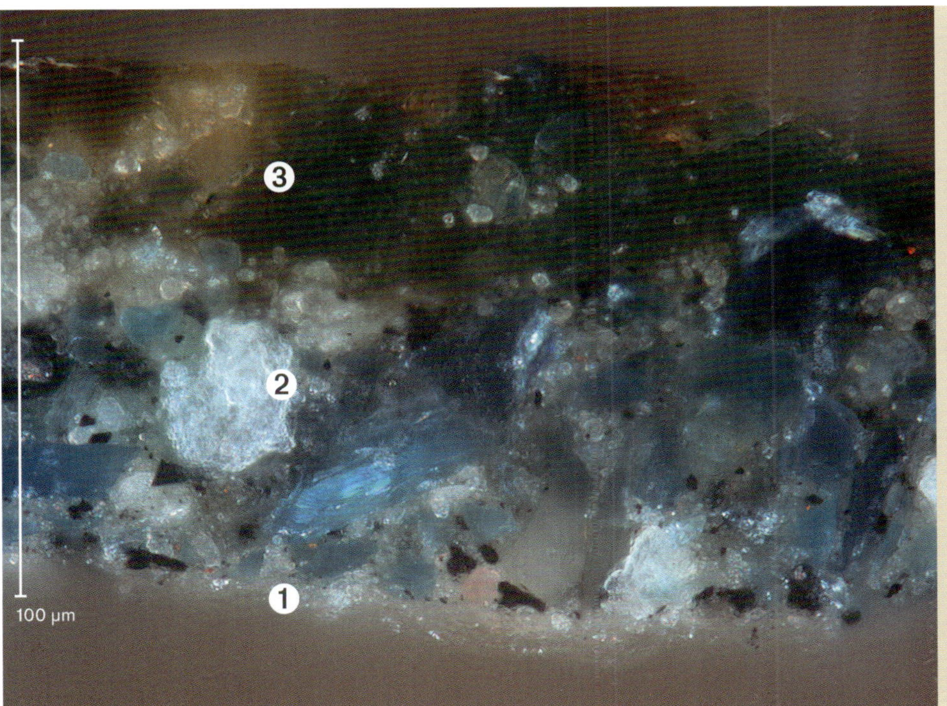

FIGURE 42

Cross-section sample from the now-dark-brownish tunic of the central figure between Christ and Pilate, viewed with visible light

- **3** Transparent copper-based green glaze that has severely discolored to brown, especially toward the upper surface
- **2** Thick underpainting composed of azurite, lead white, charcoal, and a little red lake
- **1** Thin layer of ground

The green glaze used for the central figure's tunic, which is now severely discolored to brown, contains a copper-based colorant together with minor inclusions of lead white and azurite. Similar copper-based glazes are found elsewhere on the interior paintings, most notably in the green scale armor of the soldier at the lower right of the central panel, and the tablecloths beside the donors on the wings. Most of these paints appear depleted in (green) particulates, albeit to varying extents: some are almost completely devoid of any discernible particles, while others show distinguishable large copper-rich particles in greater or lesser abundance. Taken together, these occurrences point toward the transparent copper-green colorant being not copper resinate but verdigris (basic copper acetate) that has over time become dissolved in situ in the oil medium to form copper carboxylate salts, causing the depletion of particulates of the verdigris, of which only the larger ones remain, in some cases.[32] Many of these glazed areas appear to have been dabbed on with pieces of fabric, as the impression of the weave can be discerned.[33] This technique would have allowed for judicious use of material, an appealing manner of application for cost savings.

It is evident even from normal viewing of the painting that the passages that consist of green glazes are to varying degrees discolored toward brown. In some cases, however, such as the tablecloth on the right wing, cross-section samples show that the transparent green glaze has retained a relatively vivid green color in the lower part of the layer, and that discoloration is concentrated toward the upper surface. An interesting finding connected with transparent copper-green glazes occurred in a sample from the scale armor of the soldier (fig. 43) in the lower right of the central panel: a thin layer of an intermediate varnish had been applied between two transparent green paints. Varnishing a copper-green (i.e., verdigris-based) glaze immediately after drying was one way of supposedly preventing or retarding discoloration, a strategy that is mentioned variously in manuscripts from the beginning of the sixteenth century through the seventeenth century,[34] and it is tempting to regard this instance as intending to have a protective function.

As noted earlier, several samples from the painting showed that Heemskerck exploited combinations of smalt and red lake pigment in many passages, and red appears now as something of a dominant hue in both flesh and draperies. Samples from areas of flesh, for example, the right leg of Christ, show relatively simple combinations of lead white, calcium carbonate, vermilion, and reddish iron oxide earth, but it is interesting to note the variation in proportion of these constituents as the paint varies from pale highlight to shadow: the paint of the highlight contains essentially just lead white and vermilion with a trace of calcium carbonate, while the light halftone and shadow respectively show increasing proportions of iron oxide earth, with vermilion diminishing to a trace amount.

The matching sleeves of the donors' clothing are especially saturated passages of red, with shadows of deep, transparent reddish black (fig. 44). A sample from the scarlet midtone of Jan's sleeve (figs. 45a and 45b) shows that it was rendered in two applications of paint of nearly identical composition: red lake, vermilion, and lead white, plus a transparent, colorless extender substance. The deep, reddish-black shadow is a single application of paint (figs. 46a and 46b) that includes the same two red pigments, but with the proportion of red lake increased and that of vermilion

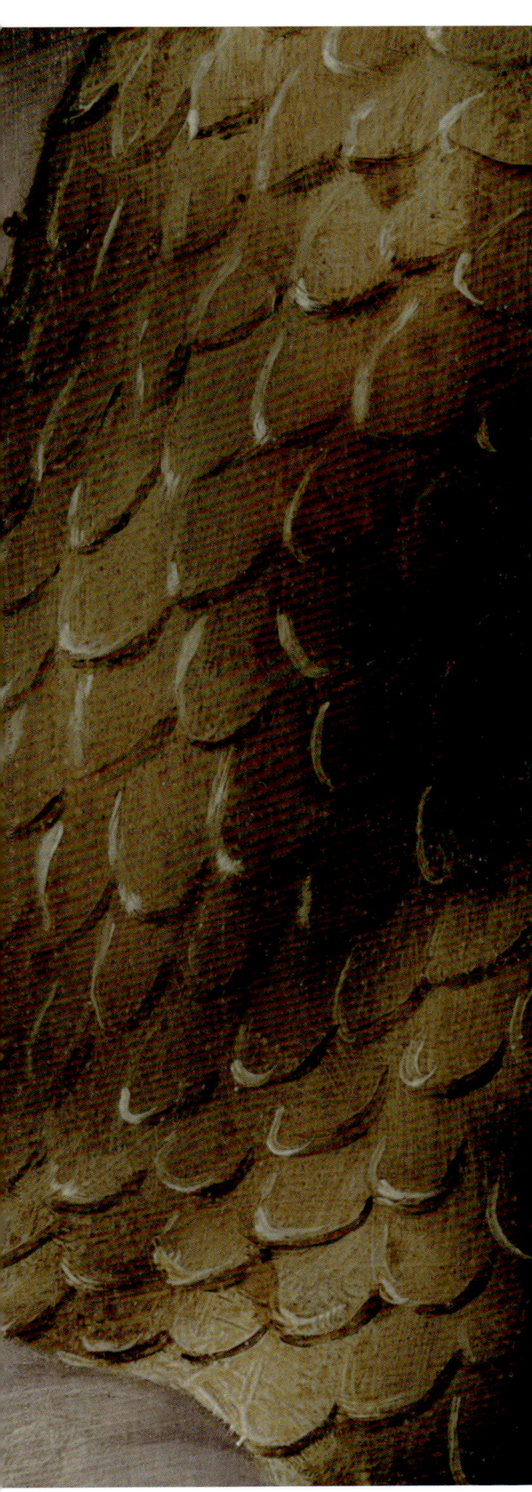

FIGURE 43 The green scale armor has discolored to a browner hue.

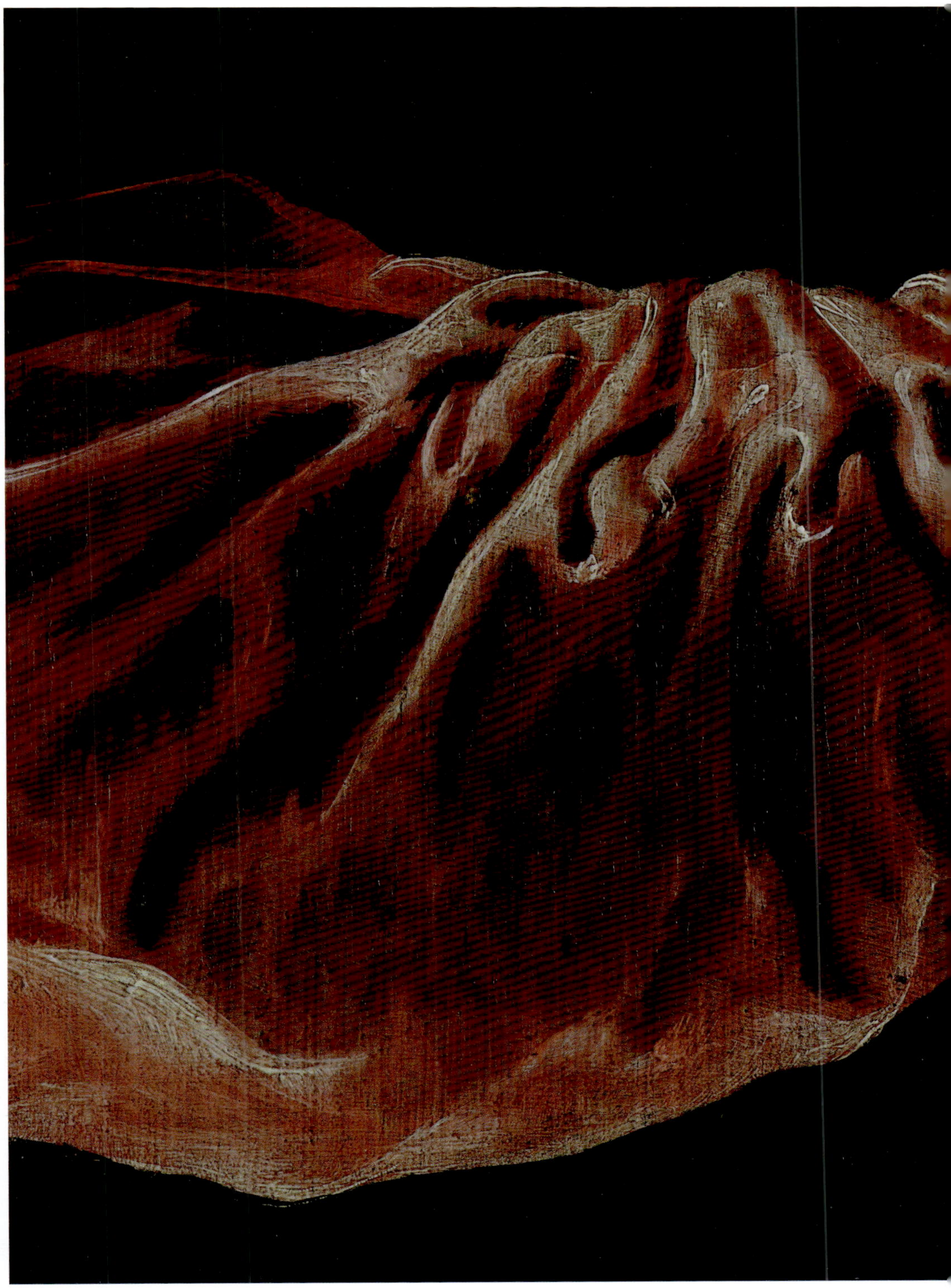

FIGURE 44 Heemskerck's masterful and quick methods are particularly evident in his painting of the red fabric.

FIGURE 45A

A cross-section sample from the scarlet midtone of Jan van Drenckwaerdt's sleeve shows it is rendered in two applications of paint (**3** and **4**) of nearly identical composition—red lake, vermilion, and lead white—plus a transparent colorless extender substance that has been identified as glass. The calcium carbonate ground (**1**) and the pale-gray (**2**) priming underlie the applications of red paint.

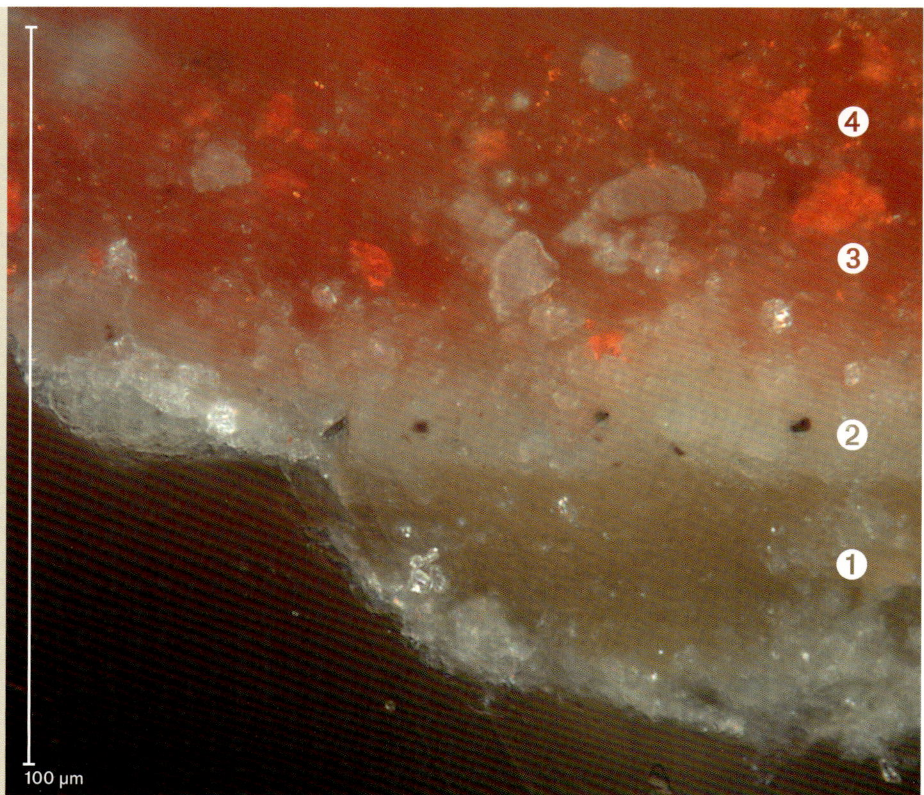

FIGURE 45B

The same sample as in fig. 45a, viewed by ultraviolet fluorescence. The two applications of similarly composed red paint (**3** and **4**) can be seen more distinctly, as can the abundant particles of the glass extender substance, which appear gray under ultraviolet fluorescence.

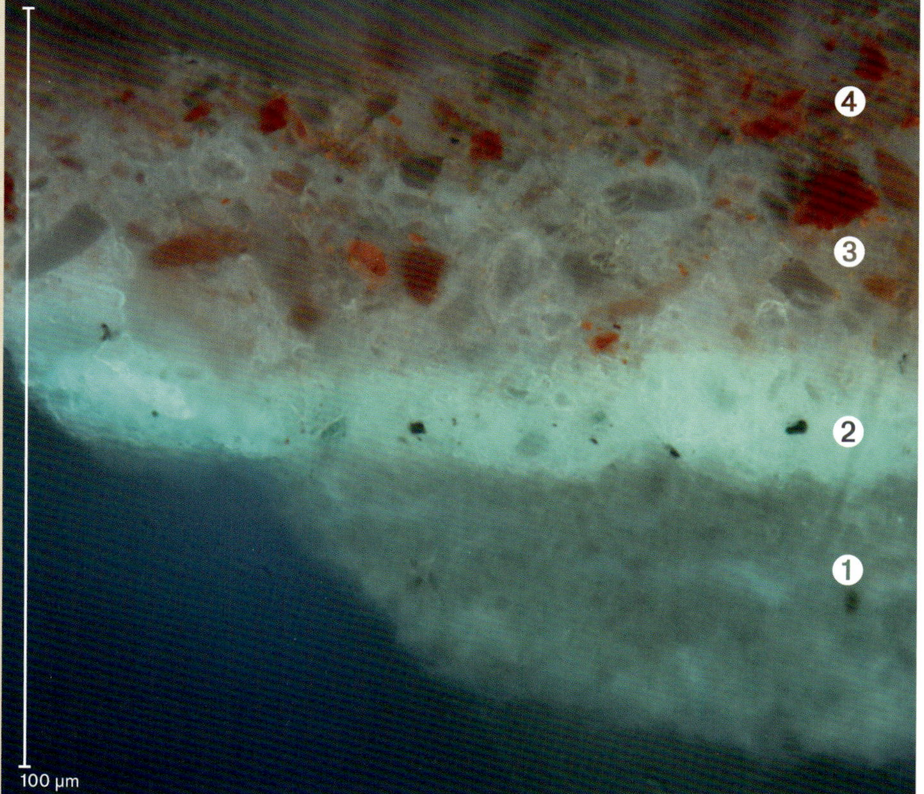

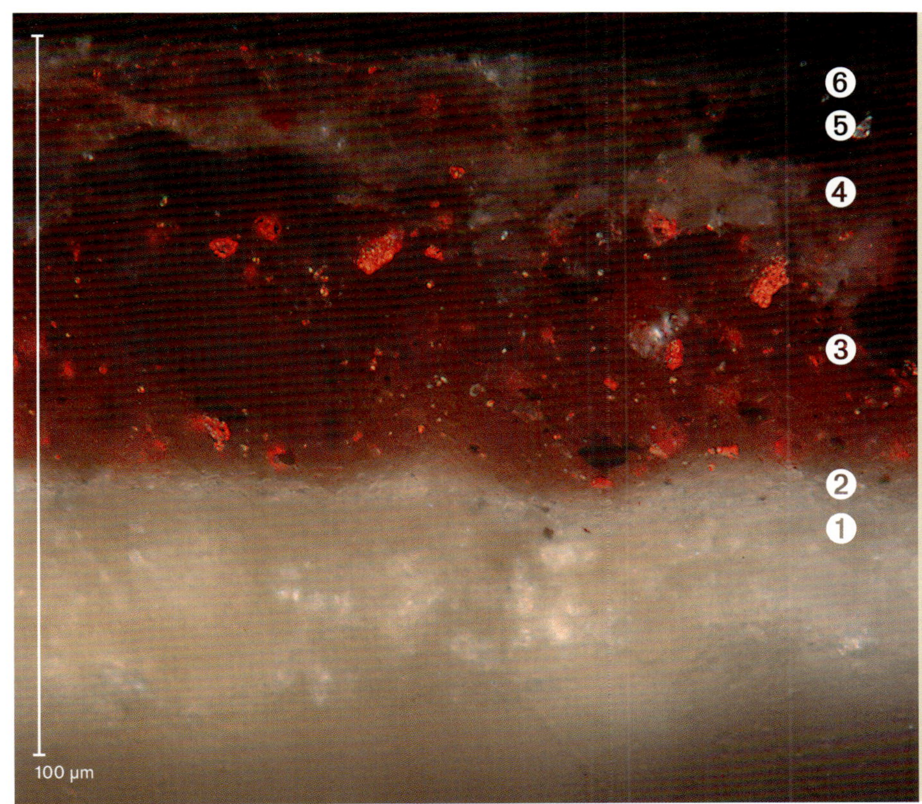

FIGURE 46A

Cross-section sample from a reddish-black shadow of Jan van Drenckwaerdt's sleeve

6 Varnish
5 Dark-brown paint: nonoriginal restoration/retouching
4 Varnish
3 Dark transparent red-brown paint rendering the shadow of the sleeve: composed mostly of red lake, vermilion, and carbon black, plus the same glass extender as used in the scarlet midtone (figs. 45a–b).
2 Pale gray priming
1 Ground

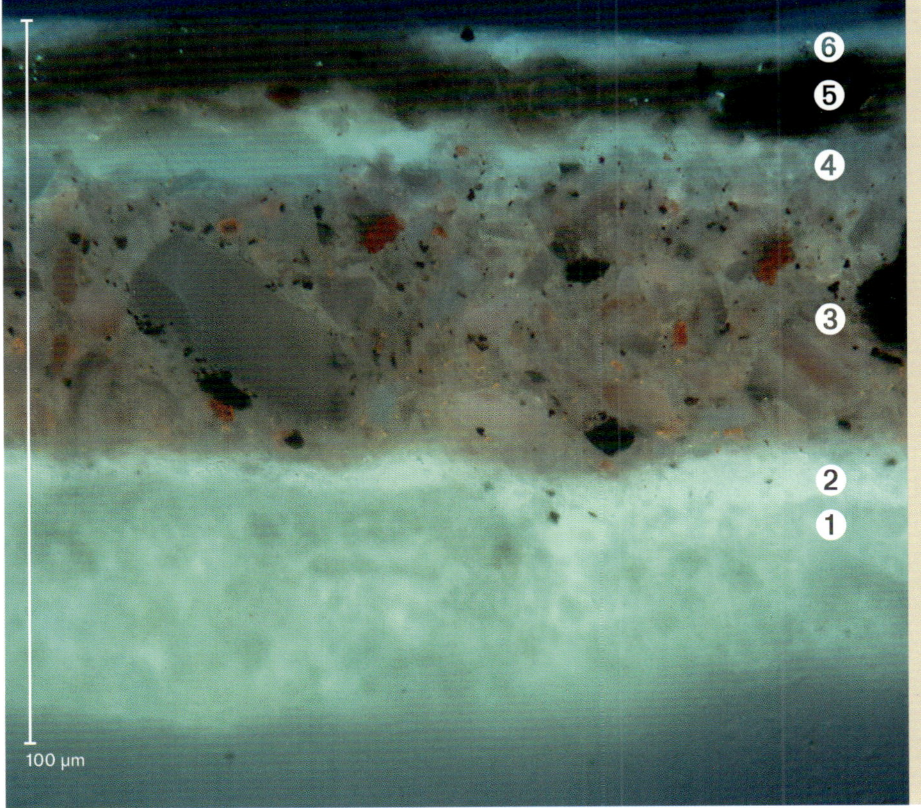

FIGURE 46B

The same sample as in fig. 46a viewed by ultraviolet fluorescence

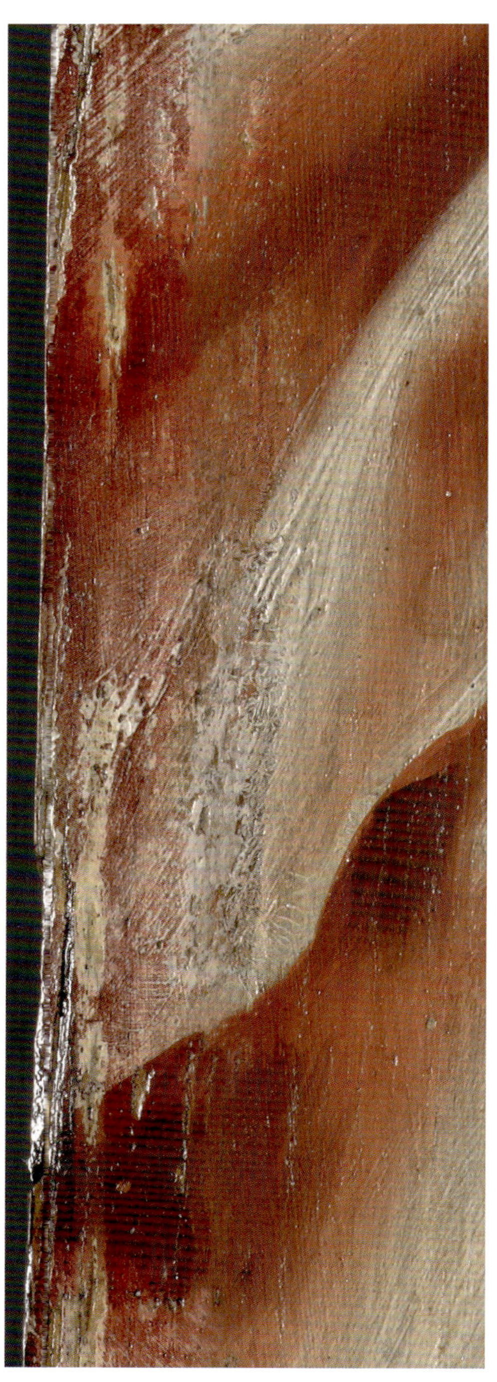

FIGURE 47 Where the drapery was protected from light by the frame, the red hue has remained vibrant.

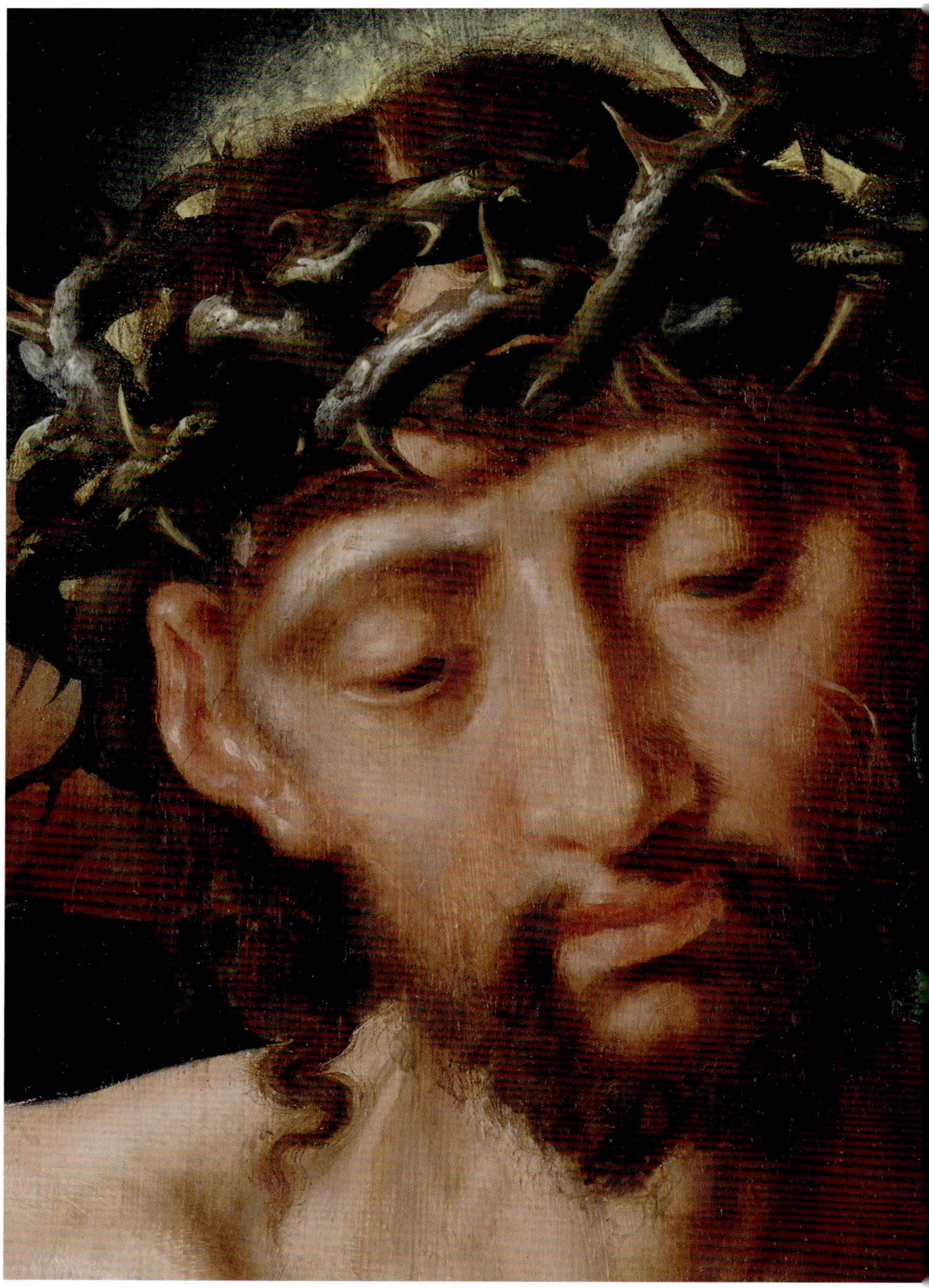

FIGURE 48 Paint used to depict red blood has now faded completely; all that remains visible are pale lines of the pigments' gray substrate on Christ's proper left cheek.

reduced, and the white removed and carbon black added; the dark, reddish-black glaze also contains the same transparent, colorless extender substance as the scarlet midtone, which will be discussed below. The precise identity of the red lake pigments remains somewhat elusive pending further analytical work.[35]

The fading of red lake pigment in Pilate's tunic has already been noted, and there are other occurrences of faded red lake, most notably in the cloak of the figure in the lower left of the central panel. Where this drapery was protected from light by the frame, the hue has remained bright and colorful (fig. 47). The most severe instance of fading may be in the figure of Christ, where rivulets of blood running down his body have lost their red color. Samples could not be taken from these areas to confirm this visual observation, but the blood must have been painted with a red lake or another organic red colorant that has faded to such an extent that all that remains visible is the residue of the substrate onto which the organic dyestuff was applied (fig. 48).[36]

The transparent, colorless substance in the red and black paints of Jan van Drenckwaerdt's sleeve was also found in several other samples that included red lake. This transparent, colorless material has a distinctive appearance and elemental composition (figs. 49a and 49b), in which calcium is the most abundant element after silicon; it is almost certainly pulverized glass. Clearly, this was a conscious addition to the paint, or to the dry pigment precursor, to serve as what is known as an extender: to add bulk and make the pigment go farther, to promote transparency, and possibly even to improve the drying properties of the pigment when used in an oil medium. Pulverized glass with a similar composition to that found in the triptych has also been identified in Heemskerck's *Virgin and Saint John the Evangelist* in the National Gallery, London. A good number of other occurrences of ground glass have now been identified in Netherlandish, German, and Italian paintings of the fifteenth and sixteenth centuries in that collection, and similar findings have also been reported recently in paintings from these regions and time period housed in German collections.[37]

Another, different colorless extender pigment was identified in a passage of blue azurite-based underpainting; in this case, the extender was bone white or bone ash, the principal constituent of which is hydroxyapatite.[38] Whether these extenders were added intentionally within Heemskerck's studio or were already in pigment he purchased cannot, of course, be determined from these few isolated observations, but they are certainly curious findings when set against Van Mander's comments regarding the artist's supposed thriftiness.

A distinctive pictorial feature of the *Ecce Homo* triptych is the relative lack of any large yellow local color fields among the more dominant purple, red, green, and blue passages; Heemskerck seems to have used yellow paint and yellow pigment in a relatively restricted manner. Undoubtedly, yellow (ocher-type) iron oxide earth pigment occurs as a staple in warm yellow-brownish passages such as the hair of the figures, and lead-tin yellow provides opaque, cool yellow highlights, as on Pilate's turban, Saint John's chalice, and the brocades on his purple undergarment and the bands decorating Saint Margaret's bodice; otherwise, the use of yellow pigment seems relatively restricted.[39]

62

FIGURE 49A

The same sample as in figs. 46a–b, viewed by energy-dispersive X-ray spectroscopy (ESEM-EDS) backscattered electron image, showing the location of the particle used for the spectrum in 49b below

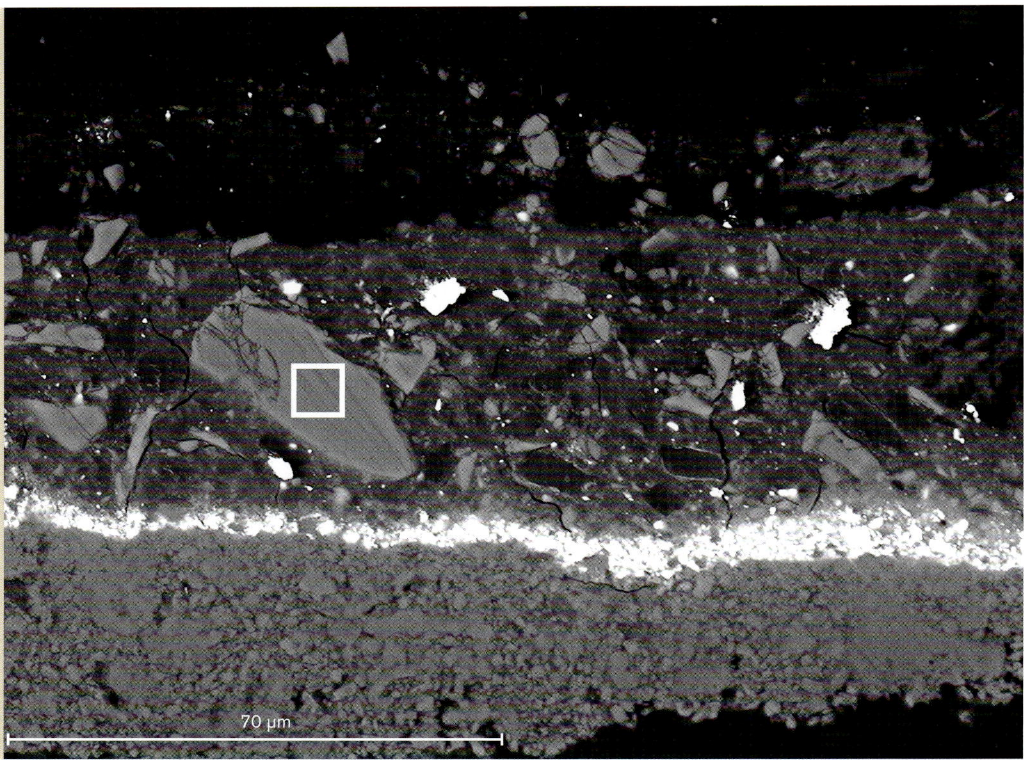

FIGURE 49B

The ESEM-EDS X-ray spectrum obtained from the transparent, colorless extender particle shown in 49a above reveals the elemental profile typical of a calcium-rich glass.

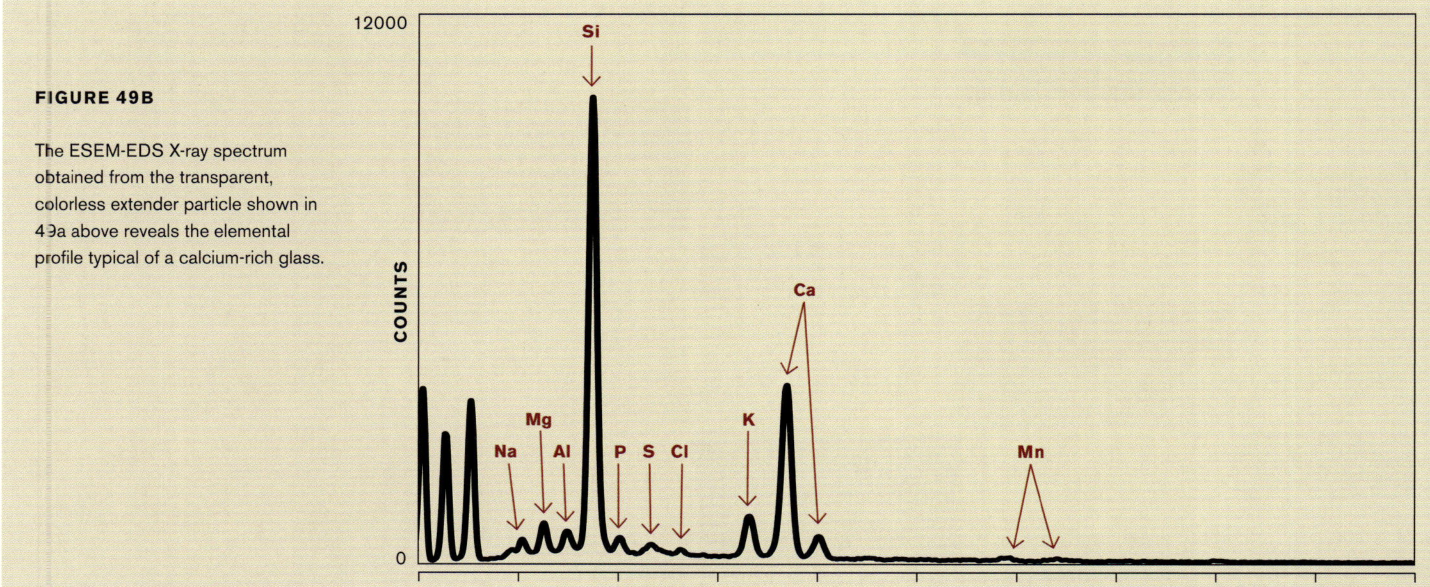

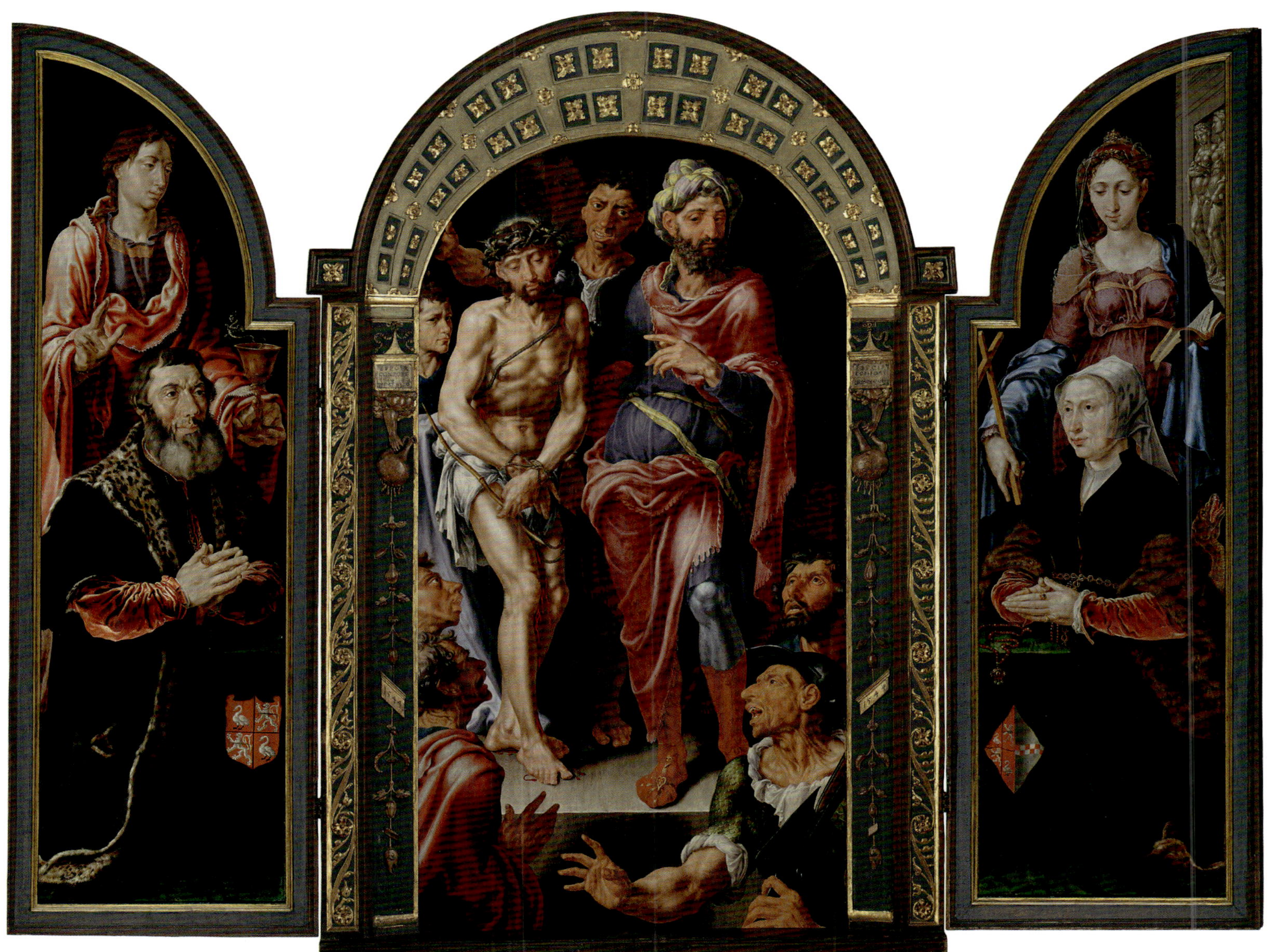

FIGURE 50 Digital color adjustments suggest the original appearance of the triptych.

It is intriguing to imagine how the painting looked before the fading and discoloration of the pigments. Digital photography and image processing make it possible to create an image that gives an idea of its original appearance (fig. 50). Heemskerck carefully orchestrated dramatic juxtapositions of color to define the spatial arrangement of the composed central scene. For example, the darkened green tunic of the figure between Pilate and Christ must have been a rich, jewel-like color of a deeper value than Pilate's tunic, pushing that figure back into space. Similar chromatic choices in other originally richly colored areas (now faded or darkened) would have emphasized the important spatial relationships of the figures.

PAINT MEDIUM

Analysis of paint samples from the *Ecce Homo* triptych by GC-MS demonstrated that, apart from the instance already noted of the priming layer, the binding media in each case is a drying oil. It is known that Heemskerck used both linseed and walnut oils,[40] presumably choosing the latter for its paler tonality when painting lighter colors (a common Italian practice). While the findings on the triptych do not unequivocally prove the use of walnut oil in these passages, it does give strong hints of more than one type of oil vehicle: linseed oil, and walnut oil either used alone or added to linseed oil.[41]

BUILDING THE FORMS

Close viewing of Heemskerck's paintings suggests that he worked extremely quickly, as noted by Van Mander, "There would be no end to recounting all the panels, paintings, epitaphs, and portraits he made because as he was by nature diligent he worked steadily and was very quick in execution."[42] His speedy and brushy application of paint was quite different from the more studied and careful approach of most of his predecessors. (His application of paint was so quick and direct that a number of brush hairs were embedded in the wet paint of the triptych and are still present.) Some of his finishing details are often particularly spontaneous and free, suggesting an impulsive decision to add them as the painting neared completion. For example, the darkened heads of the figures in the background—hardly visible now due to the dark underpaint showing through the extreme thinness of the top paint layers that have become more transparent over time—are painted in a very bold and almost expressionistic manner (figs. 51, 52, and 53). Similarly, the sculpted figures in the background of both wings—those in the left wing hardly visible (fig. 54), again due to the increased transparency of the paint over time—are an impressive example of quick but well-executed forms, using little paint but freely applied strokes to create a convincing illusion of three-dimensionality (fig. 55). The scalloped edge of Pilate's red drapery must have been added at the moment of painting, as it was clearly not present when the shape of it was originally blocked in. The forms of this initial blocking-in are now visible again, due to the age-induced increased transparency of the paint on top (fig. 56). The dragons emerging from Saint John's goblet (fig. 57) and from behind Margaretha (fig. 58) are both fantastic examples of brilliant spontaneity. Upon close examination even the precious jewels worn by Saint Margaret, which seem so carefully painted, reveal an extremely fast and confident execution (fig. 59).

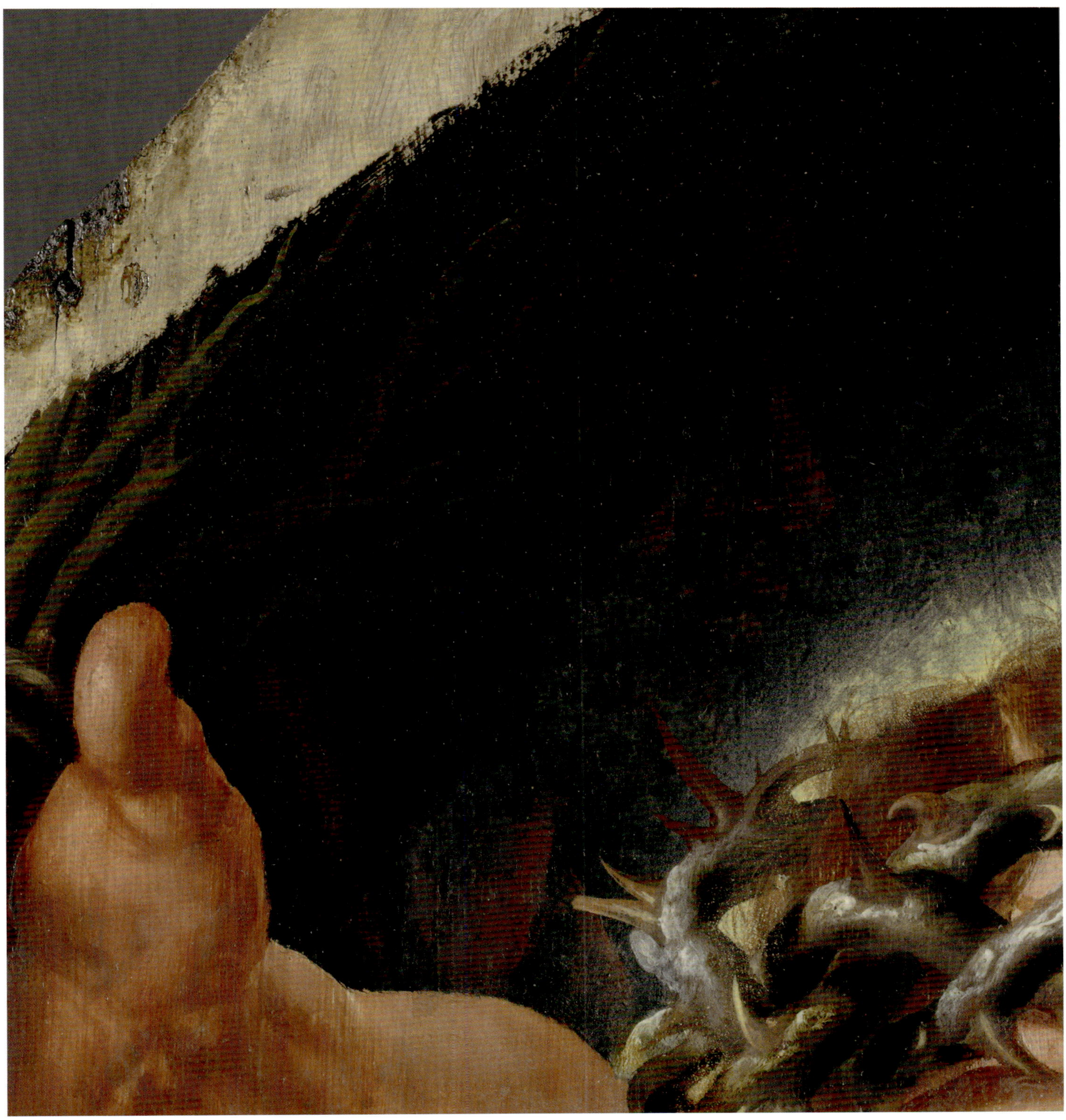

FIGURE 51 This digitally enhanced image reveals a face in the upper left background of the central panel.

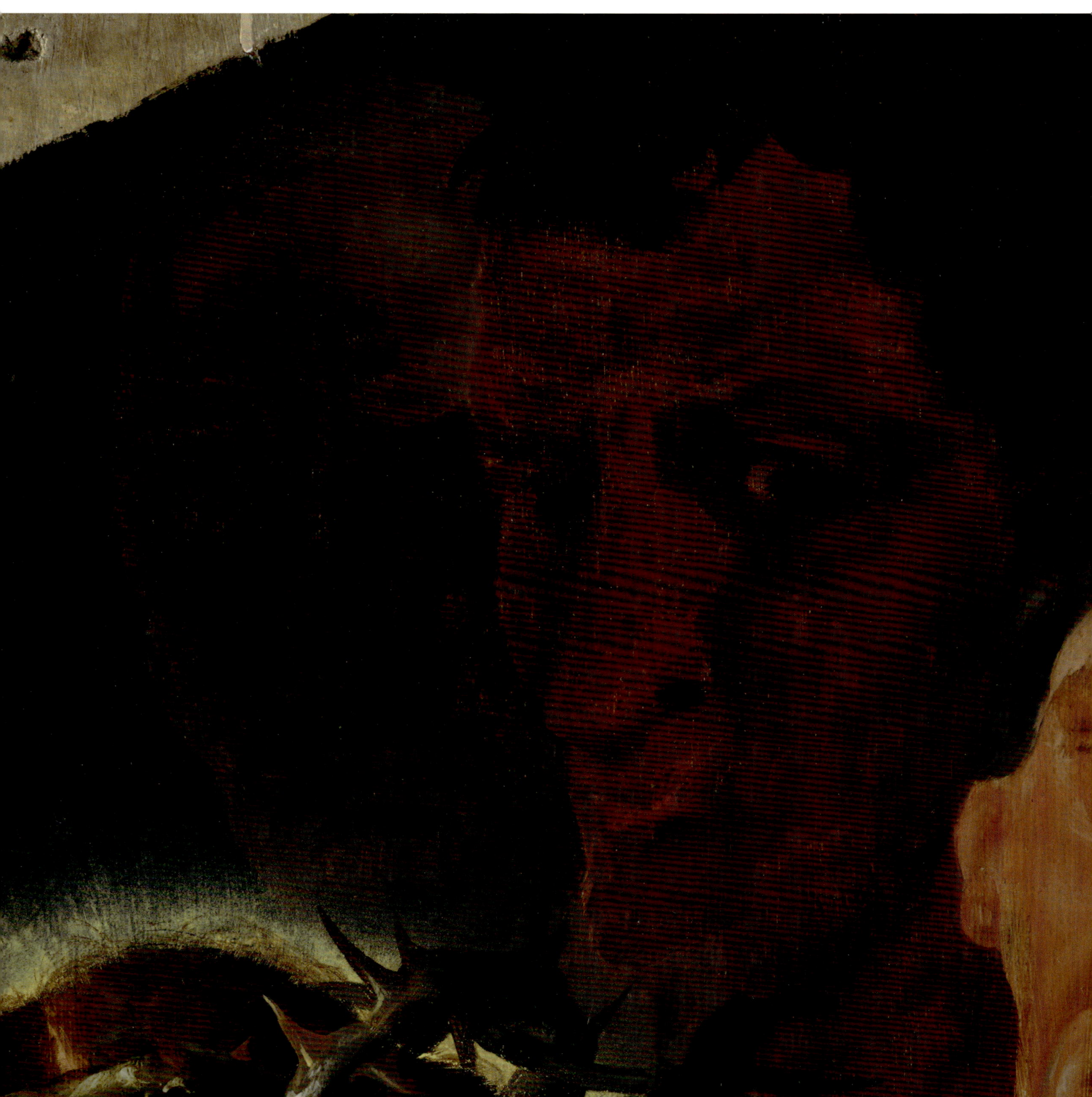

FIGURES 52 and 53 Sketchily painted faces reflect a spontaneity in Heemskerck's approach.

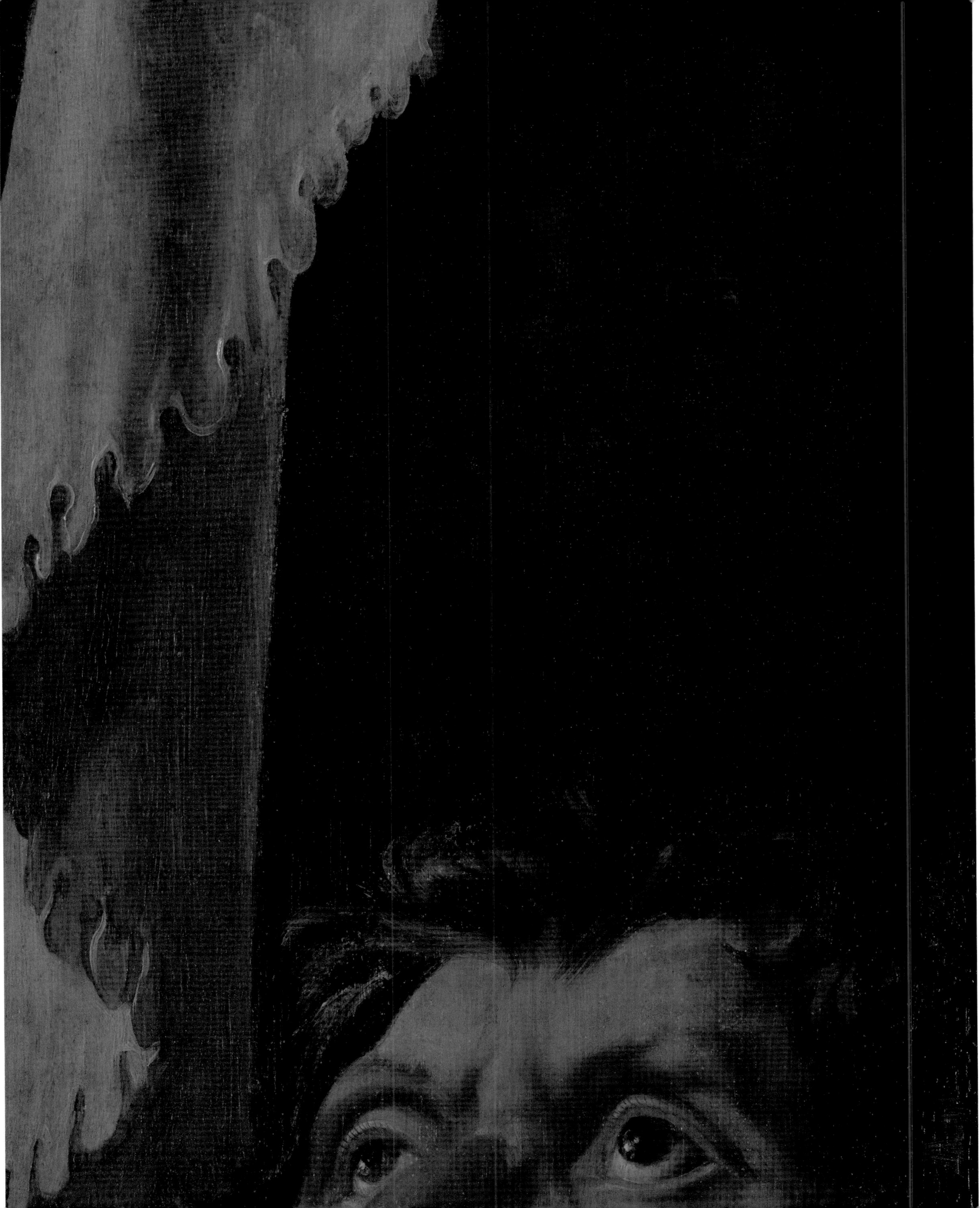

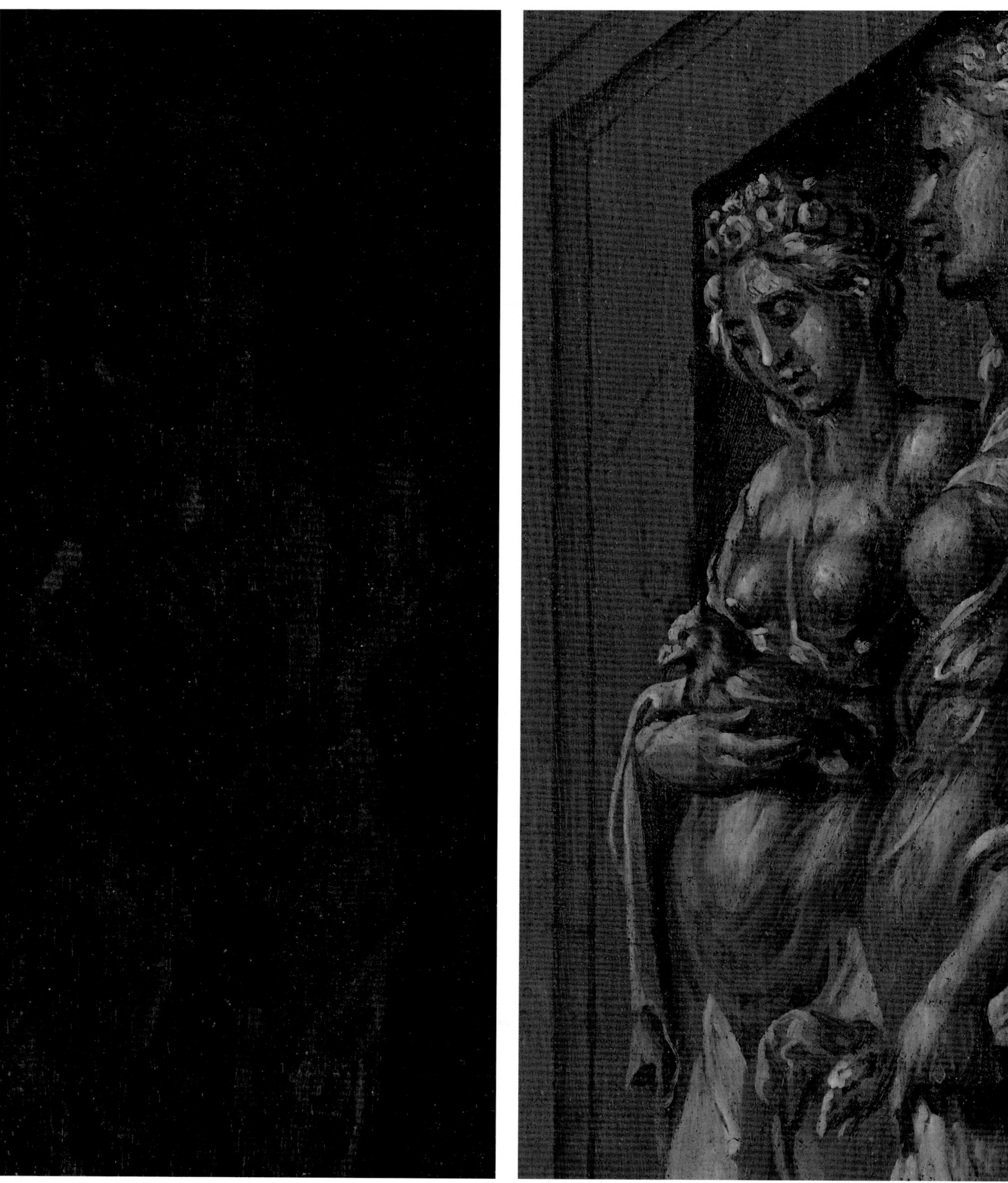

FIGURES 54 and 55 Sculpted figures in the background of both wings were painted quickly using little paint. Due to changes in the paint over time, those on the left panel are only revealed through digital image enhancement.

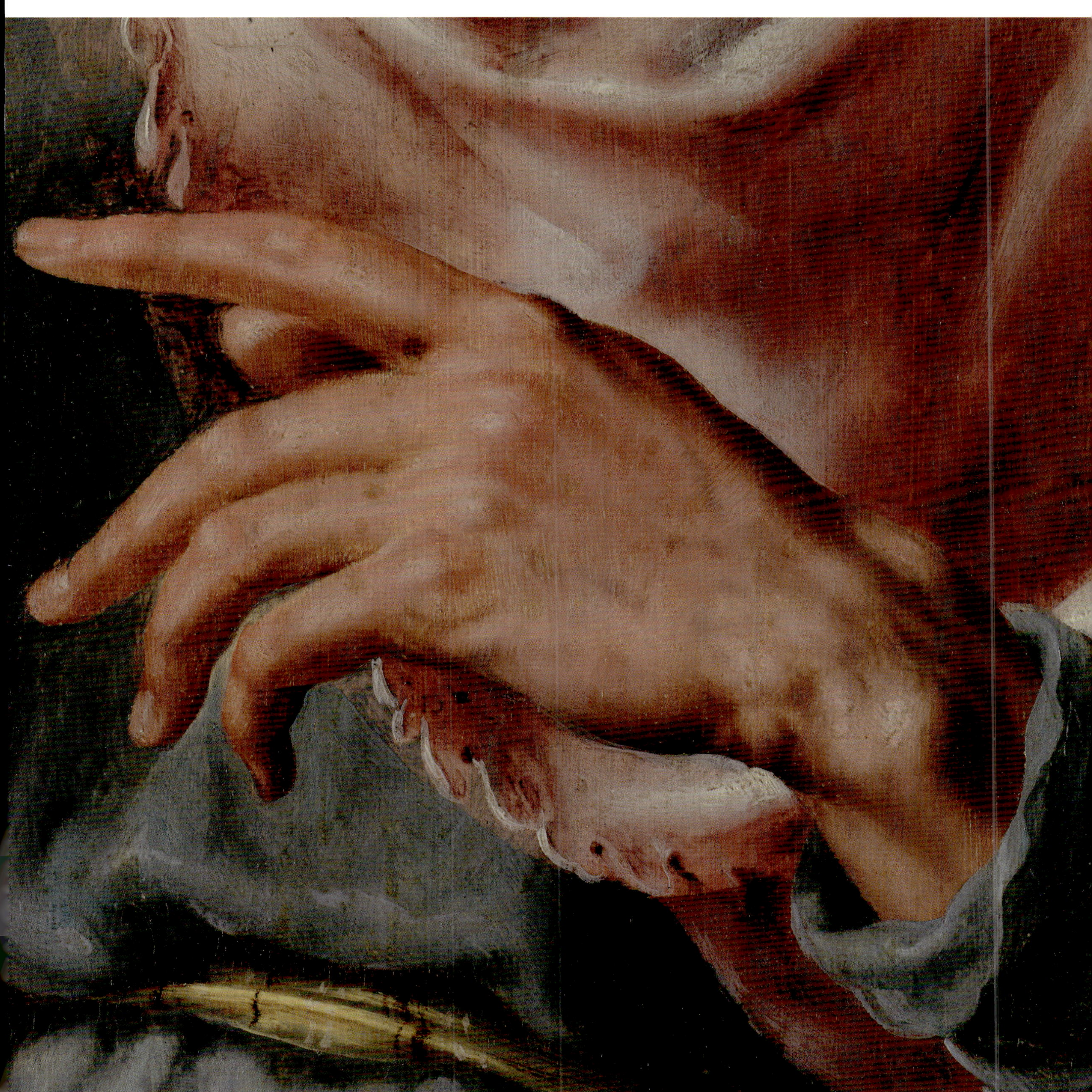

FIGURE 56 The scalloped edge of Pilate's drapery was created at a late stage in the painting process.

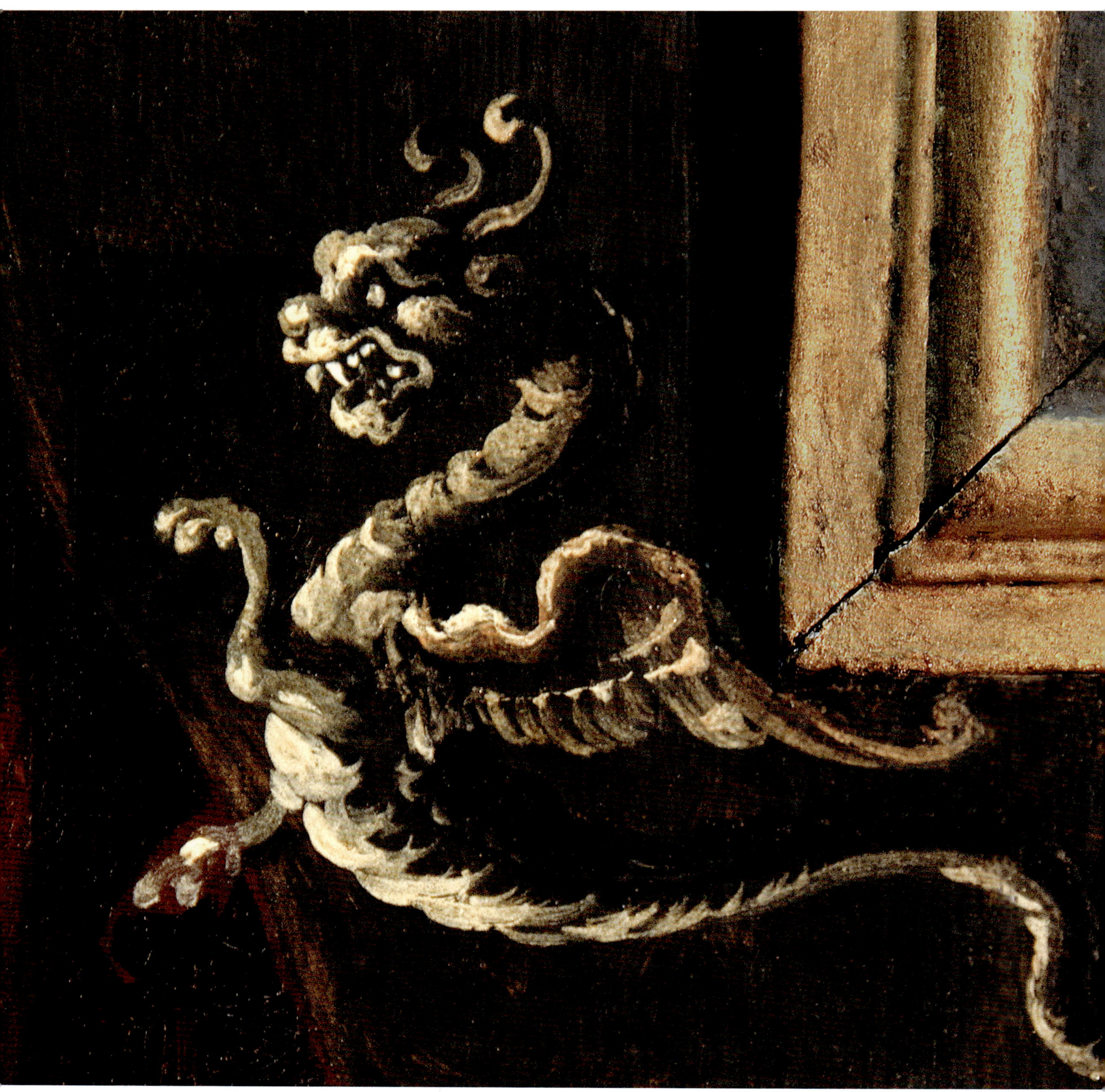

FIGURES 57 and 58 The dragons emerging from Saint John's goblet and from behind Margaretha are additional examples of the artist's distinctive approach.

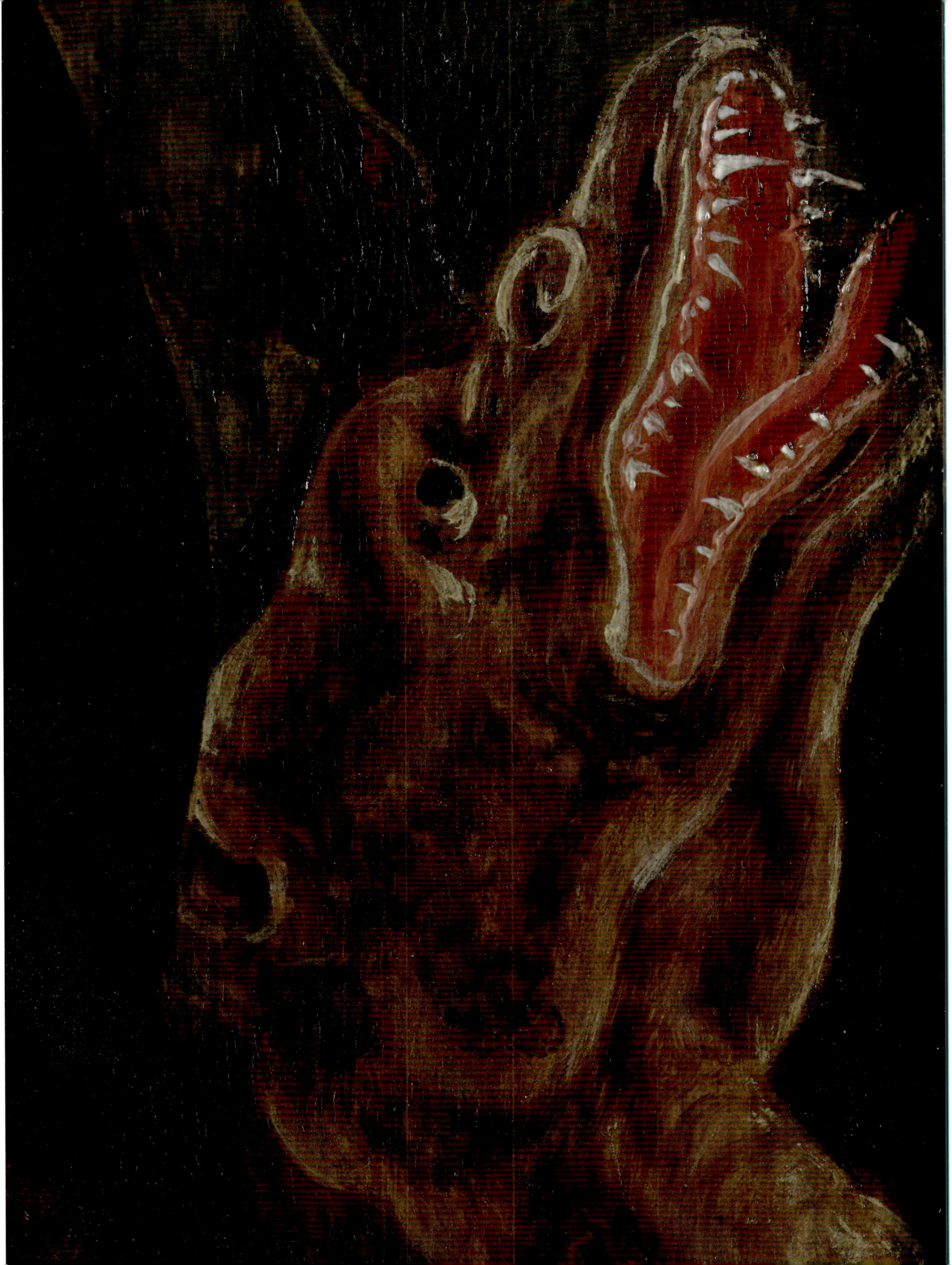

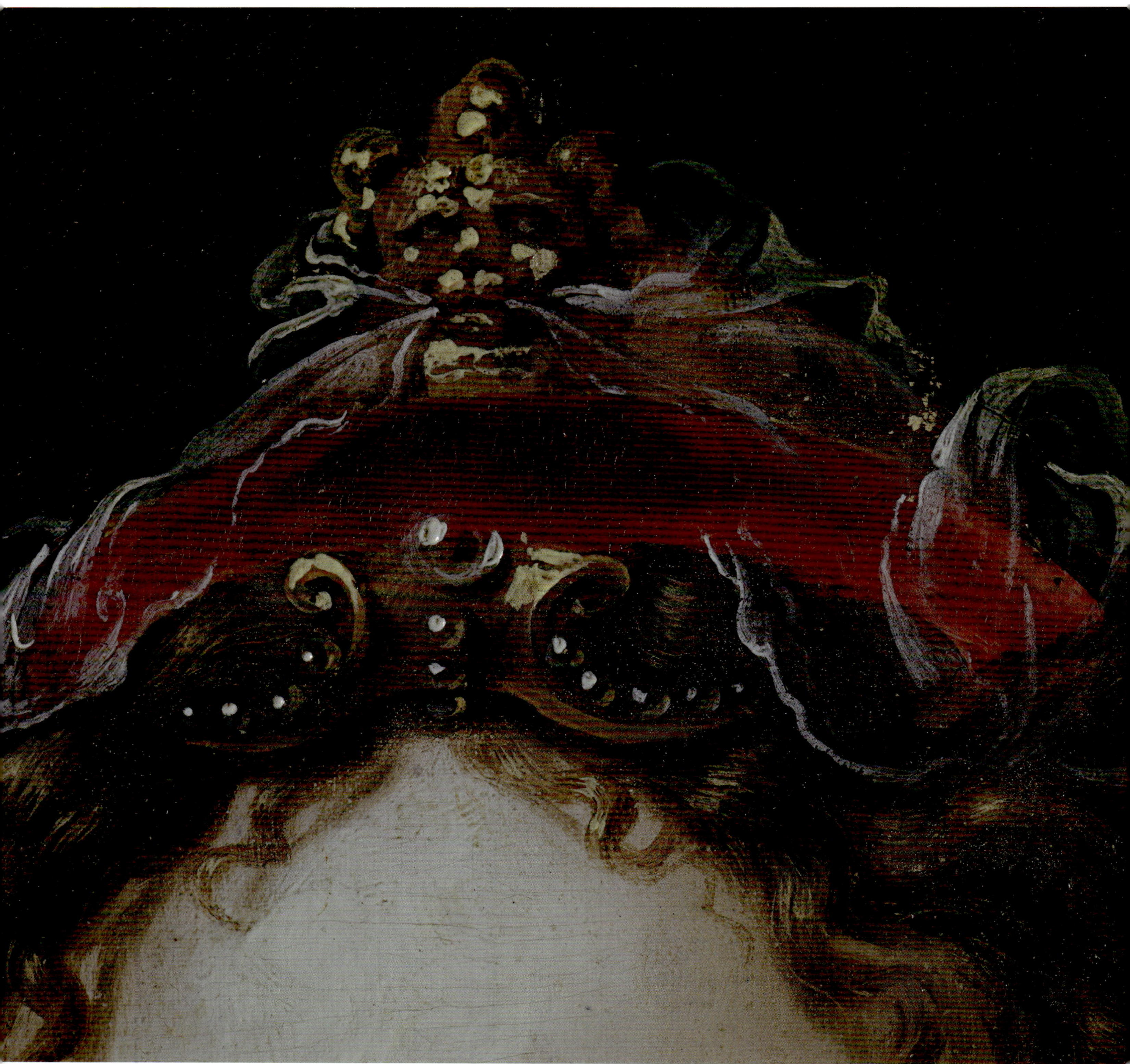

FIGURE 59 The jewels worn by Saint Margaret demonstrate an extremely fast and confident execution.

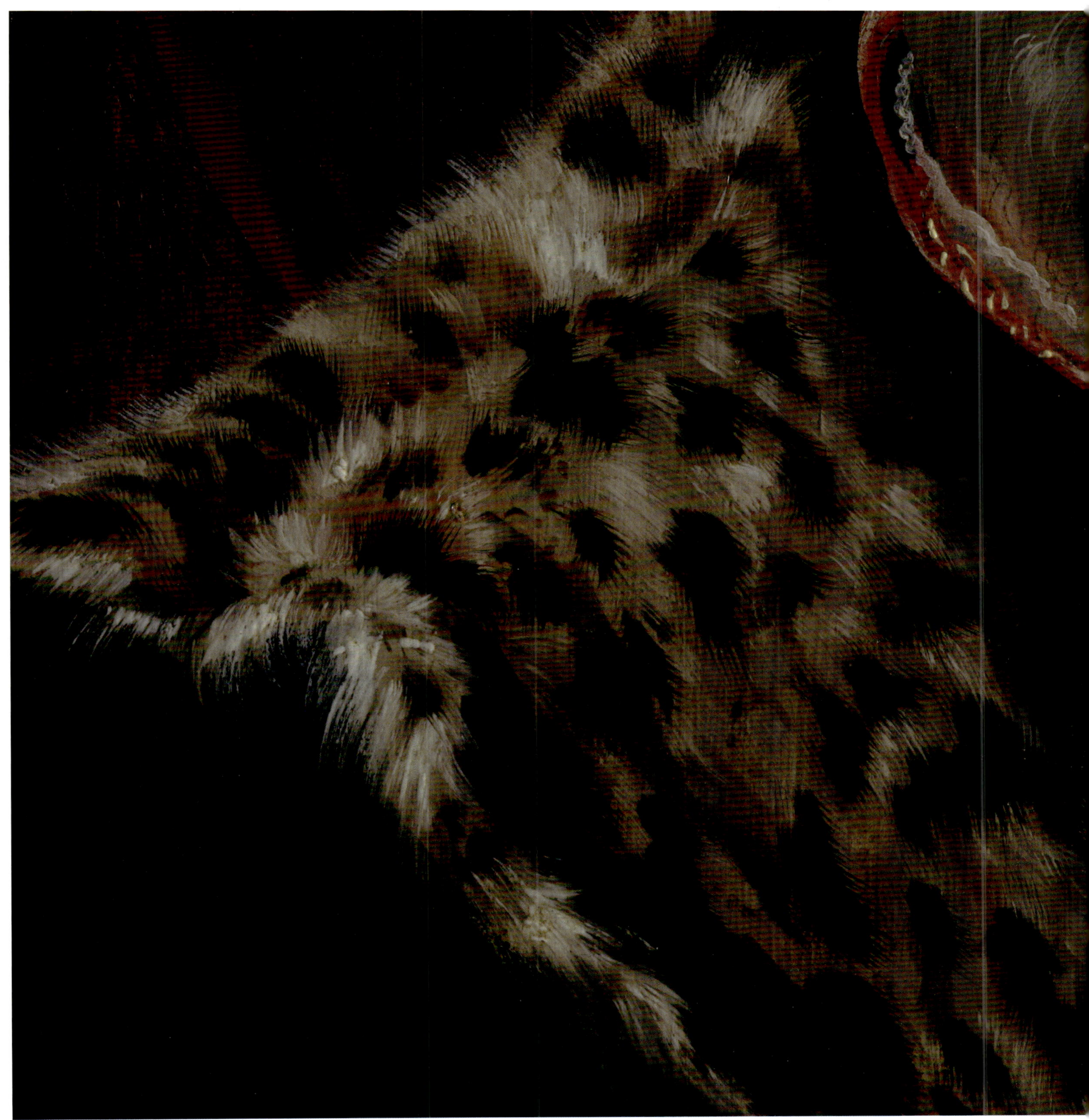

FIGURE 60 Close examination of the fur of Jan's *tabbaard* shows quickly applied dabs of paint.

FIGURE 61A The background above the left exterior figure in its final painted state

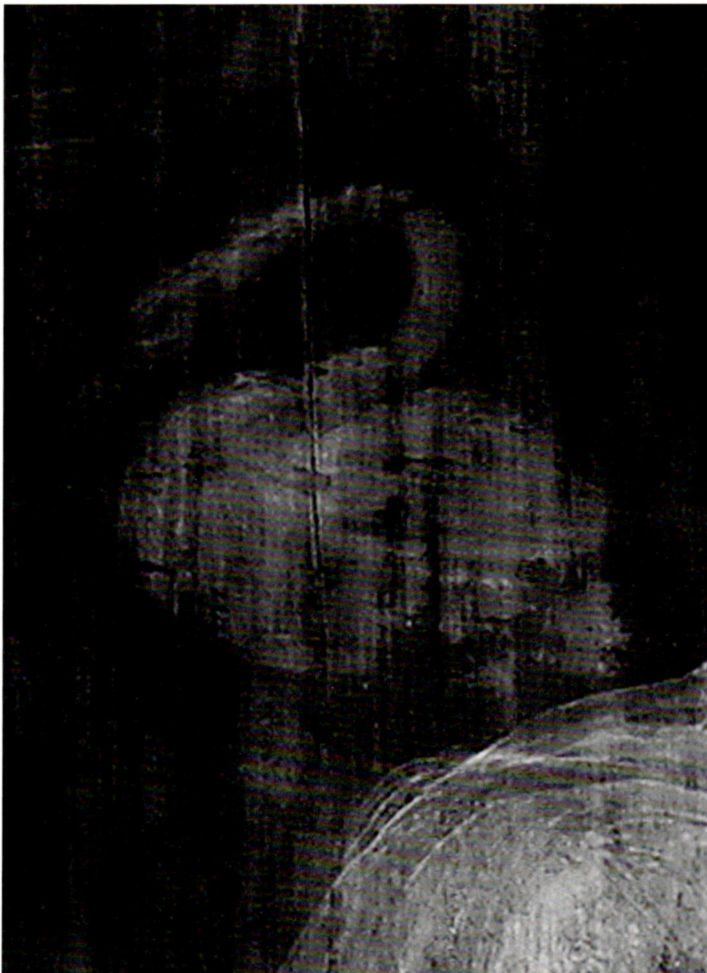

FIGURE 61B The figure of a swan, not visible to the eye, shows in the X-radiograph.

It appears that Heemskerck first painted the dark background, leaving the forms of the main figures in reserve. This can be seen in the infrared reflectogram and in the X-radiographs (see figs. 24 and 26).[43] Working loosely, thinly, and efficiently, using small amounts of paint, the artist in some areas used a colored wash as a midtone. For example, the flesh tones were started with a thin, warm, somewhat translucent layer, followed by more opaque colors mixed with lead white for the lighter areas. Other details, such as the eyes, were added at the end. Draperies were similarly modeled with glazes on top for the deeper shadows.[44]

The garments worn by both Jan and Margaretha are a tour de force of Heemskerck's simple but effective approach. Close examination of Jan's cloak edging, for example (fig. 60), shows that the majority of it is blocked in with a warm, transparent glaze directly on top of the priming, the defining dabs of black and white painted quickly and confidently to give the successful illusion of

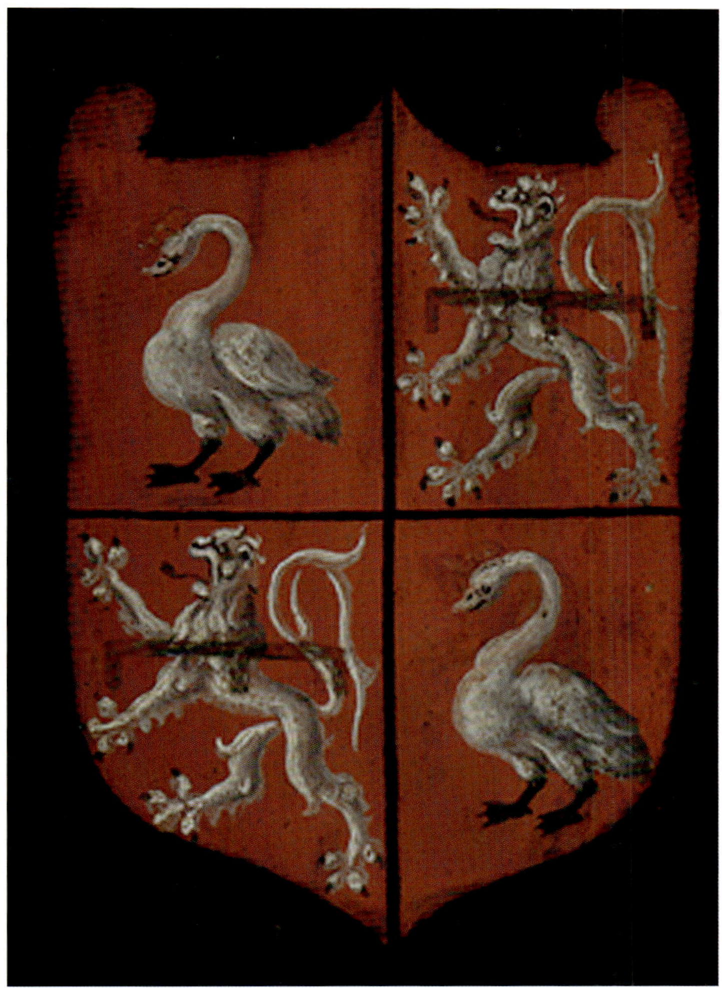

FIGURE 62A The final appearance of the coat of arms on the left interior wing

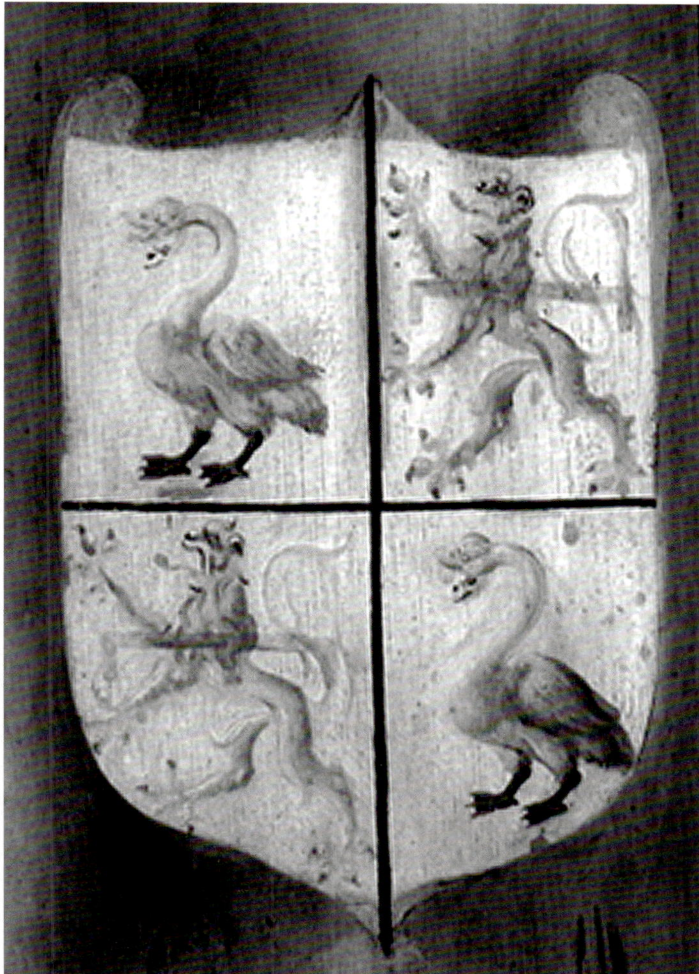

FIGURE 62B Infrared reflectogram showing forms in earlier stages

an expensive lynx fur. He must have had specific brushes to help him easily achieve various effects, much like the ones Saint Luke holds in his left hand (see detail, p. 28), and it is likely that the one he used to render the fur had divided bristles.

The only changes of note are those involving elements of the coats of arms of the donors on the grisaille exteriors. These were originally positioned in the upper inner corners at the base of the curved edge but are now visible only in the X-radiograph,[45] as their presence was eliminated at some point during the painting process (figs. 61a and 61b). Additionally, the swans on the donor sides have been changed; they were originally conceived with their heads raised higher with open beaks, different from the finished painting, which depicts them in a downward, closed-beak position (figs. 62a and 62b). For the most part, however, it can be said that once Heemskerck started painting, he made very few changes from his planned composition.

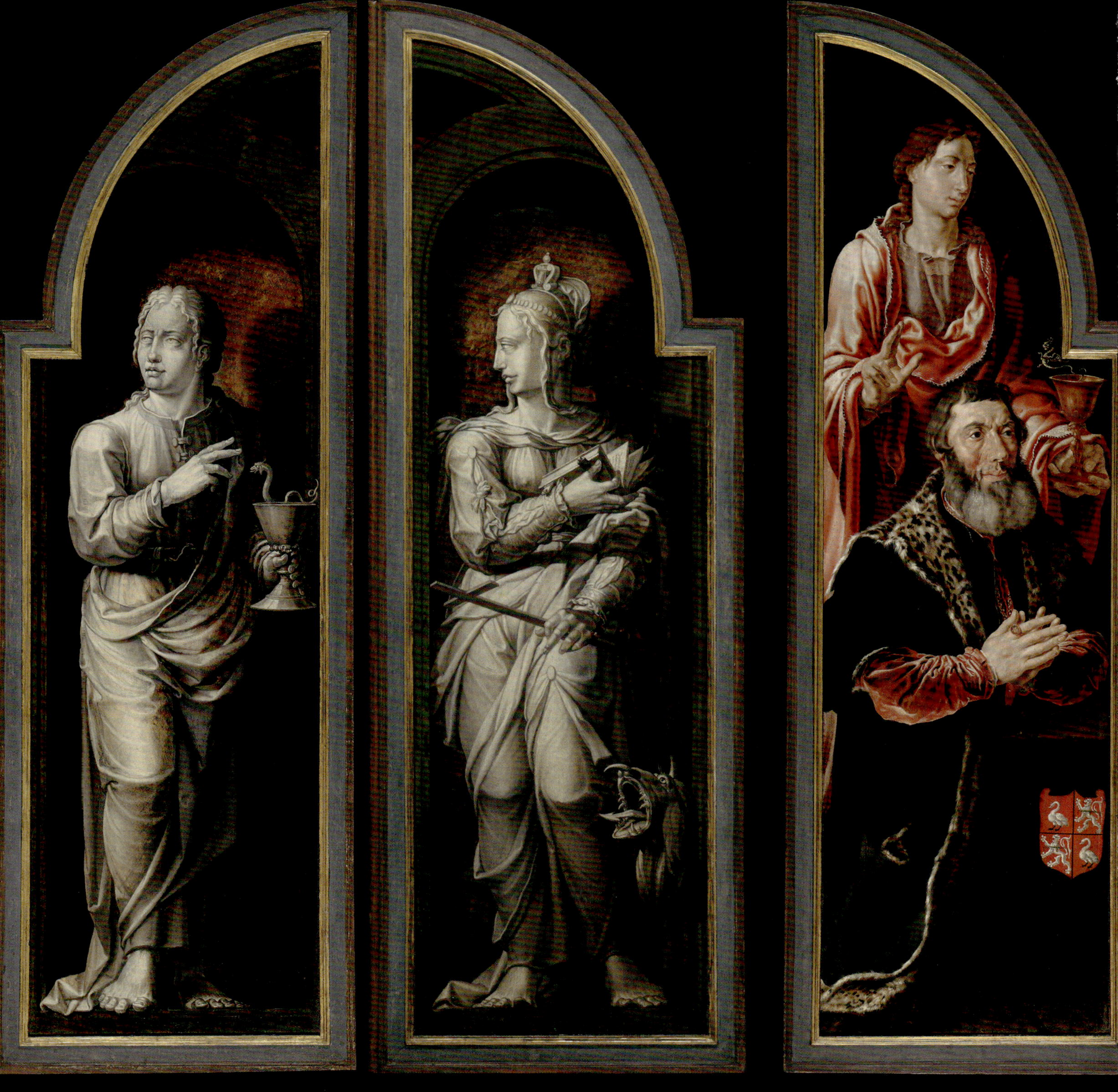

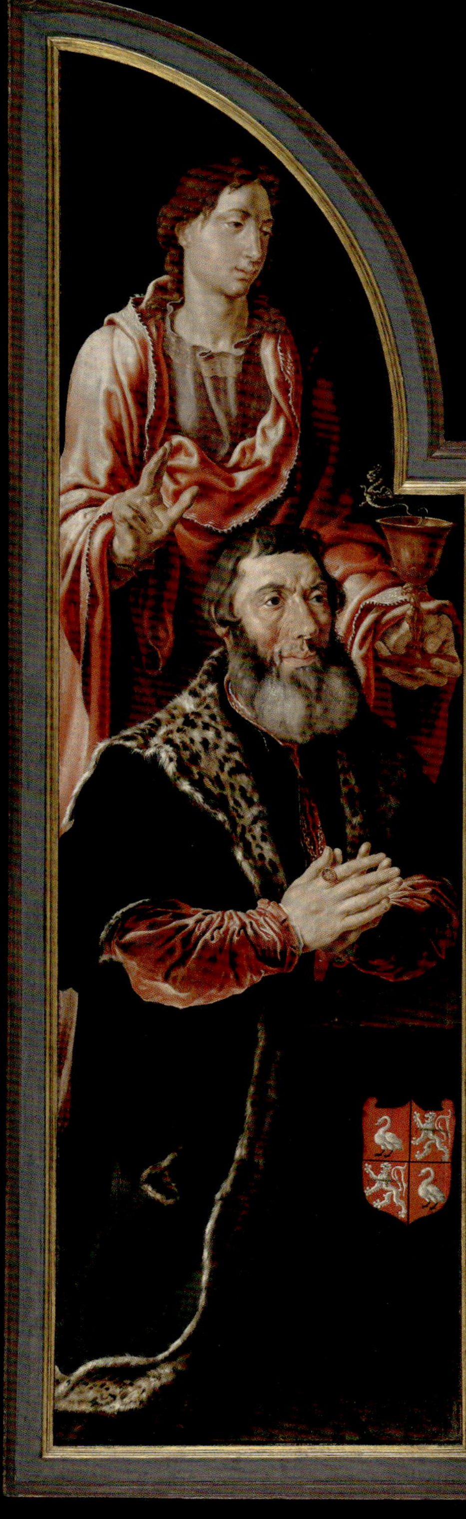

FIGURE 63 **AFTER CONSERVATION**

Heemskerck's *Ecce Homo* triptych cleaned and restored, before reassembly with its central frame

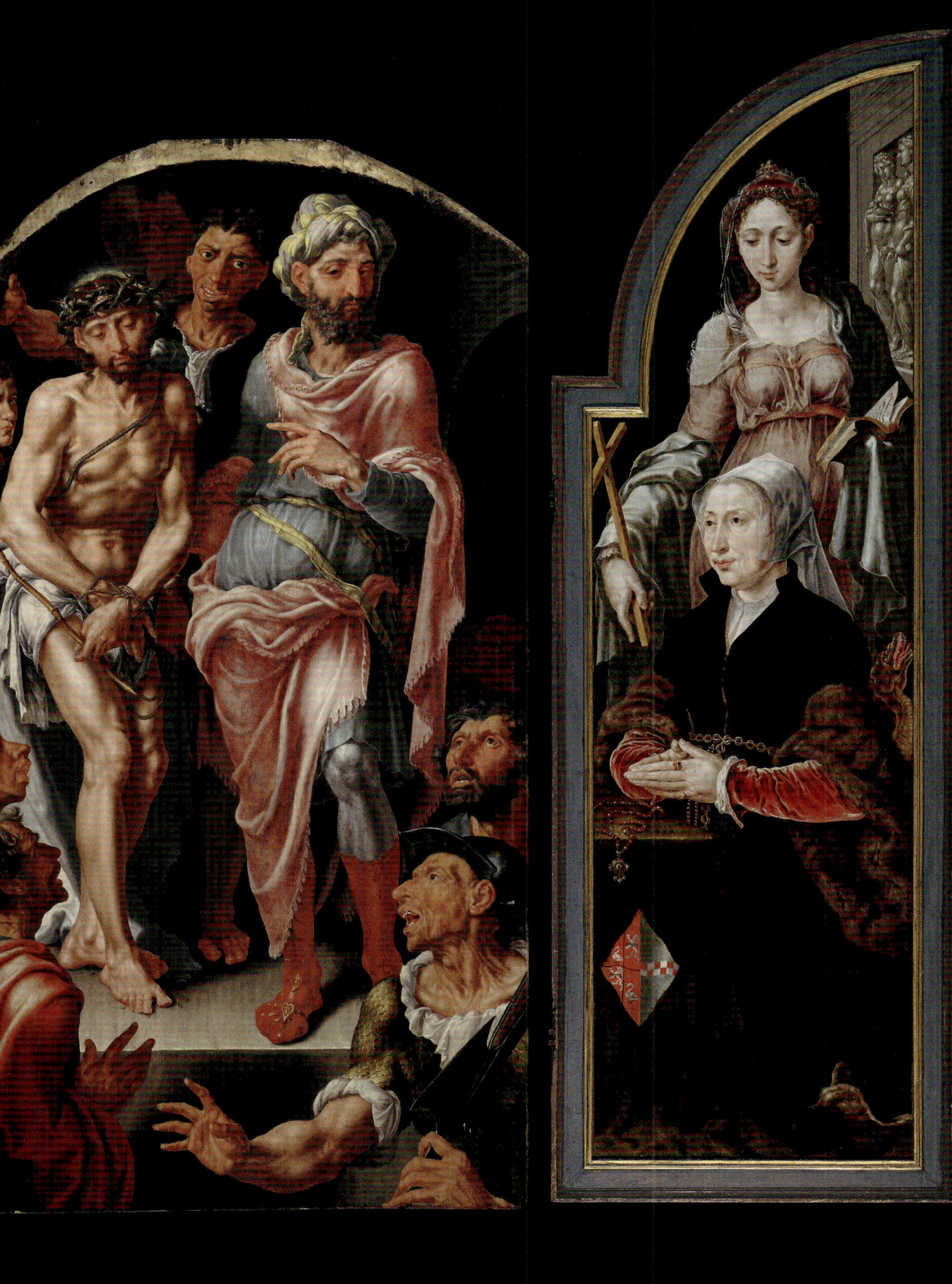

CONCLUSION

Analysis and examination of the *Ecce Homo* triptych confirm that Heemskerck painted in a straightforward and direct manner. Using fairly simple layers to build up the forms, he exploited a reflective ground by using a fairly restricted palette (similar to Saint Luke's palette) of both translucent and opaque pigments, in this respect following the established tradition of oil painting in Northern Europe. However, there are also a few variations in his method that allowed him to work in a brushier and faster way than the more considered and precise manner of painting that is more typical of his predecessors. His clever use of glue in his priming layer meant his panels were ready for painting much sooner than if he had used a more traditional oil priming. His approach to modeling forms, using single colors alone or in simple mixtures, modulated with white and enhanced with directly painted highlights as well as translucent glazes, has more in common with Italian painting of the period, as does his use of different oils. His addition of glass and other extenders not only allowed him to minimize the amount of the more expensive pigments needed but also may have decreased the paint's drying time, and while he was certainly not the only artist at the time exploiting such materials, Heemskerck appears to have used them extensively here, especially the pulverized glass. This simplified, economical approach was well suited to his brushy, confident style, allowing him to rapidly achieve rich and brilliant effects with a minimum of material, creating the wonderfully engaging altarpiece that has been the subject of this in-depth study (fig. 63).

NOTES

1. Hessel Miedema, "De St. Lucasgilden van Haarlem en Delft in de Zestiende Eeuw," *Oud Holland* 99, no. 2 (1985), pp. 77–108.

2. For an overall review of these sources, see Lorne Campbell, Susan Foister, and Ashok Roy, "Methods and Materials of Northern European Painting in the National Gallery, 1400–1550," *Early Northern Painting, National Gallery Technical Bulletin* 18 (1997), pp. 6–55.

3. Hessel Miedema, ed., *Karel van Mander: The Lives of the Illustrious Netherlandish and German Painters from the First Edition of the Schilder-boeck (1603–1604): Preceded by the Lineage, Circumstances, and Place of Birth, Life, and Works of Karel van Mander, Painter and Poet, and Likewise His Death and Burial, from the Second Edition of the Schilder-boeck (1616–1618),* translated by Derry Cook-Radmore (Doornspijk: Davaco, 1997), vol. 4, p. 67.

4. Complete records of the treatment by Yvonne Szafran, Iwona Stefanska, Laura Rivers, and Tiarna Doherty are on file in the J. Paul Getty Museum Paintings Conservation Department.

5. Among the studies are J. R. J. van Asperen de Boer, "A Technical Study of Some Paintings by Maarten van Heemskerck," in *Color and Technique in Renaissance Painting, Italy and the North,* edited by Marcia B. Hall (Locust Valley, NY: J. J. Augustin, 1987), pp. 105–14; Jill Dunkerton, Aviva Burnstock, and Alistair Smith, "Two Wings of an Altarpiece by Martin van Heemskerck," *National Gallery Technical Bulletin* 12 (1988), pp. 16–32; E. Melanie Gifford, "Maarten van Heemskerck's *Panoramic Landscape with the Rape of Helen:* Preliminary Report on the Analysis and Treatment," in *American Institute for Conservation Paintings Specialty Group Postprints* (Washington, DC: Paintings Specialty Group, American Institute for Conservation of Historic and Artistic Works, 1990), pp. 36–40; Ella Hendriks and Koos Levy–van Halm, "Technical Developments in a 16th-Century Netherlandish Altarpiece by Maarten van Heemskerck and Cornelis Cornelisz van Haarlem," in *Preprints of ICOM Committee for Conservation 10th Triennial Meeting: Washington, D.C., 22–27 August 1993,* edited by Janet Bridgland (Paris: ICOM Committee for Conservation, 1993), pp. 75–81; Molly Faries, "Attributing the Layers of Heemskerck's Cologne *Lamentation of Christ,*" in *Le Dessin Sous-Jacent dans la Peinture, Colloque X, 5–7 Septembre 1993,* edited by Hélène Verougstraete and Roger Van Schoute (Louvain-La-Neuve: Collège Érasme, 1995), pp. 133–41; Molly Faries, Christa Steinbüchel, and J. R. J. van Asperen de Boer, "Maarten van Heemskerck and Jan van Scorel's Haarlem Workshop," in *Historical Painting Techniques, Materials, and Studio Practice: Preprints of a Symposium, University of Leiden, the Netherlands, 26–29 June 1995,* edited by Arie Wallert, Erma Hermens, and Marja Peek (Marina del Rey, CA: Getty Conservation Institute, 1995), pp. 135–39; Ella Hendriks and Arie Wallert, "Orpiment Used in Paintings by Maarten van Heemskerck (1498–1574): Degradation of the

Pigment and Related Conservation Problems," in *Art et chimie, la couleur, International Congress on the Contribution of Chemistry to Works of Art, Paris, 16–18 September 1998: Conference Abstracts,* under the direction of Jacques Goupy and Jean-Pierre Mohen (Paris: Centre national de la recherche scientifique, 2000), pp. 111–12.

6. Infrared reflectograms were made using an Osiris infrared camera (InGaAs detector) operating in the wavelength range 0.9–1.7 μm.

7. XRF analyses were performed using a handheld Keymaster X-ray fluorescence spectrometer: rhenium (Re) tube, 40 kV excitation voltage, 1 μA current, 60-second accumulation.

8. The fragments of samples selected for examination as cross sections were mounted in Technovit 2000 LC UV-curing acrylic resin, ground and polished by hand with abrasive cloths without any liquid lubricant or polishing compound. The prepared cross-section samples were examined under visible light and by ultraviolet fluorescence using a Leica DM4000 microscope.

9. ESEM-EDS was performed using a Philips XL30 ESED-FEG instrument fitted with an Oxford INCA EDS analysis system. The EDS analysis was done under standard ESEM conditions: H_20 mode, 10.5 mm working distance, 20 kV accelerating voltage, 0.8–1.0 torr water vapor pressure.

10. Raman microspectroscopy was performed by Catherine Patterson and Karen Trentelman of the Getty Conservation Institute using a Renishaw InVia Raman spectrometer coupled to a Leica DM LM microscope: 50X objective, 785 nm laser excitation, calibrated using silicon 520.5 cm^{-1} Raman band. Laser power and spectrum collection times were adjusted for each particle examined to optimize the signal while avoiding sample degradation. The vibrational signatures presented in the resulting spectra allow compound-specific identification of pigments through comparison to reference spectra.

11. Seven samples from the central panel were analyzed by gas chromatology–mass spectroscopy (GC-MS) for identification of the organic binding media. These analyses were carried out by Joy Mazurek of the Getty Conservation Institute. All seven samples were first analyzed using established protocols for identification of oils, waxes, and resins, which involved preliminary derivatization (methylation/transesterification) using the reagent Meth-Prep II (methanolic [*m*-trifluoromethyl phenyl] trimethylammonium hydroxide). One sample, which consisted of the priming layer only, from the initial group analyzed for oils, waxes, and resins showed no oil component; this sample was subsequently analyzed using standard protocols for proteins by GC-MS involving ethyl chloroformate derivatization of the constituent amino acids. See Michael R. Schilling and Herant P. Khanjian, "Gas Chromatographic Analysis of Amino Acids in Ethyl Chloroformate Derivatives, Part 3. Identification of Proteinaceous Binding Media by the Interpretation of Amino Acid Composition Data," in *Preprints of ICOM Committee for Conservation, 11th Triennial Meeting, Edinburgh, 1–6 September 1996,* edited by Janet Bridgland (London: James and James, September 1996), pp. 211–19.

12. For example, see Dunkerton et al., "Two Wings of an Altarpiece," pp. 16–32.

13. Paul Mitchell and Lynn Roberts, *A History of European Picture Frames* (London: Paul Mitchell Ltd. with Merrell Holberton, 1996), p. 77.

14. After the exhibition *Kunst voor de Beeldenstorm: Noordneder-Landse Kunst, 1525–1580,* at the Rijksmuseum in Amsterdam, September 13–November 23, 1986, a number of corrections to the exhibition catalogue were published in 1987. It was proposed that the frame for the middle panel was produced in Dordrecht, and it was surmised that the polychromy of the frame was original. Jan Piet Filedt Kok, J. C. H. Buijs, and Wouter Th. Kloek, "Kunst voor de Beeldenstorm 1986: Aanvullingen en correcties op de catalogus," in *Bulletin van het Rijksmuseum* 35 (1987), pp. 252–63.

15. X-ray fluorescence (XRF) analysis on the blue-gray painted border of the interior of the left wing showed calcium, lead, and zinc as the most abundant metallic elements, with traces of copper and antimony. The abundant presence of zinc, in particular—probably present as zinc white (zinc oxide)—suggests that this section of the frame was repainted, possibly over original layers, in the nineteenth century or later.

16. Similar nails and holes on the *Ecce Homo* in the Frans Hals Museum suggest that the painting was possibly nailed into its frame. For a description, see Ella Hendriks, "Haarlem Studio Practice," in Pieter Biesboer et al., *Painting in Haarlem, 1500–1850: The Collection of the Frans Hals Museum,* edited by Neeltje Köhler, translated by Jennifer Killian and Katy Kist (Ghent: Ludion, 2006), p. 67.

17. Analysis by GC-MS of a sample of priming from the exposed, unpainted border at the top of the central panel showed that oil was not present; subsequent analysis for protein by GC-MS gave a positive result for protein, with an amino acid profile that had very high correlation (0.996) to collagen/gelatin, characterized by high relative proportion of hydroxyproline. In Heemskerck's altar wings in the National Gallery, London, a proteinaceous binder for the priming layer was also inferred from staining tests on paint cross sections, which produced a positive result for the priming with acid fuchsin; see Dunkerton et al., "Two Wings of an Altarpiece by Martin Van Heemskerck," p. 28.

18. For a recent exploration of such priming layers, see Abbie Vandivere, "In Search of Van Mander's *Primuersel*: Intermediate Layers in Early Netherlandish Paintings," in *Preprints of ICOM Committee for Conservation, 16th Triennial Meeting, Lisbon, 19–23 September 2011,* edited by Janet Bridgland, Working Group: Art Technological Source Research (Paris: International Council of Museums, September 2011), CD-ROM (unpaginated).

19. Campbell et al., "Methods and Materials," p. 25.

20. Van Asperen de Boer, "A Technical Study," pp. 105–14.

21. Nor was there evidence for drawing media applied to the ground in microscopical examinations of the cross-section samples.

22. Dunkerton et al., "Two Wings of an Altarpiece," p. 26.

23. Hendriks and Wallert, "Orpiment Used in Paintings," pp. 111–12.

24. The red lake pigment(s) in the triptych have not been studied in detail and remain incompletely characterized. Analysis of the organic dyestuff(s), for example, by high-performance liquid chromatography–mass spectrometry, has not been carried out; however, some analytical findings point tentatively to the presence of insect-derived red dyestuff (i.e., kermes, lac, or cochineal), rather than a plant dye (e.g., madder). Perhaps the most significant observation regarding the red lake pigment was the occurrence of particles showing a distinctive morphological feature, visible especially in ESEM backscattered electron images, that has been reported as a characteristic of protein-containing red lake pigments in which the colorant has been extracted from dyed wool or silk textile. See Jo Kirby, Marika Spring, and Catherine Higgitt, "The Technology of Red Lake Pigment Manufacture: Study of the Dyestuff Substrate," in *National Gallery Technical Bulletin* 26 (2005), pp. 71–87. Red lake particles throughout the painting generally show a high abundance of organic material (dyestuff) compared to inorganic substrate, and usually both calcium and aluminum are present together with sulfur. The abundance of this last element may also be a reflection of dye extraction from textile, while the calcium and aluminum may be weak indicators of an alum-derived substrate and lime as extracting alkali.

25. While natural ultramarine is reported to have been used by his master, Jan van Scorel, in whose Haarlem studio Heemskerck worked in the late 1520s, ultramarine does not appear in the *Ecce Homo* triptych, nor is it reported in other technical studies of the painter's methods and materials.

26. Van Mander, *Schilder-boeck,* fol. 247r; translation from Miedema, ed., *Karel van Mander,* vol. 1, p. 246.

27. Bruno Mühlethaler and Jean Thissen, "Smalt," in *Artists' Pigments: A Handbook of Their History and Characteristics,* vol. 2, edited by Ashok Roy (Washington, DC: National Gallery of Art; Oxford: Oxford University Press, 1997), pp. 113–30. More recent studies indicate that in the sixteenth century (and earlier), smalt was not necessarily an inexpensive pigment. For a good review of the early use of smalt, see Heike Stege, "Out of the Blue? Considerations on the Early Use of Smalt as Blue Pigment in European Easel Painting," *Zeitschrift für Kunsttechnologie und Konservierung* 18, no. 1 (2004), pp. 121–42.

28. These passages of painting appear to present the typical features of discolored smalt, characterized by loss of color in the pigment (by leaching of cobalt and potassium ions) in combination with discoloration of the (oil) paint medium. On the deterioration of smalt in oil paint, see Marika Spring, Catherine Higgitt, and David Saunders, "Investigation of Pigment-Medium Interaction Processes in Oil Paint Containing Degraded Smalt," *National Gallery Technical Bulletin* 26 (2005), pp. 56–70.

29. Heemskerck used smalt in other paintings; see, for example, the wings of the Drapers' altarpiece: *Annunciation to the Virgin* (exterior), *Adoration of the Shepherds* (interior left), and *Adoration of the Magi* (interior right), 1546–47. Oil on panel; two panels, each 261.5 × 122.5 cm (102⅞ × 48¼ in.); Haarlem, Frans Hals Museum, inv. OSI-136; in Biesboer et al., *Painting in Haarlem,* pp. 502–5, cat. 202 (entry by Epco Runia). The authors wish to thank Maryan Ainsworth for her insightful comments on this topic.

30. The finding of smalt and red lake in the uppermost paint layer of Pilate's tunic is unexpected, given the now-greenish tone of this drapery.

31. Van Mander, *Schilder-boeck,* fol. 200v. See also J. R. J. van Asperen de Boer, Molly Faries, and Jan Piet Filedt Kok, "Painting Technique and Workshop Practice in Northern Netherlandish Art of the Sixteenth Century," in *Kunst voor de Beeldenstorm: Noord-Nederlandse Kunst, 1525–1580; Catalogus,* exh. cat., edited by Jan Piet Filedt Kok, Willy Halsema-Kubes, and Wouter Th. Kloek, with an appendix by Peter Klein (Amsterdam: Rijksmuseum, 1986), pp. 106–16; Dunkerton et al., "Two Wings of an Altarpiece," pp. 16–32.

32. Dehydroabietic acid (derived from conifer resin) was identified in a sample of transparent green glaze from the tunic of the figure in the central panel holding the scourge, but at a very low level relative to the amount of drying oil and at a level comparable with instances of dehydroabietic acid in other paint that was not green. This finding points away from the transparent green being a true copper resinate pigment and toward verdigris in an oil medium containing a little resin. Additionally, copper sulfate was identified by ESEM-EDS and Raman spectroscopy as a trace inclusion in a copper green glaze from the scale armor of the soldier in the lower right of the central panel; copper chloride, again at the trace level, was tentatively indicated by ESEM-EDS in the green glaze used for the tunic of the figure holding the scourge in the central panel. Both of these other copper salts are known to occur as minor side products in old methods of making verdigris.

33. Several references in historical technical treatises to the application of glazes with the aid of fabric, often filled with cotton, are given by Margriet Henritha van Eikema Hommes, *Changing Pictures: Discoloration in 15th–17th Century Oil Paintings* (London: Archetype, 2004), p. 72.

34. Van Eikema Hommes, *Changing Pictures,* p. 68.

35. See note 24 above.

36. A faded madder lake used for blood was also found on the *Ecce Homo* triptych in the Frans Hals Museum. Maerten van Heemskerck, *Ecce Homo* triptych, 1559–60. Oil on panel; central panel: 218 x 150 cm (85¾ × 59 in.); wings: 218 × 67 cm (85¾ × 26¼ in.); Haarlem, Frans Hals Museum, inv. OSI-140; see Biesboer et al., *Painting in Haarlem,* p. 508 (entry by Epco Runia).

37. Personal communication to the authors from Marika Spring, National Gallery, London, September 2011. See also Marika Spring, "Pigments in Sixteenth-Century Painting of the German School," in *La technique picturale de Grunewald et de ses contemporains: Proceedings of an International Colloquium, Colmar: January 24–26, 2006,* edited by Pantxika Béguerie–De Paepe and Michel Menu (Paris: Centre de recherche et de restauration des musées de France; Colmar: Musée d'Unterlinden, 2007), pp. 136–44; Marika Spring, "Raphael's Materials: Some New Discoveries and Their Context within Early-Sixteenth-Century Painting," in *Raphael's Painting Technique: Workshop Practice before Rome; Proceedings of*

the EU-ARTECH Workshop, London, November 11, 2004, edited by Ashok Roy and Marika Spring, *Kermes quaderni* (Florence: Nardini, 2007); and Karin Lutzenberger, Heike Stege, and Cornelia Tilenschi, "A Note on Glass and Silica in Oil Paintings from the 15th to the 17th Century," *Journal of Cultural Heritage* 11, no. 4 (2010), pp. 365–72. Many of these reported instances of ground glass are in red or violet glazes, similar to the occurrences in the *Ecce Homo* triptych. In the Heemskerck painting, the distinctive elemental profile of the glass features calcium in relative abundance compared to other alkali metals (sodium, magnesium, and potassium), suggesting a high-lime glass, or a glass bordering between high-lime and mixed-alkali types; these are the more common types in paintings from north of the Alps. Glass found in Italian paintings has been exclusively of the soda lime (also called soda ash) type. Spring suggested that improving drying properties might also have been a reason for adding glass to oil paint; indeed, references to the practice of adding glass to oil paint to promote drying of particular pigments known to dry slowly (lakes, indigo, and lamp black) occur in early- to mid-sixteenth-century treatises on painting. The manganese content in glass of the type observed in the triptych has been suggested as a possible reason for the siccative properties of uncolored glass (not including, for example, lead or cobalt), but Lutzenberger et al. discounted this suggestion on grounds of the low mobility of manganese ions in the glass.

38. Bone white (or bone ash) was identified by ESEM-EDS by virtue of the characteristic elemental composition of calcium, phosphorus, and fluorine, with traces of manganese.

39. The possibility that Heemskerck used an organic yellow lake pigment, say, on a calcitic substrate, that has now faded cannot, however, be entirely ruled out, though evidence for such a practice has not been observed in the paint samples.

40. Faries et al., "Heemskerck and Scorel's Haarlem Workshop," pp.135–39. See also Van Asperen de Boer, "A Technical Study," pp. 105–14.

41. Ratios of the two fatty acids palmitic (P) and stearic (S) acid are to some degree indicative of the type of vegetable oil: linseed oil typically shows a P/S ratio in the range of approximately 1.2–1.9, while walnut oil is characterized by a higher P/S ratio, in the range of ca. 2.3–3.3. P/S ratios between 2.0 and 2.3 are in awkward overlap territory between linseed and walnut oil. The six paint samples analyzed that showed the presence of drying oil clustered into two distinct groups in terms of P/S ratio. Three showed P/S ratios of 1.6–1.7, which are strongly indicative of linseed oil. Three other samples, however, including the bright white of a highlight on the cloth of honor, showed higher values of P/S ratio, between 2.1 and 2.3, which is the lower P/S ratio margin associated with walnut oil.

42. "Daer waer qeen eyude te verhalen al de Tafelen, Taferaelen, Epitaphien en Conterfeytsels die hy gedaen heeft want hy van natueren vlijtigh weseude, al stadich uraccht en seer veerdich van handelingh was." Van Mander, *Schilder-boeck*, fol. 246r-v; translation from Miedema, ed., *Karel van Mander*, vol. 1, p. 242, 245.

43. This technique has been observed in other paintings by Heemskerck, including the left interior wing of the Drapers' altarpiece, *The Adoration of the Shepherds*, 1546–47, now in Haarlem, Frans Hals Museum. See Biesboer et al., *Painting in Haarlem*, pp. 503, 505 (entry by Epco Runia).

44. Heemskerck's directness and economy of process are to some degree reflected in the cross-section samples, which rarely, if at all, include more than three paint layers over the priming for the complete rendering of any given passage of painting.

45. To image these well, a stratiradiograph was taken. The project was undertaken by Getty Conservation Institute graduate intern Peter Reischig, and full details of this process are on file in the Getty Conservation Institute Collections Research Laboratory.

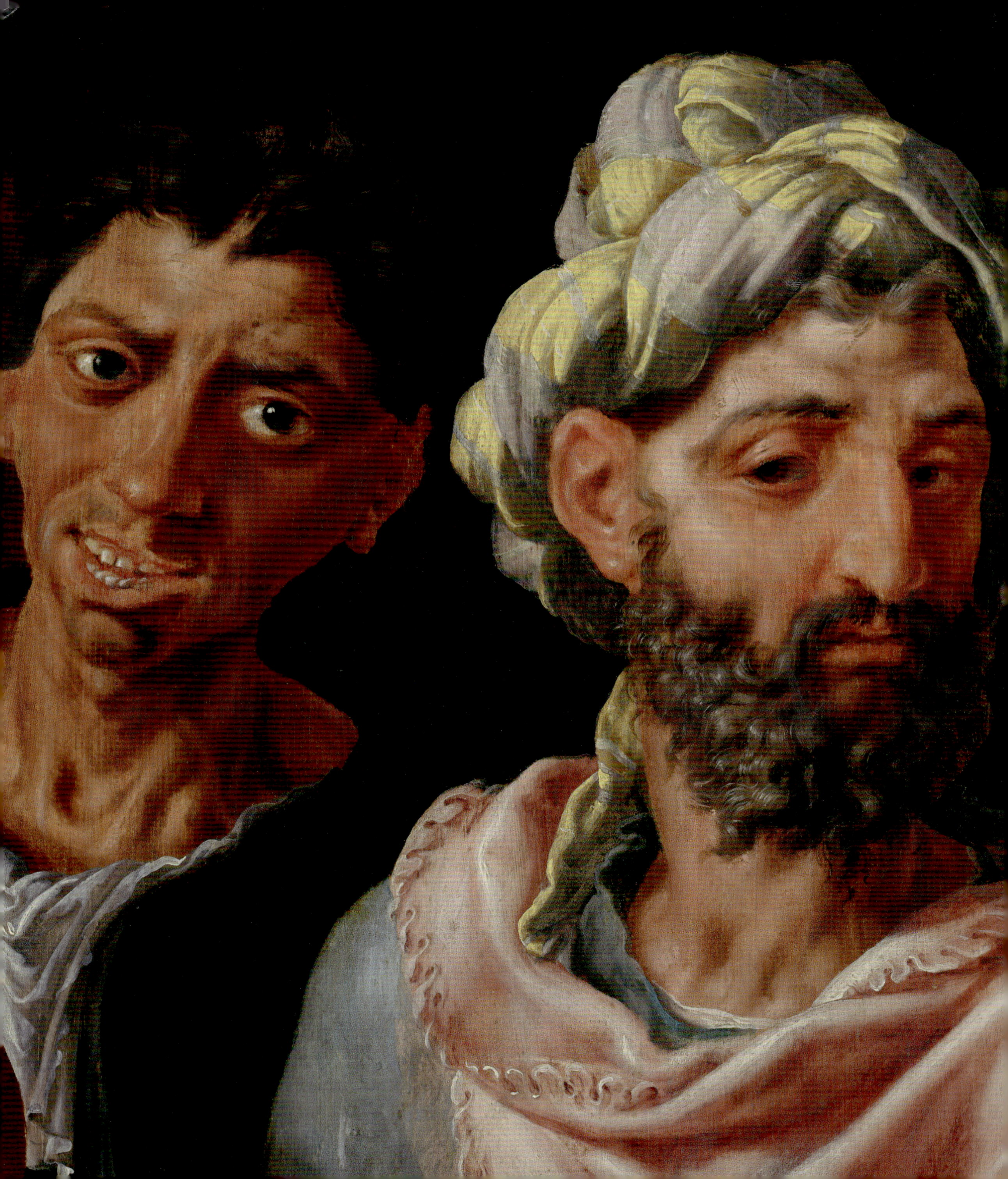

BIBLIOGRAPHY

Van Asperen de Boer, J. R. J. "A Technical Examination of the Frame of Engebrechtsz's *Crucifixion* and Some Other 16th-Century Frames." *Nederlands Kunsthistorisch Jaarboek* 26 (1975), pp. 73–87.

———. "A Technical Study of Some Paintings by Maarten van Heemskerck." In *Color and Technique in Renaissance Painting, Italy and the North,* edited by Marcia B. Hall, pp. 105–14. Locust Valley, NY: J. J. Augustin, 1987.

Van Asperen de Boer, J. R. J., Molly Faries, and Jan Piet Filedt Kok, with an appendix by Peter Klein. "Painting Technique and Workshop Practice in Northern Netherlandish Art of the Sixteenth Century." In *Kunst voor de Beeldenstorm: Noord-Nederlandse Kunst, 1525–1580; Catalogus.* Edited by Jan Piet Filedt Kok, Willy Halsema-Kubes, and Wouter Th. Kloek, pp. 106–16. Exh. cat. Amsterdam: Rijksmuseum, 1986.

Balen, Matthys. *Beschryvinge der stad Dordrecht: Vervatende haar begin, opkomst, toeneming, en verdere stant... Als mede een verzamelinge van eenige geslachtboomen, der adelijke, aal-oude, en aanzienlijke heeren-geslachten, van, en in, Dordrecht, enz.* .. Dordrecht, 1677.

Van Beverwijck, Jan. *'t Begin van Hollant in Dordrecht: Mitsgaders der eerster Stede beschrijvinge, regeringe, ende regeerders: Als oock de gedenckvaerdighste geschiedenissen aldaer gevallen.* Dordrecht, 1640.

Bierens de Haan, David. *Het Houtsnijwerk in Nederlanden Tijdens de Gothiek en de Renaissance.* The Hague: Martinus Nijhoff, 1921.

Biesboer, Pieter, et al. *Painting in Haarlem, 1500–1850: The Collection of the Frans Hals Museum.* Edited by Neeltje Köhler. Translated by Jennifer Killian and Katy Kist. Ghent: Ludion, 2006.

Bober, Phyllis Pray, and Ruth Rubinstein, with contributions by Susan Woodford. *Renaissance Artists and Antique Sculpture: A Handbook of Sources.* London: Harvey Millar; Oxford: Oxford University Press, 1986.

Campbell, Lorne, Susan Foister, and Ashok Roy. "Methods and Materials of Northern European Painting in the National Gallery, 1400–1550." *Early Northern Painting, National Gallery Technical Bulletin* 18 (1997), pp. 6–55.

Caspers, Charlotte, and Kate Seymour. "A Reconstruction of Maerten van Heemskerck's *De Calvarieberg* (1543): Accuracy and Visual Interpretation." In *Art, Conservation, and Authenticities: Material, Concept, Context; Proceedings of the International Conference Held at the University of Glasgow, 12–14 September 2007,* edited by Erma Hermens and Tina Fiske, pp. 115–24. London: Archetype Publications, 2009.

Cnattingius, Bengt. *Maerten van Heemskerck's St. Lawrence Altar-Piece in Linköping Cathedral: Studies in Its Manneristic Style.* Stockholm: Almqvist and Wiksell, 1973.

Van Duinen, Herman A. *De Koorbanken van de Grote- of Onze Lieve Vrouwekerk te Dordrecht.* Leiden: Primavera Pers, 1997.

———. "Een Augustijnenklooster van Aanzien: Conventus Sancti Augustini Dordracencis, 1275–1572." In *Jaarboek Historische Vereniging Oud-Dordrecht,* edited by Herman A. van Duinen and C. Esseboom. Dordrecht: Oud-Dordrecht, 2010.

Detail, *Ecce Homo* altarpiece

Dunkerton, Jill, Aviva Burnstock, and Alistair Smith. "Two Wings of an Altarpiece by Martin van Heemskerck." *National Gallery Technical Bulletin* 12 (1988), pp. 16–32.

Dunkerton, Jill, Susan Foister, and Nicholas Penny. *Dürer to Veronese: Sixteenth-Century Painting in the National Gallery.* London: National Gallery Publications, 1999.

Van Eikema Hommes, Margriet Henritha. *Changing Pictures: Discoloration in 15th–17th Century Oil Paintings.* London: Archetype Publications, 2004.

Elliott, John Paul. "Protestantization in the Northern Netherlands: A Case Study; The Classis of Dordrecht, 1572–1640." Ph.D. diss., Columbia University, 1990.

Faries, Molly. "Attributing the Layers of Heemskerck's Cologne *Lamentation of Christ.*" In *Le Dessin Sous-Jacent dans la Peinture, Colloque X, 5–7 Septembre 1993,* edited by Hélène Verougstraete and Roger van Schoute, pp. 133–41. Louvain-La-Neuve: Collège Érasme, 1995.

———. "Some Results of the Recent Scorel Research: Jan van Scorel's Definition of Landscape in Design and Color." In *Color and Technique in Renaissance Painting: Italy and the North,* edited by Marcia B. Hall. Locust Valley, NY: J. J. Augustin, 1987.

Faries, Molly, Christa Steinbüchel, and J. R. J. van Asperen de Boer. "Maarten van Heemskerck and Jan van Scorel's Haarlem Workshop." In *Historical Painting Techniques, Materials, and Studio Practice: Preprints of a Symposium, University of Leiden, the Netherlands, 26–29 June 1995,* edited by Arie Wallert, Erma Hermens, and Marja Peek, pp. 135–39. Marina del Rey, CA: Getty Conservation Institute, 1995.

Filedt Kok, Jan Piet, J. C. H. Buijs, and Wouter Th. Kloek. "Kunst voor de Beeldenstorm, 1986: Aanvullingen en correcties op de catalogus." *Bulletin van het Rijksmuseum* 35 (1987), pp. 252–63.

Filedt Kok, Jan Piet, Willy Halsema-Kubes, and Wouter Th. Kloek, eds. *Kunst voor de Beeldenstorm: Noord-Nederlandse Kunst, 1525–1580; Catalogus.* Exh. cat. Amsterdam: Rijksmuseum, 1986.

Filippi, Elena. *Maarten van Heemskerck: Inventio urbis.* Milan: Berenice, 1990.

Folga-Januszewska, Dorota, and Antoni Ziemba. *Transalpinum: From Giorgone and Dürer to Titian and Rubens; Painting from the Collections of the Kunsthistorisches Museum in Vienna, the National Museum in Warsaw, and the National Museum in Gdansk.* Lesko: Bosz, 2004.

Freedberg, David. "Aertsen, Heemskerck en de crisis van de kunst in de Nederlanden." *Bulletin van het Rijksmuseum* 35 (1987), pp. 224–41.

———. "Art and Iconoclasm, 1525–1580: The Case of the North Netherlands." In *Kunst voor de Beeldenstorm: Noord-Nederlandse Kunst, 1525–1580; Catalogus,* edited by Jan Piet Filedt Kok, Willy Halsema-Kubes, and Wouter Th. Kloek. Exh. cat. Amsterdam: Rijksmuseum, 1986.

———. "Iconoclasm and Painting in the Revolt in the Netherlands, 1566–1609." Ph.D. diss., Oxford University, 1972. *Outstanding Theses in the Fine Arts from British Universities.* New York: Garland, 1988.

Gifford, E. Melanie. "Maarten van Heemskerck's *Panoramic Landscape with the Rape of Helen*: Preliminary Report on the Analysis and Treatment." In *American Institute for Conservation Paintings Specialty Group Postprints,* pp. 36–40. Washington, DC: Paintings Specialty Group, American Institute for Conservation of Historic and Artistic Works, 1990.

Grosshans, Rainald. *Maerten van Heemskerck: Die Gemälde.* Berlin: Horst Boettcher Verlag, 1980.

Harrison, Jefferson Cabell, Jr. "The Paintings of Maerten van Heemskerck: A Catalogue Raisonné." 2 vols. Ph.D. diss., University of Virginia, 1987.

Helmus, Liesbeth M. *Schilderen in Opdracht: Noord-Nederlandse Contracten voor Altaarstukken, 1485–1570.* Utrecht: Centraal Museum, 2010.

Hendriks, Ella. "Haarlem Studio Practice." In Pieter Biesboer et al., *Painting in Haarlem, 1500–1850: The Collection of the Frans Hals Museum,* edited by Neeltje Köhler, translated by Jennifer Killian and Katy Kist, pp. 65–96. Ghent: Ludion, 2006.

Hendriks, Ella, and Koos Levy–van Halm. "Technical Developments in a 16th-Century Netherlandish Altarpiece by Maarten van Heemskerck and Cornelis Cornelisz. van Haarlem." In *Preprints of ICOM Committee for Conservation 10th Triennial Meeting: Washington, D.C., 22–27 August 1993,* edited by Janet Bridgland, pp. 75–81. Paris: ICOM Committee for Conservation, 1993.

Hendriks, Ella, and Arie Wallert. "Orpiment Used in Paintings by Maarten van Heemskerck (1498–1574): Degradation of the Pigment and Related Conservation Problems." In *Art et chimie, la couleur, International Congress on the Contribution of Chemistry to Works of Art, Paris, 16–18 September 1998: Conference Abstracts,* under the direction of Jacques Goupy and Jean-Pierre Mohen, pp. 111–12. Paris: Centre national de la recherche scientifique, 2000.

Hoogewerff, Godfridus Joannes. *Nederlandsche Schilders in Italië in de XVIe Eeuw: De Geschiedenis van het Romanisme.* Utrecht: A. Oosthoek, 1912.

Hülsen, Christian, and Hermann Egger. *Die römischen Skizzenbücher von Marten van Heemskerck im Königlichen Kupferstichkabinett zu Berlin.* 2 vols. Berlin: Julius Bard, 1913–16.

Junius, Hadrianus. *Batavia: In qua praeter gentis et insulae antiquitatem originem.* Leiden, 1588.

Kirby, Jo, Marika Spring, and Catherine Higgitt. "The Technology of Red Lake Pigment Manufacture: Study of the Dyestuff Substrate." *National Gallery Technical Bulletin* 26 (2005), pp. 71–87.

Lurie, Ann Tzeutschler. "Heemskerck's *Portrait of Machtelt Suijs* at the Cleveland Museum of Art." *Burlington* 134 (November 1992), pp. 698–706.

Lutzenberger, Karin, Heike Stege, and Cornelia Tilenschi. "A Note on Glass and Silica in Oil Paintings from the 15th to the 17th Century." *Journal of Cultural Heritage* 11, 4 (2010), pp. 365–72.

Van Mander, Karel. *Het schilder-boeck, waerin voor eerst de leerlustighe iueght den grondt der edel vry schilderconst in verscheyden deelen wort voorghedraghen. Daer nae in dry deelen t'leuen der vermaerde doorluchtighe schilders des ouden, en nieuwen tyds. Eyntlyck d'wtlegghinghe op den Metamorphoseon Pub. Ouidij Nasonis. Oock daerbeneffens wtbeeldinghe der figueren. Alles dienstich en nut den schilders, constbeminders en dichters, oock allen staten van menschen.* Haarlem, 1604.

Marijnissen, Peter, et al., eds. *De Zichtbaere Werelt: Schilderkunst uit de Gouden Eeuw in Hollands Oudste Stad.* Exh. cat. Dordrechts Museum, 1992.

Miedema, Hessel. "De St. Lucasgilden van Haarlem en Delft in de Zestiende Eeuw." *Oud Holland* 99, no. 2 (1985), pp. 77–108.

———, ed. *Karel van Mander: The Lives of the Illustrious Netherlandish and German Painters from the First Edition of the Schilder-boeck (1603–1604); Preceded by the Lineage, Circumstances, and Place of Birth, Life, and Works of Karel van Mander, Painter and Poet, and Likewise His Death and Burial, from the Second Edition of the Schilder-boeck (1616–1618).* Introduction and translation by Hessel Miedema. 6 vols. Doornspijk: Davaco, 1994–99.

Mitchell, Paul, and Lynn Roberts. *A History of European Picture Frames.* London: Paul Mitchell Ltd. with Merrell Holberton, 1996.

Mühlethaler, Bruno, and Jean Thissen. "Smalt." In *Artists' Pigments: A Handbook of Their History and Characteristics,* vol. 2, edited by Ashok Roy, pp. 113–30. Washington, DC: National Gallery of Art; Oxford: Oxford University Press, 1993.

Nelemans, A. *De Augustijnenkerk van Dordrecht.* Dordrecht: Kerkvoogdij Hervormde Gemeente van Dordrecht, 1993.

Nelemans, A., and K. Blokland. *Sepulture Augustijnenkerk Dordrecht.* Sliedrecht: Oudheidkundige Vereniging "Sliedrecht," Werkgroep Genealogie, 1998.

Van Nierop, Henk F. K. *The Nobility of Holland: From Knights to Regents, 1500–1650.* Translated by Martin Ultee. Cambridge and New York: Cambridge University Press, 1993.

Plomp, Nico, and Truus van Bueren. "Luiken met gebedsportretten van Maarten van Heemskerck." *Genealogie* 5 (1999), pp. 88–91.

Schilling, Michael R., and Herant P. Khanjian. "Gas Chromatographic Analysis of Amino Acids in Ethyl Chloroformate Derivatives, Part 3. Identification of Proteinaceous Binding Media by the Interpretation of Amino Acid Composition Data." In *Preprints of ICOM Committee for Conservation 11th Triennial Meeting, Edinburgh, 1–6 September 1996,* edited by Janet Bridgland, pp. 211–219. London: James and James, 1996.

Serlio, Sebastiano. *Generale reglen der architectvren op de vyve manieren van edificien: Te vveten Thvscana, Dorica, Ionica, Corinthia, ende composita, metden exemplen der antiqviteiten die int meeste deel concorderen metde leeringhe van Vitrvvio.* Antwerp, 1539.

Spring, Marika. "Pigments in Sixteenth-Century Painting of the German School." In *La technique picturale de Grünewald et de ses contemporains: Proceedings of an International Colloquium, Colmar, January 24–26, 2006,* edited by Pantxika Béguerie-De Paepe and Michel Menu, pp. 136–44. Paris: Centre de recherche et de restauration des musées de France (CNRS-UMR 171); Colmar: Musée d'Unterlinden, 2007.

———. "Raphael's Materials: Some New Discoveries and Their Context within Early-Sixteenth-Century Painting." In *Raphael's Painting Technique: Workshop Practice before Rome; Proceedings of the EU-ARTECH Workshop, London, November 11, 2004,* edited by Ashok Roy and Marika Spring. *Kermes quaderni*, pp. 77–86. Florence: Nardini, 2007.

Spring, Marika, Catherine Higgitt, and David Saunders. "Investigation of Pigment-Medium Interaction Processes in Oil Paint Containing Degraded Smalt." *National Gallery Technical Bulletin* 26 (2005), pp. 56–70.

Stege, Heike. "Out of the Blue? Considerations on the Early Use of Smalt as Blue Pigment in European Easel Painting." *Zeitschrift für Kunsttechnologie und Konservierung* 18, no. 1 (2004), pp. 121–42.

Steinbüchel, Christa. "The Investigation and Restoration of Maarten van Heemskerck's *Lamentation of Christ*." In *Le Dessin Sous-Jacent dans la Peinture, Colloque X, 5–7 Septembre 1993*, edited by Hélène Verougstraete and Roger van Schoute, pp. 143–47. Louvain-La-Neuve: Collège Érasme, 1995.

Tracy, James D. *A Financial Revolution in the Habsburg Netherlands:* Renten *and* Renteniers *in the County of Holland, 1515–1565*. Berkeley and Los Angeles: University of California Press, 1985.

Turner, Nicholas, Lee Hendrix, and Carol Plazzotta. *European Drawings: Catalogue of the Collections* 3. Los Angeles: J. Paul Getty Museum, 1997.

Vandivere, Abbie. "In Search of Van Mander's *Primuersel*: Intermediate Layers in Early Netherlandish Paintings." In *Preprints of ICOM Committee for Conservation, 16th Triennial Meeting, Lisbon, September 19–23, 2011*, edited by Janet Bridgland. Working Group: Art Technological Source Research. Paris: International Council of Museums, September 2011. CD-ROM.

Vasari, Giorgio. *Le vite de' piu eccellenti pittori, scultori e architecttori. . . .* 9 vols. Edited by Gaetano Milanesi. Florence: G. C. Sansoni, 1906.

Veldman, Ilja M. "Heemskerck's Romeinse Tekeningen en 'Anonymous B.'" *Nederlands Kunsthistorisch Jaarboek* 38 (1987), pp. 369–82.

———, compiler. *Maarten van Heemskerck: The New Hollstein; Dutch and Flemish Etchings, Engravings, and Woodcuts, 1450–1700*. 2 parts. Edited by Ger Luijten. Roosendaal: Konink-lijke van Poll in cooperation with the Rijksprentenkabinet, Rijksmuseum, 1993.

———. *Maarten van Heemskerck and Dutch Humanism in the Sixteenth Century*. Translated by Michael Hoyle. Maarssen: Gary Schwartz, 1977.

———. "Maarten van Heemskerck und die römische Kunst." In *Hoch Renaissance im Vatikan: Kunst und Kultur im Rom der Päpste*, 1, Giancarlo Alteri et al., pp. 417–20. Exh. cat. Vatican City: Vatican Museums and Biblioteca Apostolica, 1999.

Voragine, Jacobus de. *The Golden Legend: Readings on the Saints*. 2 vols. Translated by William Grainger Ryan. Princeton, NJ: Princeton University Press, 1993.

Van der Willigen, Adriaan. *Geschiedkundige aanteekeningen over Haarlemscshe schilders en andere beoefenaren van de beeldende kunsten: Voorafgegaan door eene korte geschiedenis van het schilders-of St. Lucas Guild Aldaar*. Haarlem: De Erven F. Bohn, 1866.

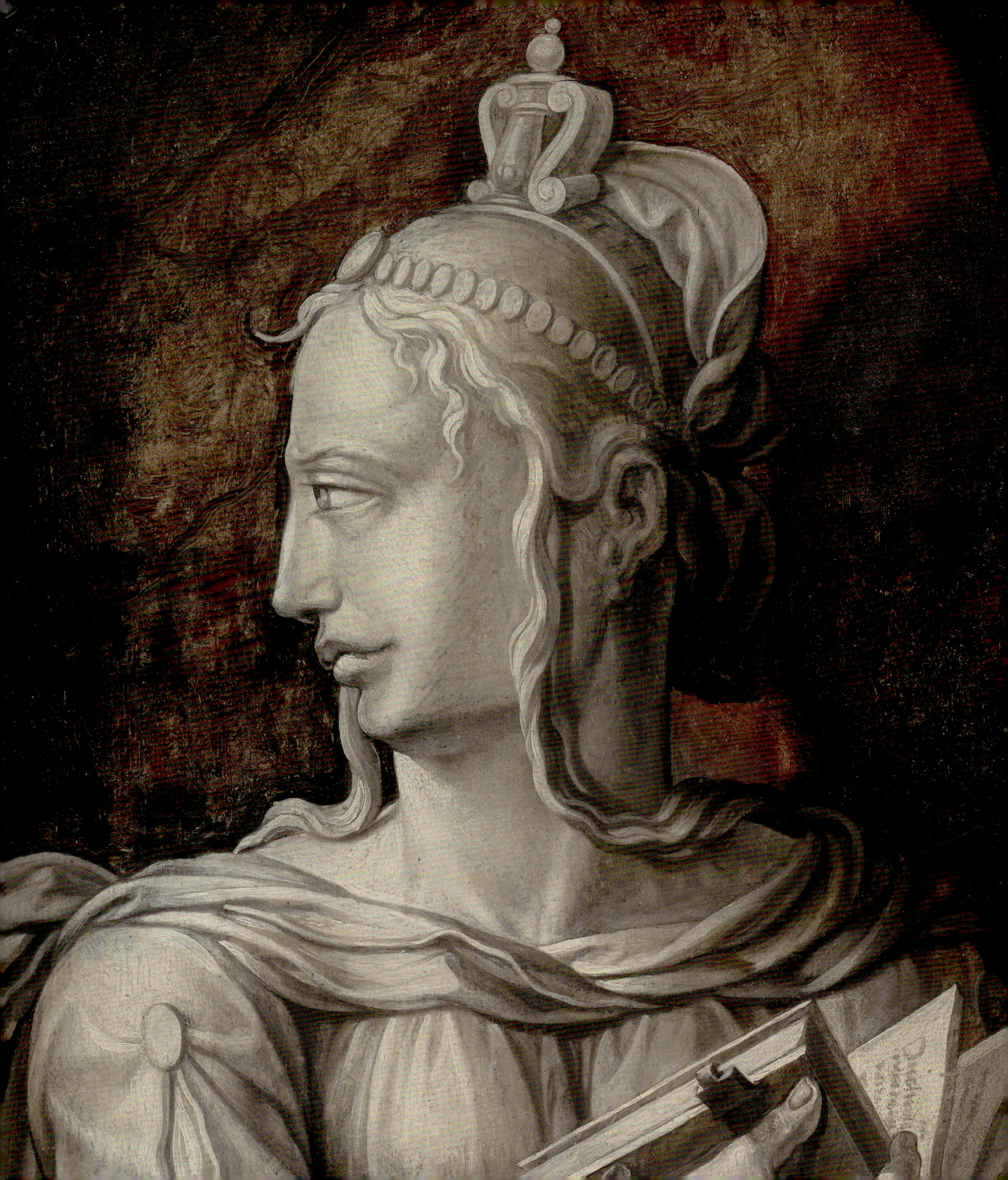

ILLUSTRATION LIST

Frontispiece (p. v); Figures 22, 23, 25, 27, 29, 30, 31, 35, 40, 43, 44, 47, 48, 51–60, 61A, 62A, 63; Details pp. ii, iii, 82, 88, 90
Maerten van Heemskerck (Dutch, 1498–1574), *Ecce Homo* triptych, 1544. Oil on panel, central panel unframed 167 × 88.9 cm ($65\frac{3}{4}$ × 35 in.), framed 188.6 × 132.7 cm ($74\frac{1}{4}$ × $52\frac{1}{4}$ in.), left wing framed 183.5 × 62.5 cm ($72\frac{1}{4}$ × $24\frac{5}{8}$ in.), right wing framed 183.5 × 64.8 cm ($72\frac{1}{4}$ × $25\frac{1}{2}$ in.). Muzeum Narodowe w Warszawie. Photos: Jack Ross, Rebecca Vera-Martinez, and Gary Hughes, J. Paul Getty Museum

Figure 1
Maerten van Heemskerck (Dutch, 1498–1574), *Self-Portrait, with the Colosseum, Rome*, 1553. Oil on panel, 42.2 × 54 cm ($16\frac{1}{2}$ × $21\frac{1}{4}$ in.). Fitzwilliam Museum, University of Cambridge, UK, 103 / The Bridgeman Art Library

Figure 2
Maerten van Heemskerck (Dutch, 1498–1574), *Saint Luke Painting the Virgin*, 1532. Oil on panel, 168 × 235 cm (66 × $92\frac{1}{2}$ in.). Frans Hals Museum, Haarlem, OS I-134. Photo: Tom Haartsen

Figure 3
Maerten van Heemskerck (Dutch, 1498–1574), *The Statue Court of the Casa Sassi at Rome*, ca. 1535. Pen and ink, 23 × 21.5 cm (9 × $8\frac{1}{4}$ in.). BPK, Berlin / Kupferstichkabinett, Staatliche Museen, Berlin, 2783 / Jörg P. Anders / Art Resource, NY

Figure 4
Maerten van Heemskerck (Dutch, 1498–1574), *The Arch of Constantine*, ca. 1535. Pen and brown ink, 20.9 × 13.3 cm ($8\frac{1}{4}$ × $5\frac{1}{4}$ in.). BPK, Berlin / Kupferstichkabinett, Staatliche Museen, Berlin, 79D2 69r / Jörg P. Anders / Art Resource, NY

Figure 5
Maerten van Heemskerck (Dutch, 1498–1574), *Panorama with the Abduction of Helen amidst the Wonders of the Ancient World*, 1535. Oil on canvas, 147.3 × 383.5 cm (58 × 151 in.). Baltimore, Walters Art Museum, 37.656. Acquired by Henry Walters with the Massarenti Collection, 1902. © Walters Art Museum, Baltimore, USA / The Bridgeman Art Library

Figure 6
Maerten van Heemskerck (Dutch, 1498–1574), *Passion* triptych with scenes from the life of Saint Lawrence, 1538–42. Oil on panel, framed 405 × 790 cm (159 × 311 in.). Linköping Cathedral, Sweden

Figure 7
Maerten van Heemskerck (Dutch, 1498–1574), *Portrait of Machtelt Suijs*, ca. 1540–45. Oil on panel, 85 × 74 cm ($33\frac{7}{16}$ × $29\frac{1}{8}$ in.). The Cleveland Museum of Art, Leonard C. Hanna, Jr. Fund 1987.136. © The Cleveland Museum of Art

Figure 8
Maerten van Heemskerck (Dutch, 1498–1574), *The Parable of the King Who Prepared a Wedding*, 1555. Pen and brown ink, brush and wash over black chalk, heightened with white gouache on green prepared paper; incised; 20.3 × 26.4 cm (8 × $10\frac{3}{8}$ in.). Los Angeles, J. Paul Getty Museum, 2003.18

Figure 9
Maerten van Heemskerck (Dutch, 1498–1574), *Judith*, 1560. Pen and dark brown and light brown ink over black chalk; incised for transfer; 19.8 × 25.2 cm ($7\frac{13}{16}$ × $9\frac{15}{16}$ in.). Los Angeles, J. Paul Getty Museum, 91.GG.17

Figure 10
Dirck Volkertsz Coornhert (Dutch, 1522–1590) after Maerten van Heemskerck, *Ecce Homo*, 1544, from the series The Fall and Salvation of Mankind through the Life and Passion of Christ, 1548. Etching, 24.5 × 19.2 cm ($9\frac{2}{3}$ × $7\frac{1}{2}$ in.). British Museum, London 1949.0709.157. © The Trustees of the British Museum / Art Resource, NY

Figure 11
Hieronymus Bosch (Netherlandish, ca. 1450–1516), *Christ Mocked*, ca. 1490–1500. Oil on panel, 73.5 × 59.1 cm (29 × $23\frac{1}{4}$ in.). National Gallery, London 4744. © National Gallery / Art Resource, NY

Figure 12
Jan Sanders van Hemessen (Flemish, active 1519–1556), *Mocking of Christ*, 1544. Oil on panel, 123 × 102.5 cm ($48\frac{1}{2}$ × $40\frac{1}{3}$ in.). BPK, Berlin / Alte Pinakothek, Bayerische Staatsgemaeldesammlungen, Munich, 1408 / Art Resource, NY

Figure 13
Dirck Volkertsz Coornhert (Dutch, 1522–1590) after Maerten van Heemskerck, *Faith Engendering Persecution*, 1550, from the series The Road to Eternal Bliss, 1550. Etching, 21.9 × 14.2 cm ($8\frac{1}{2}$ × $5\frac{1}{2}$ in.). Collection Rijksmuseum, Amsterdam RP-P-BI6546X

Figure 14
North choir stalls, 1538–39, Grote Kerk, Dordrecht. History Heritage Center DiEP - Dordrecht/the Netherlands 552_401101

Figure 15
Entrance to the Mint, 1555, Dordrecht. Photo: Yvonne Szafran, J. Paul Getty Museum

Figure 16
Schematic ground plan of the Augustinian church, Dordrecht. Based on an illustration in *Jaarboek Historische Vereniging Oud-Dordrecht*, edited by Herman A. van Duinen and C. Esseboom (Dordrecht: Oud-Dordrecht, 2010).

Figure 17
Exterior of the Augustinian church, Dordrecht. Photo: Aart de Boon

Figure 18
Interior of the Augustinian church, Dordrecht. Photo: Yvonne Szafran, J. Paul Getty Museum

Figure 19
Pieter Bruegel the Elder (Flemish, ca. 1525/30–1569), *Faith*, 1559. Pen and brown ink; contours indented for transfer; 22.5 × 29.5 cm ($8\frac{7}{8}$ × $11\frac{5}{8}$ in.). Collection Rijksmuseum, Amsterdam RP-T-1919-35

Figure 20
Maerten van Heemskerck (Dutch, 1498–1574), *Saint Luke Painting the Virgin*, ca. 1545. Oil on panel, 205.5 × 143.5 cm (81 × $56\frac{1}{2}$ in.). Rennes, Musée des Beaux-Arts, inv. 1801.1.6. ©C2RMF / Pierre-Yves Duval

Figure 21
Maerten van Heemskerck (Dutch, 1498–1574), *The Erythraean Sibyl*, 1564. Oil on panel, 126 × 76.2 cm (50 × 30 in.). Collection Rijksmuseum, Amsterdam SK-A-1910. Gift of the heirs of Jonkheer J. P. Six

Figures 24, 26, 28, 32, 35, 61B, 62B
X-radiographs and infrared reflectography: Paintings Conservation, J. Paul Getty Museum

Figure 33
Maerten van Heemskerck, *Saint Luke Painting the Virgin*, 1532 (detail of figure 2)

Figure 34
Maerten van Heemskerck, *Saint Luke Painting the Virgin*, ca. 1545 (detail of figure 20)

Figure 36
Summary of pigment occurrences: J. Paul Getty Museum and Getty Conservation Institute

Figure 37
Photos: Yvonne Szafran and Rebecca Vera-Martinez, J. Paul Getty Museum

Figure 38
Photo: Yvonne Szafran, J. Paul Getty Museum

Figures 39A, 39B, 41, 42, 45A, 45B, 46A, 46B, and 49A
Cross-section samples: Alan Phenix, Getty Conservation Institute

Figure 50
Digital reconstruction of Heemskerck's *Ecce Homo* triptych: Authors with Imaging Services, J. Paul Getty Museum

Detail, *Ecce Homo* altarpiece

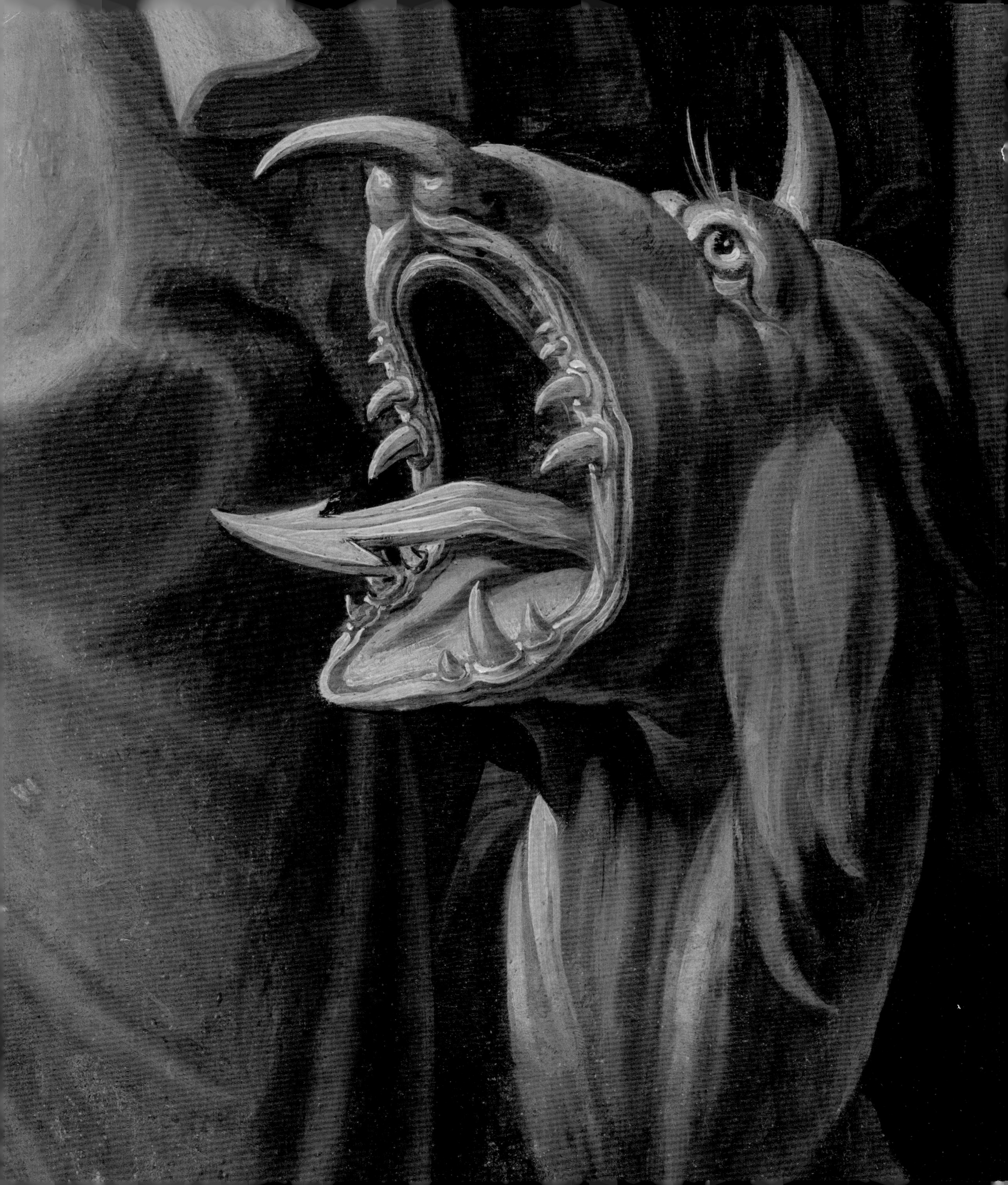

INDEX

Note: Page numbers in *italics* refer to illustrations.

Adrian VI, Pope, 2
Alkmaar, Sint-Laurenskerk, 4, 25n13
Allegory of Prudent Sincerity (Heemskerck), 26n35
altarpieces, by Heemskerck, 1, 4–9, 11–12, 18, 26n44. *See also specific works*
Amsterdam, 4
Apollo *Citharoedos*, 26n27
The Arch of Constantine (Heemskerck), 4, *5*, 16, 18
Augustinian church (Dordrecht), 1, 11, *20*, 20–23, *21*, 27n53. *See also Ecce Homo* triptych
azurite, 51, *51*, 54, 56

Bekesteyn, Josijne van, 25n20
Berck, Matthijs, 24
Van Beverwijck, Jan, 23–24
black (color), 61
black chalk, 46, 49
blue (color), 51–52, 63
bone ash, 61, 81n38
bone white, 61, 81n38
Bosch, Hieronymus, 13, *14*
Bruegel, Pieter, the Elder, 20–23, *22*

calcium, 61, *62*, 81n37
calcium carbonate, 46, 51, 56
carbon black, 46, 51, 61
charcoal, 46, 49, 54
Charles V (Holy Roman Emperor), 4, 11, 12, 18
Christ, 12–14, 56, *60*, 61
Christ Mocked (Bosch), 13, *14*
cleaning, of *Ecce Homo* triptych, 1, 29, *32–33*, *34–35*
clothing, 15, 52, 54–61, 74–75
coats of arms, 15, 75, *75*
Cock, Hieronymus, 25n15, 25n19
color, Heemskerck's use of: in *Ecce Homo* triptych, 14, 29, 51–63; fading over time, 14, 26n28, 51, 52, *60*, 61, 63; style characterized by, 1, 2, 4, 9, 51
Coornhert, Dirck Volkertsz, *13*, *17*, 25n15
Coxcie, Michiel, 4
Crabbe, Jan, 23
Crucifixion altarpiece (Heemskerck), 4
Crucifixion altarpiece (Van Scorel), 4

Daniel and Cyrus before the Idol Bel (Rembrandt), 25n19
Daniel Refusing to Worship Bel (Heemskerck), 25n19
dehydroabietic acid, 80n32
Delft, 2
Dordrecht: Grote Kerk, 18, *19*; in Heemskerck's travels, 4, 12, 25n23; importance of city, 11; Kloveniers Guild, 18; Mint of Holland, 11, 18, *19*; in Revolt of the Netherlands, 23–24, 27n58; Right of Staple, 11–12; sheriff of, 11–12, 14, 23; Smidt family, 25n23. *See also* Augustinian church
drawings, by Heemskerck, 4, 10, 16, 18, 26n27, 46–49, *49*
Drenckwaerdt, Boudewijn van, 25n13
Drenckwaerdt, Cunera van, 25n24
Drenckwaerdt, Jan van: chapels of, 1, 11, 20–23, 27n53; death of, 15, 23; *Ecce Homo* triptych commissioned by, 1, 11; family of, 11, 12, 15, 25n13, 25n20, 25n24, 26n29; as patron of Heemskerck, 1, 11, 12; portrayed in *Ecce Homo* triptych, 11, 15–16, 56–61, *58*, *59*, *73*, 74–75; as sheriff, 11–12, 14, 23
Drenckwaerdt, Willem van (father of Jan), 11, 20
Drenckwaerdt, Willem van (nephew of Jan), 23
drying oil, 64, 81n41
Duyn, Jacob van der, 26n30

Ecce Homo triptych (Heemskerck): chemical analysis of, 36; cleaning of, 1, 29, *32–33*, *34–35*; color in, 14, 29, 51–63; commission for, 1, 11; composition of, description of, 12–16; composition of, planning for, 15–16, 46–49; current condition of, 29; date on, 1, 15, 17; frame of, 1, 17–18, 26n49, 44, *45*, 79n14–16; inscription on, 17, 26n39; methods and techniques of, 1, 29–30, 64–75, *65–75*, 78, 81n44; original location of, 1, 20–23; paint of (*See* paint); panel preparation for, 46, *47*; provenance of, 24; after restoration, *76–77*; support of, *42*, *43*, 43–44; survival of, 1, 23–24; technical examination of, 29–30, 36
Enckenvoirt, Willem van, 4, 24n7
engravings, 10, 25n15, 25n19
environmental scanning electron microscopy with energy-dispersive X-ray spectroscopy (ESEM-EDS), 36, *62*
The Erythraean Sibyl (Heemskerck), 29, *31*
extender substances, 56, *58*, 61, 78
Van Eyck, Jan, 16

Faith (Bruegel), 20–23, *22*
Faith Engendering Persecution (Heemskerck), 16, *17*
The Fall and Salvation of Mankind through the Life and Passion of Christ (Heemskerck), 13, *13*
flesh tones, 56, 74
frames, 1, 17–18, 26n44, 26n49, 44, *45*, 79nn14–16

gas chromatography–mass spectroscopy (GC-MS), 36, 64, 79n11, 79n17
glass, pulverized, *58*, 61, *62*, 78, 81n37
glazes, 54, 56, *57*, 61, 74, 78
glue, animal, 46, 78
Van Gouda, Jacob, 25n14
green (color), 54, 56
Grosshans, Rainald, 26n35, 27n58
ground layer, 46, 49

Haarlem, 2, 4–10
Haarlem Drapers' Guild, 9, 26n44, 81n43
Haarlem Guild of Painters, 10
Haarlem Guild of Saint Luke, 4
Heemskerck, Maerten van: artistic technique of, 9, 29; career of, 1–10; color in style of, 1, 2, 4, 9, 51; death of, 10; destruction of works of, 1, 9; development of style of, 2–4; diligence of, 9–10, 64; education of, 2–4, 10, 29; family of, 2, 10; influence on other artists, 10; innovations of, 2, 14, 29, 51; life of, 2, 10; physicality in style of, 1, 4; studio of, 10, 25n14; travels of, 4, 12, 20, 24n7, 25n23; working methods of, 9–10, 29, 64. *See also specific works*
Hemessen, Jan Sanders van, 13–14, *14*
hydroxyapatite, 61

iconoclasts, 1, 9, 23, 27n58
infrared reflectography, 36, *40–41*, 48, 49, *49*, 74, *75*
inkijkgens (squint views), 18
inscription, on *Ecce Homo* triptych, 17, 26n39
iron oxide earth, 51, 56, 61
Italy, 2, 4, 10, 15, 16, 18, 20, 26n27, 29

Detail, *Ecce Homo* altarpiece

Jonge van Baertwyck, Margaretha de: family of, 15, 25n13, 26nn29–30; portrayed in *Ecce Homo* triptych, 11, 15–16, 64, *71,* 74
John the Evangelist, Saint, 15, 16, 52, 61, 64, *70*
Judith (Heemskerck), 10, *11*

Kies, Symon Jansz, 25n14
Kloveniers Guild, 18
Korn, Heinrich von, 24

lead white, 46, 51, 54, 56
lead-tin yellow, 51, 54, 61
light, Heemskerck's use of, 9
linseed oil, 64, 81n41
Lucasz, Jan, 2
Lumey, William de, 23
Luther, Martin, 23

madder lake, 80n36
Van Mander, Karel: on architectural skills of Heemskerck, 18; on diligence of Heemskerck, 9–10, 64; on education of Heemskerck, 2; on figures painted from life, 26n26; on Heemskerck in Dordrecht, 25n23; on Heemskerck in Rome, 4, 24n7; *Schilder-boeck,* 29; on studio of Heemskerck, 25n14; on thriftiness of Heemskerck, 51, 61
Margaret of Antioch, Saint, 15, 16, 52, 61, 64, *72*
Meerdervoort family, 12, 25n24
Michelangelo, 4
microscopical examination, 36
Mocking of Christ (Hemessen), 13–14, *14*
Mone, Jean, 18

nails, 44, 79n16

oak planks, *42, 43,* 43–44
orpiment, 51

paint, of *Ecce Homo* triptych, 51–63; binding medium of, 64, 81n41; fading of, 51, 52, *60,* 61, 63; on frame, 44, *45,* 79n15; list of pigments used in, 51; technical examination of, 36, 51–63
panel support, of *Ecce Homo* triptych, *42, 43,* 43–44, 46, *47*
Panorama with the Abduction of Helen amidst the Wonders of the Ancient World (Heemskerck), 4, *6–7*
The Parable of the King Who Prepared a Wedding (Heemskerck), 10, *10*
Passion triptych (Heemskerck), 4, *8,* 11, 12, 25n13
Philip II of Spain, 18, 23
physicality, 1, 4
pigments, in *Ecce Homo* triptych, *50,* 51–63; cost of, 51, 54, 61, 78, 80n27; extenders in, 56, *58,* 61, 78; fading of, 51, 52, *60,* 61, 63; list of, 51; original appearance of, 63, *63*; technical examination of, 36, 51–63
Pilate, Pontius: in *Ecce Homo* triptych, 12, 14, 52, *53,* 54, 61, 64, *69*; in other Heemskerck works, 13, 26n27
Portrait of Machtelt Suijs (Heemskerck), 9, *9,* 15
portraits, by Heemskerck, 1, 9, 10, 15
preparatory drawings, 46–49, *49*
priming layer, 46, 64, 78, 79n17
prints, Heemskerck's designs for, 10, 25n15, 25n19
Prudence, 16, 26n35
Prudence and Justice (Heemskerck), 26n35
purple (color), 52, 54, 61

Raman microspectroscopy, 36
Raphael, 2, 4, 12
Rauert, Jacob, 25n14
realgar, 51
red (color), 52–54, 56–61, *57, 58, 59, 60*
red chalk, 46, 48
red lake, 51, 52, *53,* 56, 61, 80n24
Rembrandt Harmensz van Rijn, 10, 25n19
restoration, of *Ecce Homo* triptych, 44, *76–77*
Revolt of the Netherlands (1566–1609), 1, 23–24
Right of Staple, 11–12
Rome, 4, 10, 16, 18, 26n27, 29

Saint Luke Painting the Virgin (Heemskerck, 1532), *3,* 4, 24n6, 29, 48, *48*
Saint Luke Painting the Virgin (Heemskerck, 1545), *28,* 29, *30,* 48, *48,* 75
Salviati, Francesco, 4
Van Scorel, Jan, 2, 4, 24n7, 29, 49, 80n25
Self-Portrait, with the Colosseum, Rome (Heemskerck), *xii, 2,* 10
Serlio, Sebastiano, 18
Sincerity, 16, 26n35
smalt, *51,* 51–54, *52,* 56, 80nn27–29
Smidt family, 25n23
soda lime, 81n37
squaring, 49
The Statue Court of the Casa Sassi at Rome (Heemskerck), 4, *5,* 16
studio, of Heemskerck, 10, 25n14
Suijs, Machtelt, 9, *9,* 15, 25n13

Van Teijlingen, Dirick, 25n13
The Transfiguration (Raphael), 4, 12

ultramarine, 51, 80n25
ultraviolet fluorescence, *53, 58, 59*
ultraviolet photography, 36, *38–39*
underdrawing, 46–49
underpainting, 29, 54, 61, 64

varnish, 29, 56, *57*
Vasari, Giorgio, 4
verdigris, 51, 56
vermilion, 51, 56–61
Virgin and Saint John the Evangelist (Heemskerck), 61
Vriese, de, family, 12, 25n24

walnut oil, 64, 81n41
Warsaw, National Museum, 1, 24
Watergeuzen, 23
Willemsz, Borritt, 25n14
Willemsz, Cornelis, 2
William of Orange, 23, 24

X-radiography, 36, *37,* 46, *47,* 74, *74,* 75
X-ray fluorescence (XRR) spectroscopy, 36

yellow (color), 61, 81n39

zinc, 79n15